CHUCK REDUCKS

CHUCK JONES™
CHUCK REDUCKS

DRAWING FROM THE FUN SIDE OF LIFE

WITH A FOREWORD BY ROBIN WILLIAMS

WARNER BOOKS

A Time Warner Company

Warner Books, Inc., 1271 Avenue of the Americas, New York, NY 10020
🅦 A Time Warner Company

Book design by Liney Li

Printed in the United States of America
First printing: October 1996
10   9   8   7   6   5   4   3   2   1

Library of Congress Cataloging-in-Publication Data
Jones, Chuck
Chuck reducks / Chuck Jones.
p. cm.
ISBN 0-446-51893-X
1. Jones, Chuck. 2. Animators—United States—Biography. I. Title.
NC1766.U52J66 1996
741.5'8'092—dc20   96-17522
                                                          CIP

This book is dedicated to Liney Li, designer,
who brought visual clarity out of the seventy-year accumulated clutter
jungle of my sketches and doodles to *Chuck Amuck* and to this effort.
and to editor Rick Ball,
who scythed away the fat adjectives and bulbous adverbs of my verbosity
and found a few sparks of lightning among the lightning bugs.
I love you both.
and to my godson, Oliver Martin Ball,
conceived and published
during the making of this curious tome.

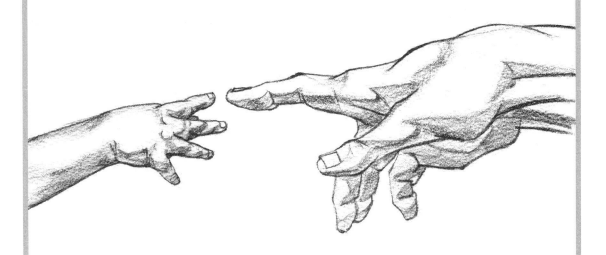

—and to John McGrew and Maurice Noble,
who together pulled the dusty brown shades aside
and thrust my head out the window into the world of color and light.

Dear Reader:

Know, as you open this book, that it would not exist
without the active help and support of many friends and colleagues.
I owe a huge debt of gratitude to John Schulman,
Terry Semel, Bob Daly, Roger Mayer, Gene Reynolds, Hugh Kenner,
Jerry Beck and Will Friedwald, Susan Suffes, Dean Diaz, Melanie Behnke,
and, particularly and especially, to Dina Andre, who has been
utterly and ever intelligently committed to this project throughout,
nurturing it from its first halting steps along the road to completion.

CONTENTS

FOREWORD

Which artistic image is more famous: the slight, enigmatic smile that da Vinci gave to Mona Lisa or the know-it-all, wisenheimer sneer that Chuck Jones gave to Daffy Duck? Which artistic image conveys more emotion: the angst-filled face in Munch's painting *The Scream* or the look of comic fear on Wile E. Coyote's face when he learns that his Acme Spring-Propelled Catapult has just flung him off a 200-foot precipice toward a certain-to-be-uncomfortable face-first rendezvous with a huge granite slab? Which artistic image most accurately conveys man's intellectualism: Rodin's *The Thinker* or Bugs Bunny?

Chuck Jones deserves a seat of honor right alongside all of those "artistes." Sure, Picasso painted some of the world's classic works of art, but he never drew a Daffy Duck tantrum. That takes real talent. Monet never turned a skunk into one of the world's most amorous and debonair gentlemen. Michelangelo never turned a meek, stuttering pig into a comic Everyman. Van Gogh probably would have given his left ear to have created such works of art as the Road Runner and Wile E. Coyote, Super Genius. If any of those artists were alive today, they'd be pea green with professional jealousy over the accomplishments of the Great Jones.

Why? Look at Chuck's body of work. Talk about prolific. I bet that if you were to watch one Chuck Jones cartoon per day, you might actually reach Duck Dodgers in the 24½th Century. Think of each painstaking drawing needed for one

Daffy Duck short film compared to one measly canvas required to paint Van Gogh's *Starry, Starry Night*. One measly canvas! Heck, Chuck probably throws away more unfinished art (animators refer to these precious gems as "mistakes") than Monet ever even attempted. Obviously Chuck didn't draw each and every panel by himself. Naturally he had help from the Animation Elves who diligently tinker away in his studio all night long with sketchpads and magical pencils while Chuck sleeps, happily dreaming of opportunities that will leave Daffy and the Coyote puzzled, bewildered, and frustrated by their own ineptitude. The point is that while Cézanne's name went on relatively few works of art, Chuck Jones's name is . . . well, it's on lots of stuff.

Best of all, you don't have to travel all the way to the Louvre in France or the Sistine Chapel in Italy to enjoy the artwork of Chuck Jones. You could if you wanted to, but you wouldn't find it there. You can, however, find Chuck's work just about anywhere else in the world. Porky Pig can be heard speaking Spanish in Spain, German in Germany, Irish in Ireland, Icicle in Iceland, Belge in Belgium, and Liecht in Liechtenstein. Chances are, if you flip on your TV right now, anywhere in the world, night or day, a Chuck Jones original is on display. You can have it right in the privacy of your own home. Can you get a da Vinci that way? Heck, no. But, then again, none of Chuck's drawings of Bugs Bunny are hanging in the Louvre.

Not yet, Doc.

—ROBIN WILLIAMS

Mural for the Museum of the Moving Image, London.

KID NIGHTWATCHMAN
M M # 6

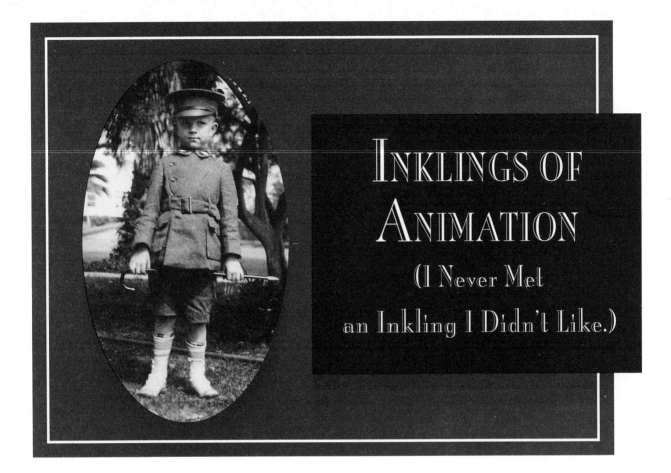

INKLINGS OF ANIMATION
(I Never Met an Inkling I Didn't Like.)

My Father, the Public Convenience

The older I get, the more individuality I find in animals and the less I find in humans. Early experiences convinced me that animals can and do have quite distinct personalities. One memorable summer Sunday morning on the beach at Ocean Park, California, an event occurred in 1921 that to this day has that mysterious, elusive quality, confirming that there are indeed stranger things than are dreamed of in my philosophy.

Left: *The cat that became a mouse.*

The Jones family were, as usual on a Sunday, encamped under their beach umbrella, backs to the low seawall that supported the boardwalk running from Santa Monica to Ocean Park to Venice. There were perhaps eighty yards of humanity between us and the water's edge—hundreds of bright beach umbrellas, blankets, backrests, picnic baskets, and the usual motley array of locals and day-visitors cluttering up the scene. To get to the wet sand and the water, one had to trip lightly and dexterously through this complicated mélange.

Presently a dog came sauntering down the beach, a dog so overtly conceited that he became the focus of all eyes.

In spite of his self-satisfied demeanor, I have never seen a more scruffy-looking dog, or a dog carry-

Above: *Off to the trenches (1918)*

There is, to me, greater individuality between dogs than between most human beings.

ing such a variegated cargo, or one who carried it with greater confidence and hauteur. He was ideally equipped to act as collector of memorabilia, being a sort of insulting caricature of a spitz with a Joseph-like pelt, comprising a variety of hues from pleasant, decayed pumpkin to blackened rust scattered in a random pattern over every part except his nose, which for some reason was of an attractive, baby-bottom pink. The scrofulous coat had with meticulous care collected the aforesaid cargo of tar, seagull feathers, bits of seaweed, broken segments of seashells, cigarette butts, and one cigar butt he had apparently in a careless moment sat upon.

He carried his possessions with world-weary confidence, trotting with an easy nonchalance and a charmingly twisted Humphrey Bogart–like grin as he surveyed the passing throng, who wisely parted in boggle-eyed reverence as he padded down the wet sand. Here obviously was a dog with a purpose. This purpose became destiny when he made an abruptly delicate and precise left turn and headed inland through the intricately packed crowd, picking his way through the awestruck masses with all the grace of a ballet-trained goat, stopped by our little gathering, lifted his leg, and peed on my father's arm.

In the cathedral-like silence and ensuing immobility of the crowd, he turned, flipped a hindfootful

of sand onto this human pissoir, trotted lightly and again with great delicacy to the exact spot he had quitted, executed another precise left turn on the wet sand, and went on his predestined way.

All this had the ethereal quality of a believably unbelievable fairy story. Why was Father selected from the thousands along that sunny beach? Why this signal honor awarded to our very own father? And from a perfect stranger. As Pogo would say, it made us all humble and sort of proud. And so my education on how to survive in a hostile world, begun by a scruffy cat named Johnson, was now continued by a scrofulous dog, who chose to remain anonymous.

This splendid animal, by his graceful and accurate movements, demonstrated the essential law of survival in his unjust climate: when you make a social statement about despotic authority (pee on an arm), do so with confidence and precise selectivity. And perform it in public.

14

It's Better to Have a Complex Father than a Father Complex.

My father was yard foreman at the Collis P. Huntington Southern Pacific yard in 1904, and he helped me well on the way to becoming an animator years before my birth by falling out of a curtained balcony during a Collis P. Huntington family wedding at Solari's restaurant on Maiden Lane in San Francisco. Pepé le Pew would have admired the self-assured elegance with which, back turned carelessly to the balcony's protective rail, he bowed gallantly—but too low—to an appealing woman, toppled over the rail, and soared dashingly into space. Fortunately for my future, he landed on a wedding cake (a Huntington wedding cake) on the table below—cushioning his fall, but not his relationship with Mr. Huntington's railroad company; they promptly shipped him off to Central America, where wedding cakes were relatively unknown and yellow fever took care of those who fell on them. My father did not get yellow fever. He got me. (Later, of course.)

Father looked like, dressed like, and moved like Rhett Butler. He was working on the Panama Canal

COME DARLING..
OBEY YOUR FOOLISH 'ART..
LOVE IS NOT A THING
TO BE ASHAMED OF ..

My father and mother were high school sweethearts—but not with each other.

and always wore white riding breeches with a string necktie and black boots, in every sartorial detail the dashing tropical adventurer. He was a stunner all right. In 1906, he appeared in his Rhett Butler guise in the village of Chanute, Kansas, where he was visiting an old school friend. He was driving—what else?—a team of spanking bays in a black surrey with, no doubt, a dashboard of genuine leather, and the belles of Chanute melted before him like crinolined tulips.

Among the more prolific of the fainters was my mother—well, she wasn't my mother quite yet—and she didn't set her sights for him so much as simply succumb to her destiny. She blushingly told me later (fifty years later, to be approximate) that she tried to seduce him, even though she didn't know how, never having gone beyond a kiss, which up to then she had parted with only as one would diamonds. Father would have none of her lust, though, probably because of all those petticoats, pantalettes, corsets, etc. (He was a "southern gentleman," with all the idiocies attendant on that peculiar state.)

When people fell in love in those prosaic times they got married, which is exactly what happened to

(MUFFLED
"BEEP!
BEEP!")

my father and mother. Mother (not yet, don't hurry me) was swept off her seventeen-year-old feet and whisked off to Niagara Falls, then to New York City (where Father proved he wasn't a prude by seducing her at the top of the Statue of Liberty), and by great, white, elegant Cunard liner to Panama City, to abide in a large, veranda-shaded white house on a green, palm-shaded hill with three servants. A company doctor helped her to bear a daughter just before her nineteenth birthday: Margaret Barbara Jones, born on June 20, 1908.

My sister Dorothy was also born in the Canal Zone, on September 27, 1910. Although I was conceived in Panama, I was—to my eternal regret— born, of all places, in Spokane, Washington, on September 21, 1912, just two years before Winsor McCay completed the first great animated cartoon— *Gertie the Dinosaur*. While my presence did little to effect McCay's film, *Gertie the Dinosaur* was to have a profound effect on me, since it was among the first and remains one of the most remarkable animated cartoons ever made.

Spokane lacks the panache of Panama as a birth-place. Bing Crosby is the only other Spokane native I know. I first noticed the Rhythm Boys with Bing Crosby because that trio, among so many others, had an oddity about it—a drunken vocalist propped up on stage between the other two. If you want to be a humorist, you have to observe such oddities.

I think I was six months old when I left Spokane.

My father told me I was run out of town for tampering with girls' diapers, but I have no memory of this.

We moved to Hollywood, where I heard echoes of life in the Canal Zone in a song with which my father used to lull me to sleep: "He has gone beyond the river, with an abscess on his liver." It was much more soothing than some buttery little "Baby Bunting."

My brother, Richard, was born in Hollywood in 1915. He soon applied for a job in the movies, as a baby in a Sam Selig film. He failed to land the part because he didn't look like a baby. History does not record what he *did* look like.

I learned to read around the time Richard appeared, just before my third birthday. I think my first book was *Uncle Wiggily* or *Peter Rabbit*, both superb volumes that I can, and do, still read for pleasure. I so enjoyed my first encounter with Uncle Wiggily that I was delighted to find what I figured must be another in the same series—a book called *Uncle Vanya*. It was hard going, and after reading a page or two, I went to my mother to complain about it.

I could read at three because my father contended that if a three-year-old could conquer the ex-

Mabel M. Jones apologizes to the infant Charles for giving birth to him in Spokane.

16

traordinary process of learning to stand up (like rid- ing a bicycle without the bicycle), learn to eat with- out putting his pudding in his eye, and learn to deposit bodily wastes into proper receptacles, then learning to read would be a snap. Anyway, he him- self saw no reason to stop reading *Don Quixote* in Spanish in order to read aloud the insipid goings-on of people named Jane, Jimmy, and Spot. Well, I knew full well—because Father told me so—that there were three-year-olds who lulled themselves to sleep in iambic-pentameter murmurings, and that people named Ludwig composed intricate cantatas and wrote things in C-sharp minor while still in their dia- pers. So no doubt as a matter of shame, I had to learn to read.

Furthermore, reading was a useful skill for a Jones child, because Father forbade any conversa- tion at the breakfast table. "In the entire history of

Why pay for models to sketch when you have grandchildren? My model cyclists were Valerie (left) and Craig (naked).

That oversized hat (left) was needed to contain all the compassion, love, and joy Mother found in all of her children.

Father encouraged us to read everything, even cereal boxes.

man," he said, "nothing worthwhile has ever been said at the breakfast table." He did not state this as an opinion, he stated it as a fact, and through my long and fairly observant life, it is one of the few "facts" I have found reason to believe in. But perhaps like all enduring philosophy, it endures because it cannot be proved.

I suppose wisdom never had a chance where no one ever said anything wise *or* foolish, but I do know that for all of us the ban on conversation gave a blessed morning respite between dreaming—over which we had no apparent control—and the so-called real world, over which we were supposed to exert control to guide our destinies to worthwhile ends. It must be generously noted that my father even curbed the privilege he lavishly indulged in at every other meal: he abstained from criticizing our table manners. This must have been a considerable strain on him.

Since we could not talk, argue, insult, or criticize one another at breakfast, we soon learned that although it was a good time for meditation, musing to oneself can become surprisingly boring, so we brought books to the breakfast table. To this day, I am always somewhat disappointed when I take a book off my shelf and don't find an ancient and fragile cornflake in it.

If you failed to bring a book and began to fidget

restlessly, Father would suggest—he had suggestions of steel—that you read the cereal boxes. I can still pretty accurately recite all that jazz about "Shot from Guns" puffed wheat and "Niagara Falls" shredded wheat.

Father encouraged us to read anything and everything. ("How can you tell what good writing is unless you've encountered bad writing?") So I became an inveterate reader long before I knew what *inveterate* meant—as did my siblings, long before they knew they were siblings.

Among the "bad" things we read was the Rover Boys Series for Young Americans. They were terrible books, so terrible in fact that we fell in love with them. The Rover Boys were Dick, Tom, and Sam, and they went to school at Putnam Hall. There was Tom, the fun-loving one (presumably the others had no love of fun); Dick was physical, and Sam was studious, and so, not being competitive, they were very happy together. Until wonderfully evil Dan Baxter appeared. He was announced—not just once but *every time he showed up*, it seemed—as "Dan Baxter—coward, bully, cad, thief, and arch-enemy of the Rover Boys." And that line reappeared in 1942 to describe Dan Backslide in my animated cartoon *The Dover Boys.* The sublimely badly written Rover Boys books were among the things that pointed me toward animation and unwittingly taught me the primary law of writing books or films that children might read or view: *never write down to anybody.*

When I became an animation writer and director for Warner Bros., I made certain that we never wrote down to children. This was not so much a matter of wisdom—although it *was* wise—as it was a matter of necessity: we simply did not know who our audience was. Since (1) *all* of our films were to be exhibited in theaters accompanying such gentle and ungentle features as *I Was a Fugitive from a Chain Gang, Little Caesar, The Public Enemy, Four Daughters, A Midsummer Night's Dream,* and *The Strawberry Blonde,* and since (2) we didn't know how to make pictures for adults of such diverse tastes, and since (3) we knew we weren't making pictures for children, therefore (4) we were forced to make pictures only for ourselves. We never stopped to analyze what made our cartoons funny. If they made us laugh, then we hoped the audience would follow. If they didn't, we would be out on the street sucking bricks.

Today, when I can afford the introspection denied me as a youth and can philosophize about the matter, I realize that we were doing exactly what Robert Louis Stevenson, Lewis Carroll, Beatrix Potter, E. B. White, T. H. White, and James Thurber did: we wrote, drew, directed only for ourselves. The rules are simple. Take your work, but never

yourself, seriously. Pour in the love and whatever skill you have, and it will come out.

As a child, I loved to draw, as do most children, and I have made at least twenty drawings every day of my life since childhood. And I intend to continue to draw and paint for the rest of my life—if I live that long. I think all children will draw naturally and beautifully if left to their own devices, but parental criticism too often makes them lose heart. When a child is doing a drawing with stick figures, "That looks like fun" is a more constructive comment than "Is that meant to be Daddy?"

A child once showed Jean Charlot—the noted teacher and painter who gave an inspirational series of lectures to the Disney animators—a drawing he was obviously very proud of. Charlot couldn't understand the drawing, but, like my mother, he would never ask a child what a drawing was supposed to be.

My parents never talked down to children, and I never wrote down to children at Warner Bros. These early drawings grew up to be Finster, who was a sort of embryonic gangster.

19

Instead he said, "I'm not sure I've ever seen one just like that." "You have, too," the kid exclaimed. "It's a spool." And he began to draw another one. He drew one end, turned the paper and drew the side, then turned it again and drew the other end. As Charlot pointed out, this is a very realistic drawing of a spool, because you can actually cut it out and fold it to make a three-dimensional spool. Similarly, the child's drawing of a table, with all four legs splayed out, is just like a carpenter's drawing of the same table.

Indiscriminate praise can be as damaging to a child as criticism. Children know that some of their drawings are better than others, and they soon lose faith in a parent whose praise is unwaveringly enthusiastic. If, every time a kid brings you a new drawing, you exclaim, "Ooo, that's wonderful!" and stick it up on the refrigerator, you are making no statement at all. All you are doing is getting rid of the child, who will begin to wonder if there is any point in drawing whatsoever.

My mother had four kids and no refrigerator magnets. Whenever we brought her a drawing, she looked at the child before looking at the drawing. Only if we seemed excited about the drawing would she become excited too. Then she might say, "Why, you used a lot of blue, didn't you?" or "I've never seen a drawing that had all those little squiggles down in the corner." But she would never criticize our efforts *as drawings*. And this method worked well. Her four children all became graphic artists. My father, who didn't care too much one way or the other about our drawings, saw to it that we had good

materials, and eventually he sent us to art school. He was certainly not an art critic.

In spite of the efforts of art critics, children (including myself as a child) ignore the rules of perspective. And quite rightly. The whole idea of perspective is no more than that—an idea, which has something to do with optics but very little to do with art. At the time perspective was developed in Italy, no other artists in the world were using it, nor did they feel any need to use it. In a Japanese painting of a city street, you can look over the fences and see what's happening, whereas perspective blocks it all out.

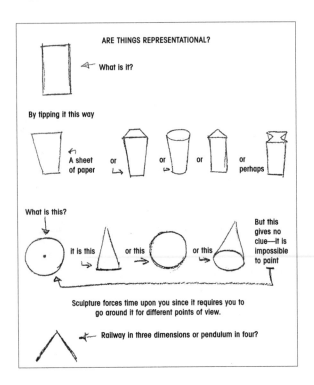

ARE THINGS REPRESENTATIONAL?

What is it?

By tipping it this way

A sheet of paper or or or perhaps

What is this?

it is this or this or this

But this gives no clue—it is impossible to paint

Sculpture forces time upon you since it requires you to go around it for different points of view.

Railway in three dimensions or pendulum in four?

20

HOPETOWN
WYONG LIMITED
INCORPORATED IN N.S.W.

19th September, 1990.

Mr. & Mrs. Chuck Jones,
Burrow No. 1
Warren No. 1
WARNER BROTHERS PATCH

Dear Mr. & Mrs. Jones,

How often has it been my duty, at the end of a long and tiring day to write a letter of appreciation on behalf of a Board, a staff or a student body?

The answer to that question is quite often - but never before with the genuine and sincere enthusiasm which is with me tonight.

I have never seen these kids, often difficult to enagage and to manage, accept two strangers with such positive warmth and in such a highly motivated manner as we witnessed throughout your visit. Their bubbly enthusiasm continued long after you left and the memory of your visit will last many lifetimes.

I tho...
littl...
culmi...
emoti...
His f...
dwarf...
clipp...
genet...
for R...

I have some delightful pictures of the day, but the kids have voted for the "group". They are:

Left Top: Bugs, Carlies's chin, Mrs. Q (Elaine), Johnathon, Daniel's ear, Mark, Matthew.

Middle: Melanie, Chuck, Marian, Nathan

Bottom: Joshua and Neville

I do apologise for the "plastic-fantastic" frame but whereas Wyong is a centre of excellence in education, it falls somewhat short in the area of photographic presentation. Los Angeles could no doubt also teach us a little bit about limousine transport.

We loved having you to visit and wish you both many long years in sharing the obvious "fun" that emanates from within.

With my warmest regards.

Yours sincerely,

Elaine Quilty

E.M. Quilty, B.A. Dip. Ed.
PRINCIPAL

Many of my trips with Marian are surprising. When we visited HopeTown, Australia, with Bugs, a small boy smiled who had never smiled before.

He did not like the grown-ups who talked down to him like a baby, but the ones who just went on talking in their usual way, leaving him to leap along in their wake, jumping at meanings, guessing, clutching at known words, and chuckling at complicated jokes as they suddenly dawned. He had the glee of the porpoise then, pouring and leaping through strange seas.

—*T. H. White*
(writing about the young King Arthur
in The Sword in the Stone)

Left: *A CONNECTICUT RABBIT IN KING ARTHUR'S COURT*

"Most powerful swimmer I ever knew," said Uncle Lynn, "was a man named Rutherford B. Klutz."

22

• • •

There can be no question that I learned practically everything I would need to know about animated cartoon writing from my Uncle Lynn Martin.

"Most powerful swimmer I ever knew," said Uncle Lynn, polishing his bald head reflectively, "was a man by the name of Rutherford B. Klutz. It took him four days to swim from Venice Beach to the Isthmus at Catalina Island: twenty-six miles. But he swam back in forty-five seconds." He checked the shine on his pants. "Caught his jockstrap on the Venice Pier."

Uncle Lynn never grew up and never talked down, and these factors alone would have made him the ideal uncle among the forest of five-and-a-half-foot to six-foot bureaucrats who cluttered our lives.

But he was far more than that to my worshiping eight-year-old self; he was a blacksmith without a forge—except, of course, for us.

He would play baseball—catcher preferably, sometimes without a glove—for any team: ten-year-old, work-up, bush, or army league. This had formed his hands into the most unusual shapes, differing enormously from each other. The left, or catching, hand was intriguingly similar to a glove filled with chunks of decomposed granite of unequal sizes, the palm tastefully covered with a surface similar to a dog's pads. The right, throwing hand was surprisingly soft, but limber and strong. His arms were those of a bowman, astonishingly powerful and sup-

Ralph Phillips in the clean-up spot for BOYHOOD DAZE (1957).

ing the Spanish-American War, after running away from home and enlisting as a drummer boy at age sixteen. The first time he ran away he was twelve, curious to see the results of the Galveston flood. (He told me in confidence that seeing one bloated man in a tree would slake even the most curious little boy's appetite for drowned people. So, he said, he returned to Chanute, Kansas, several hundred miles away.)

Never in all the years I knew him did Uncle Lynn ever muss my hair or thump my head. If he had something to say to me when I was half his height, he would sit casually down in a chair, to be level with me. He never squatted to communicate with me or

ported by a body of reassuring durability. He could stand in the sand like a squat telephone pole, those marvelous arms akimbo, two boys hanging on each one like jumping jacks, possums, or sloths.

Uncle Lynn had lost all but a flat diadem of hair around his ears when, at age seventeen, he survived a bout of dengue fever incurred in the Philippines dur-

23

If you knew nothing about baseball, you might suppose the pitcher was trying to injure the catcher, and only the batter stands to protect him with his bat. It seemed to me the manager usually got furious when the batter failed to protect the pitcher by striking out.

Never in all the years I knew him did Uncle Lynn ever muss my hair or thump my head, as six-foot bureaucrats always did.

any child—a demeaning gesture defining the difference in relative statuses. He never talked down, physically or philosophically, to any human being, any dog, cat, or housefly. He is the only person I ever knew who would talk to caterpillars, reassuring them of their thrilling future as butterflies. I have watched in fascinated attention as he spoke a word of warning to a line of ants approaching Mother's kitchen and seen them turn away from the first step. Perhaps he had smeared a bit of material obnoxious to ants on that step to ensure his warning was heeded, but I choose to believe not. He was never thought of as perfect or, for that matter, as imperfect. He was, quite simply, Uncle Lynn.

Another problem with Uncle Lynn was that he made you think. Most other adults told you what to think, which of course isn't thinking at all. But Uncle Lynn was suspicious of facts. "What about two and two equals four?" I had just discovered this mathematical dogma, which sounded about as rational as anything in an irrational world. "Isn't that a fact?"

"Two and two what?" said Uncle Lynn.

"Two and two anything makes four anything." If this wasn't a profundity, I'd never met one.

"So," said Uncle Lynn, rubbing an apple on his trousers to take the shine off, "if we have four of anything, we can take two of that anything away, leaving two, and everything will be hunky-dory." People used words like "hunky-dory" in those days. Uncle Lynn seldom did, but would occasionally throw one in to put you off guard. "Isn't that a fact?"

"Absolutely" was the word I was looking for. What I said was, "Sure."

In an effort to find some stability in a confused and unreliable world, I had independently discovered the comforting word "fact." A fact, as I understood it, or wanted to understand it, was something you could depend on. A fact was a truth, and nobody, even adults, would dare trifle with a truth/fact.

Except Uncle Lynn, who hovered like a burly, bald-headed butterfly somewhere between childhood and adulthood, never lighting firmly on either pole.

"Don't depend on it," he said, after I had confided my newfound faith in "facts." "Is an ice-cream cone a fact?" he asked.

"It sure is." I had an absolute faith in the truth and the honest integrity of an ice-cream cone. Indeed, it was a cornerstone of my belief in the rare but essential goodness of nature.

"All right," said Uncle Lynn, "an ice-cream cone is a fact only if you say what an ice-cream cone is."

"Uh ice-cream cone is uh ice-cream cone," I explained. If I'd added one more "is uh ice-cream cone" I might have grown up to be Gertrude Stein.

Uncle Lynn's troops assembled on the beach:
Chuck, Dorothy, Dick, and Peggy.

"Okay," said Uncle Lynn, "let's say we have four ice-cream cones. Two of them have just been handed over by the soda jerk and are fresh and hard and tasty beyond belief. Two of them are old and practically melted; their cones are gummy and gunky and the ice cream isn't ice cream anymore, but a gooey gucky mess. So I take two good ones and leave you the gucky mess. Is that equal? Do two and two really make four?"

"Aw," I replied.

"Look," said Uncle Lynn. "I'd say, two and two only makes four when you don't say what you're talking about."

"Aw," I commented.

"The point about all this is that you don't have to have all those things somebody calls facts and truths flopping around inside your brain trying to make sense out of nonsense."

"Yeah but," I suggested.

"Right," said Uncle Lynn. "'Yeah but' is the

whole thing. No matter what you have absolutely decided is a fact or a truth, haul back and say, 'Yeah but.' It leaves you breathing room. For instance, you're eight years old. That's a fact. Now add a 'yeah but.'"

"Yeah but." Again he was forcing me to think for myself, not forcing me to think what he thought. "Next year I won't be eight years old, I'll be nine, and last year I was seven, so eight years old is not a fact, except for now."

"Right again," said Uncle Lynn. "The only fact I know is that there are no facts."

"Is that so with *everything?*" I asked.

"Particularly true of *everything,*" said Uncle Lynn. "You said that just right. You said it in *italics.* Italics are these slanty letters that mean *'Pay attention, this is important.'* As different from capital letters, like your grandfather yelling 'PAY ATTENTION!' which is just being loud. Bullies and aunts use capital letters a lot, but italics get your attention; like,

25

The orangutan frightened Larchmont's mother when he tried to sell her an automatic coconut-crushing machine. Naturally, her child was born with arms longer than his legs.

'I wouldn't go in there if I were you' in italics makes you pretty certain that you probably don't want to go in there, it's dangerous; but 'I WOULDN'T GO IN THERE IF I WERE YOU' in capitals makes you *want* to go in there."

"How about the story?" I wanted time to digest this hot potato.

"Call out the troops," said Uncle Lynn, "while I assemble some facts."

The troops assembled. Uncle Lynn looked them over with a critical eye. "You're quite a messy lot," he said. "Two boys and two girls. That means you're actually four girlboys or gerbils for short. Two and two makes four, doesn't it?" he said, winking at me. "So you've got to be four something. That's a fact, isn't it?"

"I don't think you'd better get everybody around here messed up," I said. "Maybe you better just get on with it. The story I mean."

"Ah, yes," said Uncle Lynn. "Out of the mouth of Abes comes wisdom. Abe Lincoln's mouth anyway. I knew Abe Lincoln, you know. Fact. Met him once at a side-splitting contest."

"You couldn't have known Mr. Lincoln," said Peggy. "You're not as old as that."

"As old as *what?*" asked Uncle Lynn. Nobody else there knew how dangerous his italics were. "Abe Lincoln," my uncle said, "once observed that a man's legs only have to be long enough to reach the ground."

We four nodded to each other. Seemed reasonable.

"Trouble about a statement like that," said Uncle

Lynn, peeling an apple and eating the skin, "is that it's subject to error. Fact is, I once knew a man on Skeleton Key whose feet *didn't* reach the ground. His mother had been frightened by an orangutan who tried to sell her an automatic coconut-crushing machine, and her child was born with arms longer than his legs. Walked on his hands all his live-long life, legs swinging between them like a pair of long johns hanging from a clothesline. Often wondered what happened to him—name of Larchmont Fink. He must be quite old by now. Older than me at that time. I don't know whether he still is older or not."

"How old are you?" asked Peggy, my older sister, trying to tidy up Uncle Lynn's narratives. She always was one for difficult and impossible tasks.

"How old am I what?" was Uncle Lynn's disconcerting reply.

The Black Hole of rational uncertainty that often appeared in conversations with Uncle Lynn opened again.

"Well," said Uncle Lynn, pulling the seeds out of the apple core and popping them into his mouth like peanuts (he would later shoot them out with a collapsible peashooter he kept in his pocket). "There's no need to be baffled. Surely you're familiar with the phrase, 'You're not old enough to—'"

There was general agreement among us that such a phrase did indeed have the ring of instant familiarity.

"That's what I mean," said Uncle Lynn, tucking the seeds into his cheek for future use, looking like a muscular, bald-headed squirrel. "It isn't how old you

"What was the parrot's name?" asked brother Dick, always hungry for the latest scoop on parrots.

are, it's are you old enough to do things? Well, I'm old enough to do things I want to do without threats from the authorities, meaning parents, teachers, cobra-eyed aunts—you know the lot."

We did, but still Peggy insisted. "What year were you born?"

"As to that," said Uncle Lynn, essaying a trial apple-seed shot through his teeth and hitting our resident moosehead on the nose, "I was too young at the time to remember, but" (holding up an admonishing finger to Peggy) "I am *quite* old. In fact, I am older than some people who are a good deal older than I used to be. But to clarify matters, if all four of you stood on each other's shoulders, you still wouldn't be as old as I am right now."

There was a concerted "Hmmm" from his audience. His logic was askew; that we suspected. *How* it was askew was another matter.

"Oldest man I ever knew was a parrot. He was one-quarter woodpecker; used to stick soda crackers into telephone poles," continued Uncle Lynn. "Eighty-seven years old when he kicked the bucket. Oldest man I ever knew to actually kick the bucket: a small, white bucket that he drank whiskey out of.

Drawings by Chuck Jones, sentiments by Dick Jones.

Kicked the thing one day in a fit of frustration, emptying all the booze. Died of acute morbidity the next day. Huge funeral, attended by two Doberman pinschers and a cat, who had all along planned on eating him. They buried him in the cat. The cat became an alcoholic."

"What was the parrot's name?" asked younger brother Dick, who was insistent on that kind of thing.

"A parrot isn't a man." Peggy was still seeking order.

"Quite right," said Uncle Lynn. "A parrot isn't a man and a man isn't a parrot. I hope that answers your question." Addressing Dick: "What do you think the parrot's name was?"

"Unclebuyme," instantly replied Dick, referring to a local gimme-pig (a boy we had so named because of his constant nagging and tearful appeal to his uncle and guardian: "Uncle buy me this, Uncle buy me that—").

27

*Prince Charles had
the time to drop in
for the opening of
London's Museum of
the Moving Image,
where I did graffiti
on the outside walls.*

28   "Quite right," repeated Uncle Lynn. "How did
you know? Unclebuyme Macaw, shortened from Sea-
mus Duboru McCaw. Scottish bird. Wore the same
tartan as Bunny Prince Charlie, rabbit I once knew.
Died intestate. Ever see a macaw in kilts?"

"Where did you meet this Mr. Unclebuyme
Macaw?" I asked, ever eager, even then, to identify
the bizarre.

"Very frustrated bird. He could talk, but he
couldn't remember what he was talking about. Met
him on a riverboat that ran illicit toothpicks to the
Indians on Little Semisopochnoi Island in the Bering
Sea. Indians used toothpicks to prop their eyes open
during the three-month-long winter night. There are
no trees on Semisopochnoi Island, so you can see the
demand for toothpicks is enormous and leads to il-

licit toothpicks. Toothpick running is a thriving trade
in the Strait. Against federal law, of course. You can
make a passable toothpick out of a walrus tusk, but it
seems a shame to kill a walrus for one toothpick."

"Couldn't you take the tusk without killing the
walrus?" Dorothy asked.

"I don't know about you," said Uncle Lynn,
neatly lofting an apple seed in a graceful parabola
into the cat's dish, "but borrowing a walrus's tusk can
be a harrowing experience. Tried it once. Spent the
next six months in the hospital writing *The Decline
and Fall of the Musk Ox.*"

"Is there any place you've never been?" asked
Dick.

"You mean, is there no place I've ever *not*
been?" said Uncle Lynn. "And the answer is no. I've
been every place I've ever been. Now," he scanned
our faces, "why don't we all get together some other
time, like tomorrow, and I'll tell you of a zebra I once
met whose stripes slipped off his back."

We all agreed the next morning that interesting
and immediate dreams are stimulated by the thought
of a zebra with all of his stripes piled around his ankles. And I was hooked. The only way this marvelous
event could be accomplished would be in an art form
then only in its embryonic stage; yet animation and I
were on an irreversible collision course.

Author meets self on a Swiss train.

Laramie, Wyoming (author in hat).

Author and stave church in Norway

"Is there no place I've ever not been?"
said Uncle Lynn.

* * *

Uncle Lynn Talks to a Dead Dog

After our good dog Teddy died, we received a long letter from Uncle Lynn. How he knew of Teddy's death I do not know. Where he was I do not know. He was always "off someplace." We never knew where, and he never said until he brushed by us on his way to someplace else. He might mention Bakersfield, Kuala Lumpur, Topolobampo, Mozambique, or the Seychelles, or the Dry Tortugas, or even Hollister Drive, which was just one block over from our home on Wadsworth Avenue.

Dear Peggy and Dorothy and Chuck and Dick,

I had a telephone call last night. "Is this Uncle Lynn?" someone asked.

"Why yes," I said. "My name is Lynn Martin. Are you some unregistered nephew?"

"This is Teddy." He sounded a little impatient with me. "Teddy Jones, Teddy Jones the resident dog of 115 Wadsworth Avenue, Ocean Park, California. I'm calling long distance."

"Excuse me," I said. "I really don't mean to offend you, but I've never heard you talk before— just bark, or whine, or yell at the moon."

"Look who's talking," Teddy sniffed, a really impatient sniff if ever I've heard one. "Look. Peggy and Dorothy and Chuck and Dick seem to be having a very rough time of it because they

Teddy, the dog who cared,
and my father, who cared not quite enough.

29

think I'm dead." Hesitate. "Well, I suppose in a way I am."

I will admit that hearing a dog admit that he was dead was a new experience for me, and not a totally expected one. "If you're dead," I asked, not being sure of just how you talk to a dead dog, "how come you're calling me?" There was another irritated pause. Clearly he was getting very impatient with me.

"Because," he said, in as carefully a controlled voice as I've ever heard from a dog. "Because when you are alive, even if the kids don't know exactly where you are, they know you're someplace. So I just want them to know I may be sort of dead, but I'm still someplace."

"Maybe I should tell them you're in Dog Heaven, Teddy, maybe to make 'em feel—"

"Oh, don't be silly." Teddy cleared his throat. "Look. Where are you?"

"Oh, no, you don't. We're trying to find out where you are," I barked.

"Hey, I didn't know you could bark." He sounded impressed with my command of the language.

"Wait just a minute," I said. "You had to know where I am, or you couldn't have called me on the telephone, right?"

"Boy, you know so little," said Teddy. "I simply said I called you long distance. Who said anything about a telephone? They asked me if I knew where you were, and I said you were someplace else, besides 115 Wadsworth Avenue. So they dialed someplace else and here I am and here you are."

"Can I call you back?" I asked dazedly. "Maybe that'll give me a clue."

"Be reasonable," said Teddy. "How can you call me back when neither you nor I know where I am?"

"Oh, come on, give me a clue," I begged desperately. "For instance, are there other dogs around there? I've got to tell the kids something."

"Hold it," said Teddy, apparently looking around. "I did see a pug/schnauzer with wings a minute ago. The wings could lift the schnauzer part of him off the ground, but the pug part just sort of dragged through the grass bumping into the fireplugs."

"Fireplugs?"

"Orchards of them, hundreds of 'em. Yellow, red, white, striped. Unfortunately, I don't seem to have to pee anymore. I strain a lot, but all I get is air. Perfumed air," he added proudly.

"Sounds like Dog Heaven to me," I said. "Are there trees full of lamb chops and stuff like that?"

"You know," Teddy sighed. "For a fair to upper-middle-class uncle, you do have some weird ideas. But the reason I called you was Peggy, Dorothy, Chuck, and Dick trust you and will believe anything you say, which in my opinion is carrying the word 'gullible' about as far as it will stretch. Anyway, gullible or not, they trust you, so I want you to tell them that I'm still their faithful, noble, old dog, and—except the noble part—that I'm in a place where they can't see me but I can see them, and I'll always be around keeping an eye, an ear, and a nose on them. Tell them that just because they can't see me doesn't mean I'm not there. Point out to them that during the day you can't see the latitudes and you can't really see a star, but they're both still there. So get a little poetic and ask them to think of me as 'good-dog,' the good old Teddy, the Dog Star from the horse latitudes, and not to worry, I'll bark the britches off anybody or anything that bothers them. Just because I bit the dust doesn't mean I can't bite the devils."

That's what he said. I never did find out exactly where he was, but I did find out where he wasn't—not ever very far from Peggy, Dorothy, Chuck, and old Dick Jones.

Sincerely,
Lynn Martin, Uncle at Large

• • •

Cat, a List

Among the lavish supply of kittens who graced our manse were three whom my father immediately recognized as having learning potential. In his quaint way he named the white kitten Othello, the black kitten Desdemona, and the odd kitten—a tortoise-shell roan—Iago. Iago later had kittens, sired by

We had cats the way other people had mice.
—*James Thurber*

Albert the cat came at dawning, looking for affection and justice, having been wrongly accused of stealing the neighborhood's goldfish ("the masked raccoon did it"). Marian's love is something Albert and I shared without jealousy.

31

Desdemona. Othello couldn't have had less interest in the whole matter, at least at that time, and was content with the ménage à trois just as it was. He became a wonderful kitten-sitter too, whenever the others were out rousting.

Before all this happened, however, we came in-

dignantly to my father, grasping in our grimy paws (except my sister, Peggy, whose ten-year-old paws were never grimy, grubby, or greasy) the living proof of his mendacity: William Shakespeare's *Othello*.

"Othello was black." Dorothy shook the book at Father. "And Desdemona was his wife and she was white and Iago was treacherous, so hah! There!"

"Hah?" asked Father.

"Because we looked it up!" shouted Dorothy.

"Hm," mused Father. "Why did you look it up? What difference does it make—?"

"Because," hotly interrupted Dorothy, "we figured it might be one of your tricks and we asked Mother and she said look it up so we looked it up and found that the real Desdemona was a girl and that Iago was a boy, and that you knew it."

"You know," said Peggy thoughtfully, "I think you're a very sneaky man. Come on, gang, I think we've been hoodwinked by this Machiavellian."

"Speaking of Machiavelli," Father said, as we trooped off, "Shakespeare wrote another play about another Scotsman—Mac something. MacAroon? MacAdamia?"

"If you think we're going to look *that* one up, you, dear Father, are sadly mistaken," snarled Dorothy, who was an adept snarler even at eight.

But we *did* look it up. It was, as it turned out, actually *Macbeth*.

Just as Johnson, our intern cat of my early childhood, taught me that only in differences can we determine individual personality (Johnson swam in the ocean and relished grapefruit over all foodstuffs), so Othello, the seemingly content and most domesticated of cats, vividly demonstrated once again that you simply cannot trust appearances.

Othello was the only cat I ever knew to discover sex, consummate a lifetime of sexual experience, and reject sex all in one memorable night. Just what triggered his sudden and frantic devotion to this new hobby is hard to establish. Before this, he was an orthodox cat to an almost nauseating degree, living absolutely by the book, drowsing contentedly before the fireplace even on summer evenings, relaxed and purring more as a cat-bag full of cat than a wild animal temporarily domesticated by economic requirements.

*Complacent author and Johnson's cathouse—
pardon me: castle.*

32

Few cats fancy Claude's method of locomotion (below). Bottom: *Rani the Great Dane had large, sad eyes and a wrestler's neck. He woke me every morning by resting his head on my pillow and just staring. I could look up the long, dark tunnel of his nostrils to see his brains.*

But the love bug that mysteriously struck Othello that night changed everything. He came out of his docile nap with an unbelievably evil yell and tore furiously around the perimeter of his hooked rug with the keening roar of Ferrari-like gear changes, until centrifugal force shot him like a comet through a set of French windows, fortunately open to the summer night. Across the porch he flung himself, through an arbor of Cecil Bruner roses, then, wearing a small but stylish bonnet of tiny pink roses, he careened off in a wild and gallant effort to seduce the world.

It is a matter of record that he mounted at least eighteen cats that night, mostly female. Also, for the record, he ravished one small Boston Bull, who wore a permanent tic from that day forward, one gopher, who died either from ecstasy or terror (difficult to tell from its expression), and numerous inanimate objects of more or less catlike dimensions, including a velocipede, two teddy bears, a galosh, and a motorman's glove. He not only violently seduced everything in sight, he de-

"Great Danes peered from overturned doghouses."

scribed his revels in crude and gutter-ridden language as he went, screaming his exploits to a shocked and wondering world. He was like a siren-blasting patrol car driven by a sex-mad sergeant, ricocheting past cowering homes, his satyric screams shattering the night in hideous boasts of love, joy, and passion.

His lewd yawps echoed off into the night like a thousand demented bagpipes, taking the darkness apart with the volcanic Doppler effect of approaching and diminishing yells never heard before outside of hell. No cat ever overplayed the part of Mr. Hyde more than did our demure cat Othello that night.

Like a lightning flash, it all stopped as suddenly as it had begun. The night simply ceased being an orgy. All sounds halted in mid-yell, the breeze timidly resumed its caress of the mimosa, shell-shocked cicadas tentatively tried their quivering legs, Airedales peered apprehensively out of garbage cans, Great Danes from overturned doghouses, and terrified terriers from hastily dug fox-terrier holes.

The next morning, we fearfully and carefully awoke and dressed to find Othello peacefully curled in his cat sack, back on his hooked rug, freshly laundered and seemingly unaffected by his singular experiences or his loss of virginity. He purred in what appeared to be dreamless sleep, and until the day thirteen years later when he died thoughtfully in a shoe box, he never referred to the matter by word or deed.

33

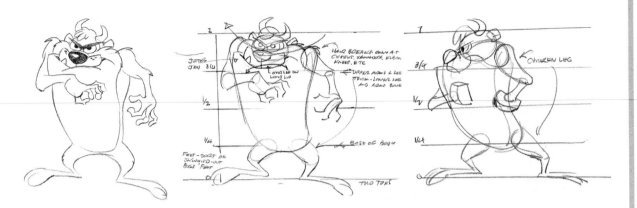

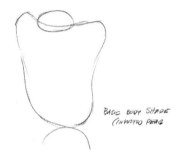

BASIC BODY SHAPE (INVERTED PEAR)

BACK VIEW

As a child I dreamed of being a track star sailing powerfully over hurdles. But good hurdlers don't sail through the air at all; they chop down over the hurdle with precision. An animator should know that the less time a hurdler spends in the air, the faster he moves, because he starts to lose speed the instant his feet leave the ground. The child, on the other hand, will leap high in the air and sail inefficiently over the hurdle, or knock it down. Running into things is quite natural for young animals.

The physical action of children is adult action over- or understated. A child will clear a corner faster and wider than an adult—or run into it. When a child is prohibited from getting rid of excesses of energy—such as when walking hand-in-hand with an adult—the child will sporadically jump up and down, pull, push, skip, and drag. This excess energy can only be bottled for very short moments. Just as a colt will bounce and buck around its mother when trotting down a pasture, so a child must bolt and buck too. Like champagne, he cannot stay bottled, and if forced to do so will develop into a very dangerous animal indeed. "God protect us from the well-behaved child" is not an aphorism but a prayer.

34

If you bottle up a child's excess energy, you can create a very dangerous animal, not unlike Bob McKimson's Tasmanian Devil—a mixture of whirlwind, chainsaw, tornado, and lightningbolt striking a TNT factory.

TOINGGG!

The layout drawings a director gives to the animators must communicate what he wants to see on screen. These drawings (below and right) show a moment from DRIPALONG DAFFY (1951), demonstrating that pallbearers are ever alert for new business.

. . . .

132 takes—Th-Th-That's All Folks!

I was raised in Hollywood when the great comedians were at the top of their power, and I soon realized that—just like our temporarily demented cat Othello—what they looked like had almost nothing to do with what they were. It was how they moved that made them what they were, and to this day and forever this will be an invaluable truth in a field where truth is rare indeed. Ed Wynn undoubtedly said it best: "Comedy is not opening a funny door, it is opening a door funny." Repeat to yourself, repeat, repeat, repeat.

From 1918 to 1920, the Jones clan (including this Jones, aged six to eight) lived in an orange grove directly across from Hollywood High School on Sunset Boulevard. If I thought about the matter at all, I would not have considered myself privileged. As far as I knew, any little boy in the world could, by the simple process of sitting down on his own front steps, watch Mary Pickford ride by on a white horse as the honorary colonel of the 160th Infantry, or could, by doing nothing whatever, have the early comedy team of Ham and Bud drop in. (This was done for the sole purpose, as far as I could discern, of letting me put on Bud's wooly cowboy chaps and gun belts. He was my size in every department but the hat; his sombrero hung on my head like a garbage-can lid.) And, as far as I knew, any other boy in the selfsame world could, by walking two blocks to Charlie Chaplin's studio at La Brea Avenue and looking through an open-link fence, watch Chaplin at work, which, I am sorry to say, I often found deadly dull. I loved his films; so easy, so natural, so appealing to my sense of rebelliousness and anarchy, they were a complete contrast to the endless repetition of the filming itself, which I found almost unbearably tiresome.

One evening I lost faith in both my father and Chaplin when my father came home to tell us that he had seen Chaplin shoot a single fifteen-second scene 132 times. He was trying to perfect the little choppy run he used when he was being chased around a corner. To simulate running on ice, he put down an oilcloth and oiled it, but his feet kept going out from under him—131 times! Either my father was lying (a possibility I could not ignore) or Chaplin didn't know what he was doing (another possibility, which observation had taught me I could not ignore either).

35

"Why," I asked myself, "not do it right in the first place? Can't he learn how to

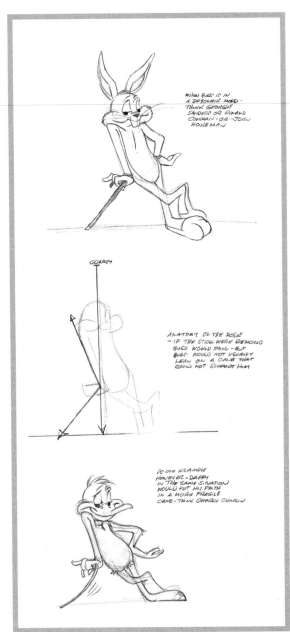

When Bugs is in a debonair mood - think George Sanders or Ronald Colman - or John Houseman

Gravity

Anatomy of the pose - if the stick were removed Bugs would fall - but Bugs would not usually lean on a cane that could not support him

As one example however - Daffy in the same situation would put his faith in a more fragile cane - think Charlie Chaplin

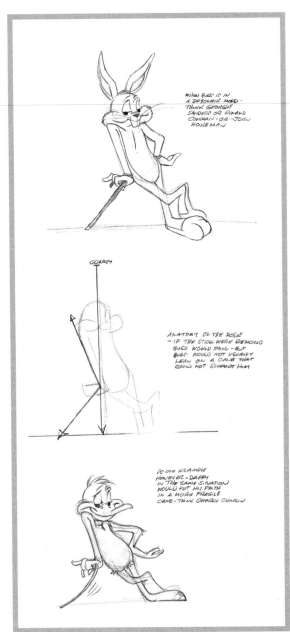

Style makes a comedian great, a style that sometimes implies great dignity coupled with impending disaster. Daffy's Chaplinesque stance when leaning on his cane is only millimeters away from the George Sanders–like Bugs's.

you birds has a hundred thousand bad drawings in you. The sooner you get rid of them, the better it will be for everybody." It was the beginning of my understanding of the two primary rules of all creativity. The first is that you must love what you are doing; the second is that you must be willing to do the often dull and tiring work necessary to bring each creative endeavor to completion, and in that endeavor only the love should show. It took Chaplin more than a hundred takes a thousand times to bring his incredible craft to the screen he loved so well, and never, never did the work show.

Style makes a comedian great, a style that implies great dignity, often coupled with impending failure. Chaplin's stance when leaning on his cane is only millimeters away from George Sanders's doing the same thing. While both show a kind of decayed elegance, Chaplin's is very close to disaster, since the cane bearing his weight is clearly not built for the job. Though it never snaps, it does fail, because Chaplin—his need for elegance contrasting with Sanders's easy and unconscious achievement of it—will plant his cane on an icy pavement, a skate, or a gangster's toe. It is not a funny cane—Chaplin uses it in a funny way.

With few exceptions, like the comic genius Emmett Kelly, great comedians, like Chaplin, are rarely clowns. They do not depend on their clothing to raise laughs, as walk-through circus clowns do. This kind of circus clown has no time to achieve style—he appears before a spectator's eyes for only a few seconds. Such a clown is to humor what Norman Rockwell is to painting. The message he is delivering must be communicated in a trice. There is no time for nuances.

The Jones family's two-year sojourn near the Chaplin studio ended in 1920, but my links with

do it by watching his own movies?" Everything was always right the first time in the movies!

But the number 132 stuck in my stubborn cerebellum like a cocklebur under a saddle, and it resurfaced when I heard a brilliant old art teacher named Francois Murphy at Chouinard Art Institute repeat to a shocked beginner class, "Every one of

When Jackie Coogan and Chaplin appeared in THE KID, something happened to me that took 50 years to bear fruit.

silent comedy were not cut. We later lived at Ocean Park, between Santa Monica and Venice, California, where the beach (about a block from our house) was constantly used as a location for the Mack Sennett bathing-beauty pictures, in which the local kids often found undemanding work as extras in crowd scenes. There was no pay, but there was a major compensation—a free lunch.

One day we heard that child star Jackie Coogan was shooting a film on the beach. He had been richly supplied with his own elegant tent, complete with shaded awning. We peered through the flap and saw this pale child in the back, all bundled up, too precious to leave out in the open. I had envied him so

much in the films, but there we were, a freckle-faced group of beach kids out in the sun chomping on hot dogs, while he was sadly drinking tea in his tent, the classic "poor little rich kid."

My allowance at eight years old was twenty-five cents a week, which was usually adequate for my simple needs. For times of extreme poverty, I had an illegal line of credit in the feeding dish of the canary cage, where my mother naively deposited any overflow of pennies in her purse. I'm quite sure we never

Bill Scott's drawing shows the canary cage in which, we contended, Leon Schlesinger confined my diminutive background artist, Bernyce Polifka, thereby saving valuable office space.

37

had a canary, but we always had a canary cage. "Just in case," I suppose. The tenant-less cage was characteristic of our household. We had dog collars of all sizes from dogs past, none of which ever fit dogs present; hamsters were not yet in fashion, but we had a dog collar that would have fitted one of those pouchy rodents—it was certainly too small for any of our cats, who would anyway have disdained such encumbering paraphernalia.

Cats did not wear collars in my day, although on days of great festivity our cat of the day was often dressed in doll's clothing (I still have the scars to prove it). We found that turtles don't take to col-

Father felt indignantly that the beach houses were too damn close to each other (300 yards). Today the land sells for $20,000 a front foot—and more!

Keaton and Lloyd could make an entire ten-minute short using only a banana skin. We were not slow to learn from them.

lars—all the turtle has to do is back out of a collar into that garage turtles leave the factory with.

My twenty-five cents a week would provide, without undue stress, an immense bag of sugary lemon drops, or equally sugary chocolate chips, or kisses (also chocolate), plus a huge "jawbreaker" about the size of a golf ball, containing succeeding lavalike linings of the most revolting colors (most attractive to a boy's furtive eyes), and still leave the funds necessary to replace a glassie or two, or maybe a metal lagger, in my marble bag and also see one or perhaps two movies a week.

The acting techniques of the silent film comedians we saw as kids reappeared in the Warner Bros. cartoons, not because we consciously imitated anyone, but because these techniques—such as the double take, or even the triple take—were simply part of the culture.

Marcel Marceau once told me that he too had learned a lot from watching Buster Keaton's movies. Since Keaton would not move his face, most of his action was done with his feet. If he felt sure of himself he would move hesitantly forward, if he was unsure he would inch back, and if he was undecided he would shuffle sideways. The comedian Jacques Tati used the same pedal technique in his magnificent Monsieur Hulot films.

The animation director needs an understanding of acting techniques, but he need not be an actor. As an animation director at Warner Bros., I would act out a cartoon's scenes in my mind before supplying the animators with drawings showing the characters' key poses. Unlike at the Disney studio, we very rarely acted out our scenes on film at Warner Bros. before animating them, although we did act in our own live-action Christmas films, which presented such dramatic episodes as "Escape to Fleischer's," in which gagman Dave Monohan attempts to break out of the studio to work on *Gulliver's Travels* in Miami and is shot by Henry Binder, our de facto business manager (Ray Katz officially held the title), who kept us from going insane and looked after our interests. Pretty broad stuff.

An animator must be able to do two things well: get inside the character, then draw it. Almost all the Warner Bros. animators used a mirror at first to check facial expressions, just as dancers will make great use of a mirror to check positions when they are studying. Eventually the tension in the muscles is enough to tell the dancer what a position *must* look like. (Dancers cannot, after all, go around with mirrors hanging around their necks all the time.) Similarly, I soon found that if

Business manager Henry Binder looked after our interests but had problems protecting his own. (Everybody thought he was rich.)

When my weight rose to almost 200 pounds, an obese Jones-like character appeared in office cartoons, such as Art Heinemann's.

I was asked to draw a look of doubt or anger, for example, I could do it without looking in a mirror. I could feel it in my fingers. There is a photograph of the great Warner Bros. animator Ken Harris with a mirror mounted behind his drawing board, although he never actually used one. Oddly enough, he always had the same twisted look on his face no matter what emotion

The great Ken Harris grimaces at the mirror he only used to comb his hair.

he was animating, and this photograph captures that strange expression.

Any acting skills I *do* have were learned from reading, from the movies, from encounters with Uncle Lynn, and from visits to vaudeville, for which I must thank my Uncle Kent. Uncle Kent was an automobile salesman in downtown Los Angeles, and whenever my brother Dick and I went to see him, he would take us to lunch and give us enough money to spend the afternoon in a theater where six or eight vaudeville acts and a film ran in the same show. Vaudeville became very important to me; watching the acts gave me a great education in gags, many of which I utilized later.

In one memorable act, the curtain rose to reveal a huge machine with countless levers, wheels, bands, and gears, all of them motionless and silent. Then the performer came on stage, carrying several drums, cornets, whistles, trombones, a concertina, and a mouth organ, and went through his one-man-band act in front of the machine, which just stood there the whole time. Throughout the performance,

39

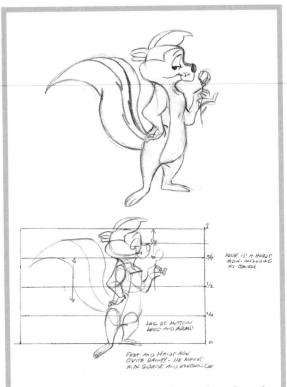

Years after I saw a vaudevillian machine
with countless levers, I used it in this 1937 Valentine
for my mother.

we wondered about that damn construction, until the music had almost finished, whereupon he pulled a lever on the machine. Instantly it sprang to life, with wheels turning and bands moving. Finally, on the far side, a tiny hammer rose and struck a small cymbal, and that was it. That was all it did; the act was over. Wonderful!

40

The author O. Henry taught me the value of the unexpected. He once wrote about the noise of flowers and the smell of birds—the birds were chickens, the flowers dried sunflowers rattling against a wall.

Bandaids decorate a plump caricature of the author, who had just come out of hospital. (We are tossing about our tiny layout artist, Bernyce Polifka.)

Reading O. Henry's short stories also developed my understanding of comedy. O. Henry taught me the value of the unexpected. For example, he wrote about being awakened in the morning by the noise of flowers and the smell of birds, then explained that sunflowers banging against the wall of the house were causing the noise, while the smell came from some odiferous chickens under the window. O. Henry is often dismissed as a sort of stand-up comedian, who could only write well enough to create clapper lines. A great deal better than that, he was one of the best raconteurs of turn-of-the-century America.

. . . .

The World Symphony . . .

The wind was from the north that bright morning in October 1922 when I set out for the Ocean Park Pier. It flattened the beach and drove curved patterns of tiny sand dunes across the great cement walk that bordered the sea.

My careful feet honored the perfection of these miniaturized dunes with as much respect as I paid to the sidewalk cracks. "Step on a line, break your mother's spine; step on a crack, break your mother's back."

I was not quite sure about the validity of this statement; many such admonitions hung uncertainly suspended in my imagination. Just *who* would break my mother's spine I had no idea. It did not require an evident executioner to justify a threat. If a threat existed, I knew too well a means would be found. So I avoided cracks and lines as a matter of caution and the dunes, I suppose, as a matter of an early love for the wonder of wild symmetry.

This caution, however, did complicate the first business of the day: acting as conductor of a world symphony, an orchestra of the cold wind, the crashing waves, and the eddying tides. The tips of the gulls' wings were black notes against the wind-white sky. I lifted my bamboo baton and cautioning hand to the elements, and each component responded to my every command, each bird hesitated, waiting for the downward slash of my wand, then sliding and swooping off into the distance: crescendos and diminuendos of such grace and beauty that my amazed heart for the first time knew that action could be translated into music. (Hello, Carl Stalling and Milt Franklyn!)

I, whose commands even dogs ignored, held the universe in the palm of my hand, the crook of my finger, the very flick of my eyebrow. All living things,

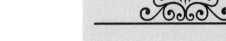

I do not know what I may appear to the world, but as to myself I seem to have been only like a boy playing on the sea-shore, and diverting myself in now and then finding a smoother pebble or prettier shell than ordinary, whilst the great ocean of truth lay all undiscovered before me.

—Isaac Newton

41

In *Baton Bunny* (1959), Bugs conducted the full Warner Bros. Symphony Orchestra in masterly fashion. Friz Freleng— who believed he could not draw well!—made a series of beautifully expressive drawings (right) during an early *Baton Bunny* story session.

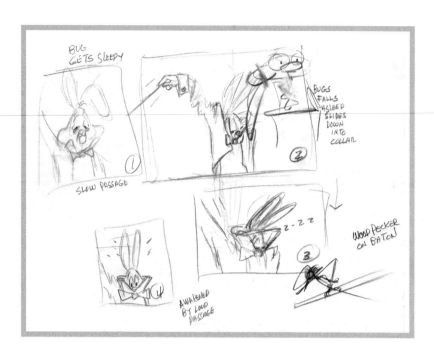

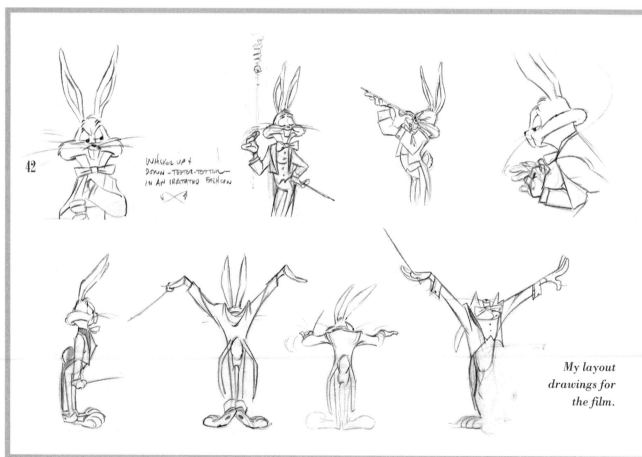

My layout drawings for the film.

including the vital and therefore living crash of the waves and the hurrying clouds were mine to command. The gulls swirling about me—diving, swerving, carving the sky—were my string section; the counterpoint a hundred sanderlings skittering along the wet sand, a multitude of tiny harps; the woodwinds sandpipers, moving as deliberately as dainty oboes. The visual bassoons were a flight of pelicans falling and rising along the wave edges to the turn of my hand, then plunging into the sea through the timpani of the breakers.

In looking back at this curiously awkward and gyrating boy conducting the universe, I cannot doubt that he was indeed one with the crying, flying gulls, the salt wind, and the triumphant crash and sobbing ebb of the great waves. Sometimes in life the ultimate triumph is the first one, and on that bright morning I was as close to being a god as I have ever since known.

· · ·

...And the Gumball Machine

I wandered out onto the pier, passing boarded-up fun houses, clangless Dodge-ems, frozen merry-go-rounds, roller coasters with cars unbothered by shrieks, quietly stabled hot dog and popcorn stands.

The clean-up crew had long ago scoured the great rough planks of the pier, clearing away all the debris of revelry. Even the air seemed somehow washed clean of the cries of the barkers, the calliope song of the carrousels, the ominous clatter of the ascending roller coaster cars, and the mutter and twitter of the crowds.

I strode penniless past sleeping kiosks, where the unheard-of wealth of nickels, dimes, and quarters would soon clash in metallic cacophony. No, not quite penniless, because I was the sole possessor of one red cent, its Indian head rubbed bright against the pocket lining of my knickerbockers. Expending this treasure most expeditiously would be the final act of my morning prowl. No candy shop was available. On Sunday on the deserted pier, the only place of business available for any purchase was a gumball machine.

The gumball machine consisted of several hundred candy-enclosed gumballs encased in a volleyball-size glass globe balanced on an iron rod protruding from a twenty-pound iron base. It would, if approached with a penny, deliver a gumball. I did not expect the gumball of my choice, but I did expect a gumball. What happened? Why, nothing! The machine ate my penny and regurgitated only air. Nothing came down the chute with the windowed door at the bottom. I had never been cheated by a gumball machine before and was stricken into momentary immobility by this monstrous injustice. Then I delivered one of my better kicks at the base of this devious fiend. This proved to be a mistake, resulting in a rather interesting one-legged dance around and about.

Squatting on the ground, I cranked my toes back to their proper, throbbing length. From this position I could, by lifting the gate of the delivery chute, peer up the tiny, dark tunnel, and to my surprise I discovered the culprit: a gumball whose crust had somehow broken and stuck to the walls of the tunnel. I carried no probing instruments of any kind about my person, but this lack of foresight was quickly remedied by a tough six-inch-long splinter torn from a pier plank. It was the inspired work of but a second to dislodge the recalcitrant gumball from its trap. I now had a shopworn but suckable, chewable bit of confection, and I

43

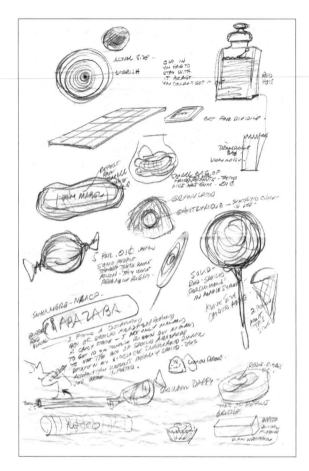

Besides gumballs, the candies of my youth included Abazabas, Red Hots, jawbreakers—some of which uncovered a tiny statue of Charlie Chaplin when you had sucked through to the core—and the strangely named chocolate bar, WHY MABEL?

turned away with renewed faith in gumball machines, giving the lever a quick, contemptuous flick for luck.

Down came a gumball! I stopped, stupefied, in mid-stride and flicked again. A whole, entire, complete, pristine gumball came rolling down the tunnel and banged against the little door. I could not believe it then; I cannot believe it now; but every time I flicked that handle—*without* the insertion of a penny—a fresh gumball emerged smiling and ille-

gally willing to be added to the trove accumulating in my pockets. Although I had pockets both fore and aft, these quickly became overstocked.

What was I to do? I was engaged in a crime of awesome proportions. I could not go publicly home with my hands openly crowded with incriminating evidence. Then, in a moment of divine inspiration, I discovered a new and surprising fact: knickerbockers could be closed tightly below the knee by the simple act of feeding a flap into a toothed metal doohickey. This was news. This was very, very, very special news. The way home was now clear. By securing my pants in this fashion, I added two new voluminous pockets, inhabited heretofore only by my legs and my underwear.

A few minutes later, a casual observer with an eye for the peculiar could have seen a small boy furtively hobbling along the sidewalk, a boy with the knees of a camel stuffed with gravel, a boy so obviously guilty of something that any passerby would have been quick to make a citizen's arrest, if there had been citizens about to do so.

I managed to reach home without accident or incident, and to get up the stairs without arousing the suspicion of my parents or the interest of my siblings, either calamity being sufficient to deprive me of some, if not all, of my ill-gotten wealth.

Propping a chair against the doorknob (there were no locks on the doors of children's bedrooms; privacy was reserved for adults), I divested myself of my treasure-laden pants, being careful not to stir the enemy by dropping any gumballs on the floor, and stored them all beneath my bed in a small chest that *did* have a lock. The only evidence of my crime I was now aware of seemed to be the palms of my hands—apparently I had anticipated Jackson Pollock by

Jones mènage (1935) carefully recorded by a grotesquely inept artist.

some thirty years. No amount of scrubbing would remove the brilliant dye intended to discolor boys' tongues, so at dinner I was careful to keep these gaily caparisoned palms flat to the table and so to momentarily escape detection.

However, Mother, in one of her more motherly moods, brought up a new book just as I was disrobing for bed. To my surprise and her horror, my exposed knees looked like they had been designed by Egon Schiele. They were garishly interwoven with all the colors of a demented rainbow: a tasteful background of blue green and brownish purple, heavily speckled with spots of bilious yellow, butterfly blue, and nacreous parsnip.

My mother seldom fainted, in an era when fainting was considered *de rigueur* in circumstances much less traumatic than these, but I think she flirted with the idea. "If I can't faint on an occasion like this," she might have said to herself, "when, may I ask, can I faint?"

I tried to persuade her that there was nothing alarming or even unusual about my knees, but, of course, this line of thought only brought Father onto the scene—a confrontation I would have cheerfully avoided. To my surprise, he laughed at my garish legs. Mother was furious with him and mentioned gangrene as a strong possibility. Father assured her

Fashion à la mode (1924).

that self-respecting gangrene would no more settle on my knees than it would on those of a skeleton. Gangrene, he said, would starve on my knees. He further said that he had never dared hope that anything or anyone could improve the looks of my knees, and here I had done it all by myself. An early admirer of Seurat, he felt only a whisper of sadness that we could not share my knees with Georges. He said my knees pursued pointillism to its logical three-dimensional extreme.

I had to bribe my brother and sisters with gumballs for almost a month to keep the truth from Mother, but never before or since have I had enough, indeed a surfeit, of something I really loved.

. . .

Several years after this juvenile crime, when I was about fourteen years old, Uncle Lynn and I had a discussion about morality. I had just discovered the Ten Commandments, and I had also just discovered that girls and adultery were both desirable and forbidden,

The house on Kulli Street, later poetically renamed Buena Vista Terrace. Kulli was more accurate.

Ali Baba Bunny (1957)

and that some of my teachers would be better off murdered, which unhappily was also unlawful. The only commandment I was certain I had not broken and probably would not break was the one forbidding the making of a graven image. (Little did I anticipate that it would take 5,000 images to make a six-minute animated cartoon.)

"Well," Uncle Lynn said, "I can give you a pretty good reason for not committing murder."

"How?" I asked. I was genuinely interested.

"Because," he replied, "according to Mark Twain, when you commit a murder, it will most certainly lead to other crimes. You might next bear false witness, or practice usury, or lift a hotel towel, and one day find yourself telling a lie, a lie that might be traced back to a murder you didn't think much about at the time."

He had a way of doing this. A way, I suppose, that helped me immeasurably toward becoming an animator, a method that started with the ridiculous and revealed a truth. So I asked him, "What is truth? What's so great about truth?"

"Truth," he said, "is great, because truth is what you cannot help thinking."

Hollow "YOU'RE GOING TO HAVE TO PAY FOR THIS, RALPH PHILLIPS!!

Truth is what you cannot help thinking. This frightened me; it still frightens me, just as always. Bare honesty is a wondrous and frightening thing.

. . .

The Nomenclature of Academics and Other Matters Academic

The vice-principal of Franklin High in Highland Park, California, was named Mr. Sniffen. Now, if you take a name like that for granted, chances are you'll never be an animator. "Mr. Sniffen." It simply won't hold up. It is a title that droops at the end. Like Cleveland Pink, whose name I stumbled happily over many years later. Pink. A sad little comma of a surname after such a grand beginning: Cleveland. Vice-Principal Sniffen. I don't recall his first name, if he had one.

But the point is: none of his students—in fact, nobody else—thought anything about it. The name aroused no feeling, no response of any kind among my fellow students. None. Zero. His surname could have been Noodlefork or Turtlehips or Pink, and I'm sure nobody would have noticed. I suppose they thought of anyone's name—if they thought of it at all—as a generic title; he was the only vice-principal they knew, and perhaps all vice-principals throughout the world were named Mr. Sniffen. Boys' vice-principals that is. We had a girls' vice-principal also: Miss Lucretia B. Van de Kamp. No kidding. *Lucretia! B.!* For *Borgia*! And no one saw anything incongruous about that either, although there was a Van de Kamp company that canned beans for a living—very popular. But no association, no perception of an oddity here among our student body. As far as I know, only my sister Dorothy and I ever envisaged Miss Lucretia B. Van de Kamp moonlighting in another career dosing bean cans with cyanide.

Mr. English taught English, and this was to me fully appropriate. He taught English the old-fashioned way: his students *earned* it. He taught them to love the English language by speaking it, by reading it, by listening to it as a music lover listens lovingly to music. Even the dullest clods found his devotion catching. It was impossible not to do so. He

47

To be filed in Department of Irrelevant Information:

MY 4½ YEAR OLD DAUGHTER HAS A TURTLE WHOSE NAME IS

GOSSAMER

Paul Julian's informative note on naming a turtle, which I found useful later for my shaggy monster.

did not teach words, he taught the *meaning* of words as a structure, how words alone meant nothing, but that the right word in the right place meant everything and was well worth searching for. "The difference between the right word and *almost* the right word," said Mark Twain's endorsement of Mr. English, "is the difference between lightning and the lightning bug." It is seldom that love and respect command our devotion to the same end, but without these two in tandem, language cannot be really understood. That is what Mr. English taught, and seventy years later his teaching remains as vivid as it was in 1926. Mr. English is not only a name, it is and will always be, to me, a proud and worthy title.

. . .

Rhett Who?

"Chuck Jones" as a name to conduct symphonies? To build empires? To win Scarlett O'Hara?

Really now, can you imagine Scarlett O'Hara falling for anybody named Chuck Jones, or even Chuck Butler, or Rhett Jones? What is it about "Rhett" that will dress up the most ordinary surnames so elegantly? But Rhett Jones? Still, better than Chuck Jones. Chuck Jones in a lovers' contest with Ashley Wilkes is no contest at all.

Another problem, of course, was that at thirteen I didn't look like Rhett Butler, unless you considered Rhett Butler's skeleton the essence of his beauty. I looked like Ichabod Crane studying to be a parsnip. "Gawky" would have been considered a compliment. "Tatterdemalion" might have worked nicely except I wasn't ragged, not much of a plus, to be sure, but anything is a plus when you're clutching at straws.

At 6'1", tipping the scales, fully clothed, at 123 pounds, I was a boy without a frontal view. All I had was a profile. As I remember it, I had only one profile. There wasn't room for two profiles on my bony skull. However, what I lacked in gladsome features I made up in Adam's apple, and, in spite of what has been aforesaid, for some illogical reason I wore a large, 7¾ hat, with a stringy number ten neck to prettily hold it up. My father also wore a 7¾ hat, but he had a seventeen-inch neck. We could companionably exchange hats, but his shirts hung over my xylophonic rib cage like Mother Hubbard's Mother Hubbard, a sight to cause trembly old ladies to tremble and miniature poodles to leave miniature puddles here and there.

"There was this friend of Bill Nye's," said Uncle Lynn in response to my complaint that I was too skeletally skinny to play football. "Man named Mick E. Morbid. Only had one leg, yet"—he scratched a bit of seaborne tar off his big toe with a Malayan dagger—"that man could play the trombone so beautifully it brought tears to the eyes of angels."

It seemed an insufficient answer to me. Uncle Lynn's rationality bordered sometimes on the ob-

48

Jones? Jones? Who's Jones?

*A director reacts
indifferently
to a story idea
promulgated by
Bill Scott.
Result: suicide.*

scure. The logic in comparing my thirteen-year-old, six-foot-tall, 123-pound frame with a one-legged man whose trombone playing sent angels a-sobbing brought no solace to my rickety frame, and I said so.

"Any tar on your toe?" asked Uncle Lynn solicitously.

I was not to be diverted by toes or tar. "What has my playing football got to do with a one-legged trombone tootler?"

Art Heinemann's flattering caricature of me and my doppelgänger.

"He didn't tootle," Uncle Lynn said reprovingly, placing a bit of tar on my big toe. "He *played* the trombone. Artists *play*, amateurs *tootle.*"

"May I borrow your knife?" I was upset about the tar, not about his response, which was always refreshingly arcane, unlike other adults' absolutes, such as: "You can do anything you want if you only try hard enough. You know what's wrong with you, don't you? You're lazy."

"It's not a knife," said Uncle Lynn, handing it to me, "it's a Swiss Army Malay kris—very useful for cutting cuticles or throats. As for rationality, I never knew anything that was rational that made any sense. But to answer your question without being rational, it may be helpful to know that he had been a slack-wire tap dancer in the center ring of the next-to-greatest-show-on-earth: The Sells/Floto Circus. And one evening, when he went out to perform, he found to his surprise that he only had one leg. Couldn't remember losing it. It's the sort of thing most people would probably notice. But he did instantly realize that his days as a slack-wire tap dancer were probably about over. Well, what to do? He suddenly remembered some-

49

old Mick E. bent a little too far down to the tanbark in one of his riffs from his seat in the orchestra and scooped up in the loop of his slide a performing fox terrier by the neck.

"The indignant yelps of the dog as it slid back and forth in the trombone's slide turned to barks of the utmost pleasure when—being a dedicated actor himself—the dog heard the roars of appreciation from the crowd, who in their innocence had never seen a flapping fox terrier as part of a one-legged slack-wire trombonist act. Novelty is the very essence of success in circus life, and **THE ONE-AND-ONLY ONE-LEGGED TERRIER-STRICKEN TROMBONIST ACT IN THE WORLD** floated Sells/Floto almost to the empyrean level of the Ringling Brothers and Barnum & Bailey Circus (separated at that time, to amalgamate later in order to meet the competition). As I said, goes to show you."

"Goes to show me *what?*" I really was confused. Enchanted, but confused.

thing that had slipped his mind (as it might naturally slip from anybody's): he'd studied trombone for fourteen years in high school (he was a little slow in academics) and graduated with honors, summa cum laude in brass accomplishment. The envy of all, he became the only slack-wire, terrier-stricken trombonist in the world. Goes to show you."

"Goes to show me what?" I was entertained, sympathetic, but puzzled. "And whattaya mean 'terrier-stricken trombonist'?"

"What happened was," said Uncle Lynn, peeling an orange skin in such a circuitous way that he could, by taking the end piece and whirling it dexterously around his head like a bolo, strip the orange clean and catch it in midair, "one day

50

"Ain't I a stinker?"

"Exactly," said Uncle Lynn, looking as though I wasn't the idiot child everyone thought me to be, but rather the idiot savant he knew me to be. "'What' is exactly what I was trying to demonstrate. You're too old to be a moppet, but if you were, you'd be a very smart one. Now then, you have two legs, so you can't be a one-legged slack-wire trombonist, with or without a fox terrier. So we must seek a more likely avocation. Now with your name—'Chuck,' that is—you can never be a concert glockenspielist or probably even a world-class kazoo artist. No, 'Chuck Jones,' I think, limits you to one of two professions: you must either be a second baseman or a cartoonist. Do you agree?"

"But, but, I can't hit, and I can't field, and I don't own a glove."

"Hm." Uncle Lynn studied me carefully. "Do you need a glove to draw?"

"No, but I thought we were talking about baseball," I protested.

"No, we were talking about what you *can* do," said Uncle Lynn, working his corkscrew magic on another orange. "You *can* draw better than a lot of your friends, even the valedictorians, who will no doubt end up as ribbon clerks."

"But I'm not in the same class as Tad Dorgan or Jimmy Swinnerton."

"And at thirteen Babe Ruth wasn't in the same class with Christy Mathewson or Ty Cobb, who preceded him."

"But, but"—I was big on "buts" that morning—"I don't have talent. You have to be born with talent."

Uncle Lynn looked at me as though my intellect was suspect, which I felt it was. "You mean Babe Ruth was born with the ability to hit home runs? He once said that when he was a pitcher he struck out or flied out 843 times before he hit his first single, and it was a bunt."

Come on. What was all the nonsense about a slack-wire trombonist act? And Babe Ruth? What did *that* have to do with *me* not being able to play baseball?

And Charlie Chaplin shooting one fifteen-second scene 132 times. Did that apply? Look, I loved Uncle Lynn—but could it be? Could it be that he knew more than any living man I ever knew? Could he flush wisdom out of the bushes where one-legged trombonists lived with talented fox terriers?

Hm.

Chuck Jones (age 4) and a pile of cobblestones.

51

WEST COAST STUDIO

Warner Club

It's Not Too Late To Give To The Red Cross

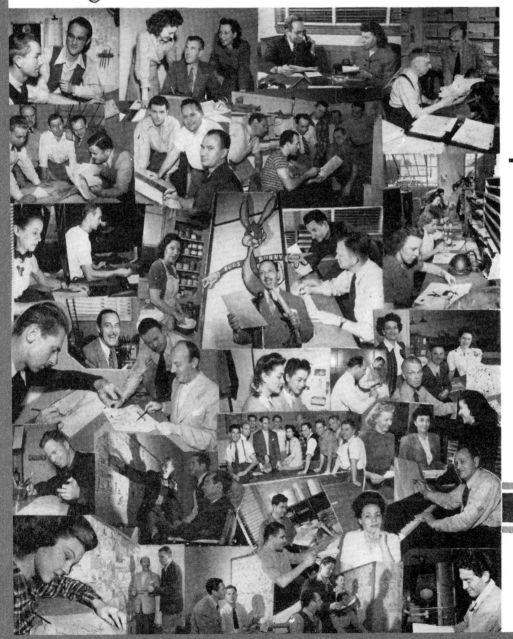

NEWS

★

**APRIL
1945**

★

**THE
CARTOON
STUDIO**

MY LIFE IN AN ANIMATION DUMP

But yield who will to their separation,
my object in living is to unite
my avocation and my vocation
as my two eyes make one in sight.

—*Robert Frost*

*I*n 1928 I was unceremoniously jerked from Benjamin Franklin High School's womb and installed equally unceremoniously into Chouinard Art Institute (pronounced "shuh-nard," as in "hunh," or "chow-nard," as in "chow-chow," the dog, and later pronounced "California Institute of the Arts"). My two sisters—Dorothy, who favored "shuh," and Peggy, who favored "chow"—accompanied me in this whim of my father's. His whimsy was usually as fragile as a butter-fly's wing; most of his whimsies fluttered along the rim of disaster. Just installing all three of us into the finest art school west of the Pecos was in his eyes all that was needed financially. I think my father's theory, as usual, was that if your foot can find the first stone, you can walk on water the rest of the way. So the subsequent sums needed for tuition and materials would obviously

be supplied by a benevolent Nature satisfied with my father's initial investment.

I don't quite remember how remaining in art school without financial support worked for my sisters, but benevolent Nature (in one of her expansive moods) secured for me a late-night job (a smidgen different from that of a Carson or a Letterman) as a janitor-third-class in a building infested with cigar-sucking and cigar-chewing real-estate men. The 2:00 A.M. streetcar took me to this malodorous monument, where I worked for four hours before school.

After the day's classes, I worked a second janitorial job, at Chouinard. Mrs. Nelbert N. Chouinard—who was always kind to dumb crea-tures—took pity on me by giving me what was called "a working scholarship" or "janitorial." Fortunately,

In 1930, *everybody* smoked cigarettes. When I was a student at Chouinard Art Institute, even the life models, with acres of non-sparkproof skin at risk, puffed a cigarette every half-hour.

54

none of the teachers or students smoked cigars, so there were no gloomy spittoons to clean out, only trash barrels. Of course, everybody smoked cigarettes. Curious but true, *everybody* smoked cigarettes. Even the life models were allowed a cigarette break every half-hour, and *every* female model I remember took it—robe loosely draped across her shoulders, carefully avoiding dropping ashes or coals on her exposed facade. This, I suppose, could be classified as a job-related hazard. Sexual harassment—the hazard that in the eyes of the public would seem to be uppermost for a nude girl—simply didn't exist. Some of my fellow students, after spending two and three years drawing unclothed models with a sexual disinterest that would have boggled the studs of the outer world, found no contradiction in spending the rest of their lives trying to get the clothes off of *all* the women in the world who were *not* models. Tomcats of some reputation have been known to tip their hats as these lascivious wolves snarled by.

After finding that I could look at a nude model with the same lack of emotional interest as I would any other object set before me to draw, one day I drew a cautious breath and looked around at my fellow students and *their* work. Jesus Christ! I was in a nest of Michelangelos, Titians, and Degases! I looked feverishly around the old carriage-house art studio and couldn't find a mouse hole small enough to accept my scarletly embarrassed carcass. The following weeks only solidified my belief that I was a left-footed bumpkin in a field of Nijinskis. I crept in humiliated despair to my friend, the classic Uncle

I remember with surprise that I spent years drawing unclothed models ("nude," not "naked") with a sexual disinterest that would have boggled the belief of the Ancient and Dishonorable Studs of the World.

Lynn, who was eating a piece of pie backward—that is, from the blunt end to the point. He listened to my pliant, sobbing dismissal of myself as a miserable midget in a field of graphic giants.

"You can't," I sobbingly pointed out with seemingly inflexible logic, "make a racehorse out of a pig!"

"True, true," responded Uncle Lynn, squashing a bit of pumpkin between the tines of his fork and disposing of same. "You

Moderately fast pig

can't, as you put it convincingly, make a racehorse out of a pig. But," he said, cutting himself another piece of pie, "you can make a mighty fast pig."

That did it. This was a destiny I could live with. *Memoirs of a Mighty Fast Pig* could well be the ideal title for this unvarnished volume.

56

. . .

I Was a Teen-Age Thumb

Why didn't I prepare myself for a career by going to an animation school? Simple. I did not go to an animation school because at that time no school in the world taught animation. What I did not know then, but do know now, is that at Chouinard Art Institute I received the best possible education for my future as an animator and an animation director.

What I did not know then, but do know now, is that the ability to draw the human body in simple graphic terms—with the simple single line—is the best possible tool for any career in graphic arts.

At Chouinard, I concentrated on drawing the human figure and getting a rough idea of the body's bone structure. I had no plans to become a doctor, but I wanted to know how the hand worked, and what it would do.

The ability to draw the human body in simple graphic terms—with the simple single line—is the best possible tool for a career in graphic arts. THE DOT AND THE LINE (1965) (drawing opposite) brought me an Academy Award and a photo opportunity (left) with Elke Sommer, Don Knotts, and my co-producer, Les Goldman.

How do you draw a hand? If you are right-handed, you use your left hand as a model, and if you are left-handed, you draw your right hand. You look at it, draw it from different angles, examine it. In learning how it works, you will learn how to draw. You will learn how to draw because you are developing the very tool that makes the drawings. Everything created by Leonardo da Vinci or Jackson Pollock, every building in the world, all depend on our ability to hold two fingers together and grasp an object. Everything we do depends on that ability to grasp, and no other animal has it, because no other animal has the opposed thumb and forefinger. And that's the magic.

When a young artist asked me for advice on drawing the human foot, I told him, "The first thing you must learn is how to take your shoe off, and then how to take your sock off, then prop your leg up carefully on your other knee, take a piece of paper, and draw your foot."

Aside from the great and legendary teacher Fran-

For a quick cure for over-sentimentalizing, remember Christopher Morley's description of the human being as "an ingenious assembly of portable plumbing."

cois Murphy, we had at Chouinard arguably the finest teacher in America—perhaps the world—of the fine art of drawing the human figure. Don Graham could, like Francois Murphy, teach without imposing or even revealing his own style of drawing. This is not an easy thing to understand, but it is the hallmark of great art teachers. I never saw a Don Graham drawing until after he died.

After I became a director of animated films, I attended Don Graham's Monday night master classes for about ten years. One evening I was struggling unsuccessfully to draw a model's leg as it faced me head on, rather like the pointing arm in the famous World War I recruiting poster: "I Want You for the U.S. Army." "Having problems?" Don asked, and I explained that I couldn't draw that leg. "Chuck," he said, "can you imagine any time, anywhere, whatever you are illustrating, when you might have occasion to draw a head-on view of a leg in that position? You are movable, and the leg is movable. Never learn to draw anything that you have no reason to need to draw." It is all too easy to drive yourself crazy trying to draw things that you will never need. It was a wonderful lesson.

Head-on views are rarely useful in animation. Even a slightly three-quarter view of the human face is more interesting. Furthermore, the chances are that you will draw a head-on face with identical left and right sides, even flipping the drawing over to be sure the eyes on the two sides match. In fact, the human face is never symmetrical. *Life* magazine once showed a series of faces they had created by replacing the left side of each face with a mirror image

of the right. They all looked either inhuman or criminally insane.

Except for their skulls, all vertebrates—including man—have pretty much the same skeletal and musculoskeletal structure. Lengthen or shorten a few bones, and man and bear are brothers under the skin. Going to the zoo to sketch animals is made a lot easier (not simpler) by this knowledge. To repeat the

words of the great illustrator Albert Hurter in a talk with Disney animators on how to draw and move dinosaurs in *Fantasia:* "Show me the skeleton of an animal, and I will tell you how it must move."

Few people realize that our bodies have a lot in common with the turtle's. The human rib cage is like the turtle's shell, and as far as the animator is concerned, it is just as rigid, as the ribs cannot move individually. The turtle's neck comes out of its shell in much the same way that ours emerges above the breastbone, and if you know this, you will never make the mistake of drawing the neck in the wrong place. Go ahead, feel your own neck. If *you* can't feel it, who can?

Feeling yourself helps you draw. It is also fun, of course. Get to know the bones of your own body, and you will find the same bones in any animal at the zoo or the natural history museum: elephant, alligator, dinosaur, or shrew.

So, as the artist saunters up to a bear cage, he is not sauntering empty-handed or empty-brained. He knows the animal (be it bear or mouse) has the follow-

58

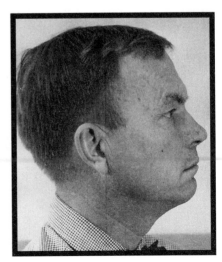

The human face is never symmetrical. If you photographically replace the left side of a face with a mirror image of the right side, it will almost certainly look inhuman or criminally insane. I could achieve the insane look even in profile.

Throughout my life, I have visited the great San Diego Zoo, watching and drawing in order to learn the intimate structure of animals.

ing equipment: a rib cage (we care not how many ribs); a backbone (with or without the extension known as the tail); usually a neck (the giraffe has the same number of vertebrae there as we have; for more, look to the owl, who, for reasons of its own, needs to look backward); a bowl-shaped pelvis to hook onto the hammock that connects to the rib cage; the hammock in which vertebrates carry around all the machinery that keeps the animal alive and in motion (but the artist can ignore the whole interior matter). Then, of course, there are the appendages, which the artist does care about—arms, legs, containing and dependent on the vari-shaped ulnas, tibias, fibulas, etc.

The artist must pay particular attention to the skull. Although most mammals have a brain pan and lower jaw, the differences pretty much start there.

From munchers to snappers to grinders, the animal's diet is valuable information to an artist. (Show me what an animal chews, and I'll show you what kind of jaw and tooth structure it must have.)

The carnivores need three-dimensional vision to pinpoint moving prey, so the eyes must be forward in the skull, with no interference from the nose: witness the hawk and the shark, as well as the wolf, the dog, the tiger, and the man. In contrast, the herbivores have two-dimensional vision—their food (grass, leaves) doesn't move, and their eyes are set far back in the skull. Why? Because the herbivores are the food source to the carnivores. With eyes near the back of the head, chickens, codfish, and deer can quickly discern who is coming up from behind to make a meal of them.

When I was making *The White Seal,* I had to find out the difference between the warm-blooded sea mammals and the fishes. It turned out to be simple: fishes' tails are in a vertical plane, whereas mammals tails are horizontal.

Wondering why, I went to the zoo to visit the seals. On a seal's tail flippers I saw little toe nails and realized that these were his feet.

Fish cannot be caricatured. Nature has already imagined every funny-looking personality. The skate family, for example, anticipated Picasso by millions of years. Although these flatfish spend their lives cruising around on their side, they are born upright, with eyes on each side of the head like any other fish. Gradually one eye crawls over to join the other, so that a diver staring down at the ocean floor sees a mouth in profile and two eyes on the same side—just like a Picasso portrait. This arrangement lets the fish look up for enemies, and if he wants to look for food, he just flips over.

60

The animator knows that an animal, be it bear or mouse, has a rib cage, a backbone (with or without a tail extension), usually a neck—and the giraffe has the same number of vertebrae there as we have—and a bowl-shaped pelvis.

If Picasso had been an animator, he might have illustrated Elmer's "Oh dear, I've killed the wabbit. Poor witto bunny . . ." from WHAT'S OPERA, DOC? *(1957) in this fashion. Bugs is pointing out to the audience the magnificence of his performance, while Elmer's eyes recall a flatfish.*

Although animals are structurally similar, it is unwise to make assumptions about any animal. Most people might believe that a snake is perfectly circular in cross-section, but its underside has to be flat to improve contact with the ground as it moves. (Similarly, an automobile tire may look round in its natural state, but it flattens down under the weight of the car to provide grip on the road surface.)

This is the type of basic knowledge an artist finds useful when sketching animals. But, as Grim Natwick once said about animation, "The animator needs about ten thousand tools—*one* of them is an understanding of how a horse trots, subdivided into fat horse, old horse, limp horse, colt—" Memory is a toolbox; creativity is something new, born through the use of the tools found inside.

Having mastered the horse and its various motions, you can consider the rabbit, instantly raising the question, "What kind of a rabbit?" Who is he? What does he have in mind? Where is he going? Is he

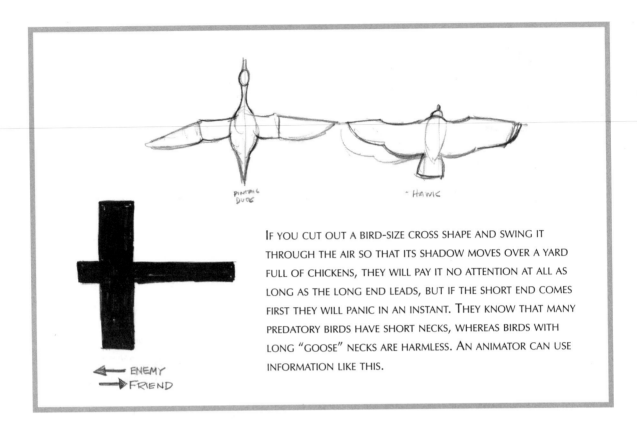

PINTAIL DUCK

~ HAWK

← ENEMY
→ FRIEND

IF YOU CUT OUT A BIRD-SIZE CROSS SHAPE AND SWING IT THROUGH THE AIR SO THAT ITS SHADOW MOVES OVER A YARD FULL OF CHICKENS, THEY WILL PAY IT NO ATTENTION AT ALL AS LONG AS THE LONG END LEADS, BUT IF THE SHORT END COMES FIRST THEY WILL PANIC IN AN INSTANT. THEY KNOW THAT MANY PREDATORY BIRDS HAVE SHORT NECKS, WHEREAS BIRDS WITH LONG "GOOSE" NECKS ARE HARMLESS. AN ANIMATOR CAN USE INFORMATION LIKE THIS.

dawdling or striding purposefully? If he is running, is he chasing or being chased? This is an important distinction, as the attitude of a character in pursuit is quite different from the same character being pursued: one is determined, the other panicky; the hunter leans forward, like an engine driving toward his victim, whereas the hunted animal arches its back as it tries to increase the distance between them.

There is no such thing as a standard walk for Bugs, for Daffy, or for anyone. Bugs strolls at about twelve frames per step, but if retreating in embarrassment from an armed adversary or a sixteen-foot abominable snowman, his first step might be twenty-four frames, speeding up to four frames before he breaks into a blur run in sheer panic.

Observation is the animator's bread and butter. The animator always keeps his eyes open and observes. Nothing can be taken for granted, and there is nothing, no matter how simple, that is not of interest to his curious mind. The only thing the animator

62

BLUE COLOR

STRIPE

GUM

INSIDE MOUTH

LIP

TONGUE

*Show me what kind of diet a carnivore enjoys, and I can make a reasonable graphic guess about the way his jaw and dental structure **must** be.*

All mammals (our chief concern) have a fairly simple brain pan, varying mainly in size. The identifying differences are in the nasal structure and the lower jaw.

takes for granted is that most people take most things for granted. The animator will never assume that he knows how Bugs Bunny—or anybody else— walks, because every walk by everybody is different every time.

In timing a film, we used to think that sneaks were basically slow. This was great for animators—thirty-six to forty-eight drawings for a single step—but it was sheer hell for the pace of the picture. And after all, what is the sneak's priority? To escape detection, and

minimal visibility offers the best chance of remaining undetected. So the fast tiptoe came into being, and the pace of what could be a lethargic sequence quickened. Going from tree to tree, doorway to doorway, in four-frame steps to the twanging of a single violin string looked, sounded, and *felt* right.

Similarly, a skip is just a step with a hop in the middle, but you can't animate the skip until you know *who* is skipping. A giant skips unlike a girl on her way to school, even though both are expressing joy. The girl will swing lightly through the movement, adding a roll from side to side, like a ship bobbing on the ocean, as she does not mind wasting energy, but the giant will land heavily on every hop.

Every great artist must begin by learning to draw with the single line, and my advice to young animators is to learn how to live with that razor-sharp instrument of art. An artist who comes to me with eight or ten good drawings of the human figure in simple lines has a good chance of being hired. But I will tell the artist who comes with a bunch of drawings of Bugs Bunny to

In this incident from BULLY FOR BUGS (1953), the difference in attitude between the pursuer and the pursued is the essence of the whole matter. In all the years I directed Bugs Bunny, I never found that I could repeat the exact same run from one picture to another.

The more weight that is exerted on a flat surface, the flatter and more distinct the base line becomes. Finster (a fake baby, below) and my grandson, Craig (right), both demonstrate this phenomenon.

All of us must learn that the **how** is what we have to learn, until action happens without thought. A baby learning to stand up and walk wonders where its hands and feet should go, and the same is true of anyone learning how to drive a car or how to draw. Eventually, it becomes second nature. Left and right: My grandson, Todd, works it out.

In timing a film, we used to assume that sneaks move slowly. This was great for animators—thirty-six to forty-eight drawings for a single step—but it was sheer hell for the pace of the picture. So the rapid tiptoe was invented.

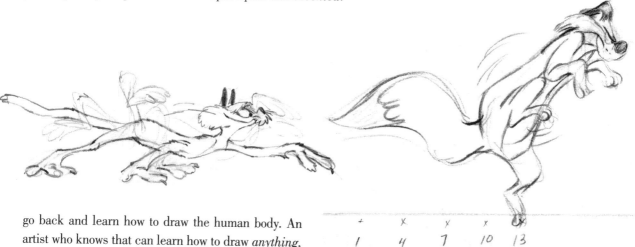

+   x   x   x   ⊗
1   4   7   10   13

go back and learn how to draw the human body. An artist who knows that can learn how to draw *anything*, including Bugs Bunny.

The *how* is the thing you have to learn until you can do it without thinking. A baby learning to stand up and walk spends its time wondering where its hands and feet go, and the same is true of learning how to ski, how to drive a car, or how to draw. Eventually it becomes second nature.

If you can draw with that vital single line, I can help you learn to animate, but I probably cannot if you come to me as a cartoonist harnessed to a graphic style. Style—essential for the strip cartoonist—is the death stroke to the animator. The animator must be able to move from style to style, with the same confidence as an Alec Guinness, a Laurence Olivier, a Helen Hayes, or a Meryl Streep moving from role to role. My animators have in their time with me found it necessary to animate in the drawing style of Dr. Seuss, of Raoul Dufy, of Walt Kelly, of Cruikshank, and of Beatrix Potter, as well as animating the antic actions of Bugs Bunny, Daffy Duck, and the myriad of other

There is no substitute for drawing.

Fiery riverboat gambler Colonel Shuffle was Bugs Bunny's adversary in MISSISSIPPI HARE (1949).
Like all Warner Bros. characters, he had his individual style of movement and thinking and was subject
to the restrictions of his skeletal structure.

Warner Bros. characters, each of whom has an individual style of movement and of thinking, all subject to the restrictions of their own skeletal structures. The same rules apply to animated characters as to all other animals, so in having gained at Chouinard a fairly solid understanding of drawing the human figure, I unknowingly was far better prepared for animation than I remotely suspected.

The thousands—the hundreds of thousands—of drawings done in art school are to the artist what the countless hours of practice are to the pianist. Without the willingness and the devotion to endure those years of repetitive frustration necessary to find the difference between surface cleverness and a visual understanding of honest draftsmanship, you are lost. Without that understanding, the chances of true graphic competence are nil. There is no substitute for drawing.

The Left Turn at Albuquerque and How I Missed It

Equipped with no practical knowledge of commercial art, I came out of Chouinard Art Institute in June 1930 into the hopeless heart of the Depression, into a world where even the most skillful of practiced workers could not find even the vestige of employment, where fine commercial artists—if they were lucky—dug ditches.

At that said time, my horizon was uncluttered by any ephemeral misconceptions about getting a job drawing. Drawing? The only thing I could draw was the human figure (undraped), and that not very well. No, what I hopelessly hoped for was a *job;* a permanent job, that fleeting, elusive, amorphous thing I had heard about but never experienced, in which some patron *paid* you to do something. In my shabby little appraisal of myself, I could discover no reason why anybody would want to avail themselves of my services.

After almost two years of being in-between—hired, fired, hired, fired—and a brush with Bohemia, I was eventually accepted as a *real* in-betweener at the Leon Schlesinger studio in Hollywood.

These were the qualifications I brought to the Schlesinger studio:

1. Six months as a first-class (perhaps world-class) cel washer for the Ub Iwerks studio. This was a humble job, and of course my friends thought I was scrubbing prison cells. At the time, art was cheap and celluloid expensive—each cel cost seven cents, and there could be four thousand reuseable cels when a film was finished. The drawings on the cels were considered worthless, and my job was to wash them off, which quickly taught me the artist's place in the pecking order. I was never tempted to keep any cels, even from the studio's Flip the Frog cartoons. The price of celluloid soon dropped, and the cel-washing craft vanished, but not before I had unknowingly added to the rarity value driving the market in animation cels today.

2. Five months as a third-class cel painter, at the increasingly dissatisfied Ub Iwerks studio. (Did you ever spell that surname backward?) The studio did not ask me to wash clean the cels I had painted; they employed somebody else to do it.

The author at Manhattan Beach, c. 1936.

3. Two months as a fourth-class cel inker. There were some great inkers, and I was not one of them. The "Nutcracker Suite" sequence in *Fantasia* includes some very precise and beautiful inking work done with fine brushes, showing the inker's art at its best. However, inkers often lost the character of an animator's line in transferring it to a cel. When the arrival of photocopying allowed the animator's drawing to be reproduced directly on the cel, the advantages in doing away with a middleman (or -woman) inker were instantly obvious. Most inking was not creative work, and I quickly decided that I did not want to be an inker. It was not for this that I had been to art school. The hypnosis of boredom forced me, in order to exist at all, to learn to ink while napping, which failed to charm Ub Iwerks, so in sheer desperation he promoted me to in-betweener (known as an assistant animator in more glorious times to come).

4. A six-month stint as an in-betweener, where finally (he was a long-suffering and kindly man, besides being a genius of animation) Ub Iwerks fired me for (again) napping.

5. The term "failure went to his head" might well have been written about this unborn animator who went, as an in-betweener, to the following animation studios:

(a) The Walt Lantz studio at Universal, where the legendary early animator Bill Nolan and the now-sainted Tex Avery resided. The embryonic genius Preston Blair was also there, sleepily brooding over his future triumphs: "Dance of the Hours" in *Fantasia*, and Tex Avery's *Red Hot Riding Hood* at MGM. I guess I wasn't a very good in-betweener, and Walt Lantz promptly fired me. In fact, he fired me twice. A few months after the initial firing, I returned to the studio to visit a friend, and Walt re-fired me. I told

him apologetically that I probably deserved to be fired twice, but that unfortunately he couldn't do it, since I didn't work there.

(b) The George Winkler studio (Felix the Cat), where I tried to pass off a sheaf of Bill Nolan's animation as my own. To nobody's surprise, I was fired again.

Warner Bros. was not alone in housing their animation units in dilapidated shacks. Even Disney's early buildings were reminiscent of Termite Terrace. MGM broke the mold, attracting animators with this fine building for their unit, photographed in 1946. Fred Quimby can be seen in the window, wondering, perhaps, why there is a gun in the foreground.

(c) The Ub Iwerks studio, where Ub, having apparently abandoned his memory when he moved to Beverly Hills from Western Avenue in Hollywood, hired (rhymes with "fired") me again to act as an inbetweener to the truly great Grim Natwick.

Besides being a great and versatile animator, creating both Betty Boop and Snow White herself, Grim was a magnificent linear draftsman (probably the first one any of us had encountered in animation), and we stood in awe of him when we weren't clandestinely rifling his wastebasket for his discards.

When we met at Ub Iwerks studio, Grim was an

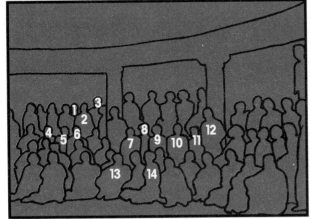

Ub Iwerks Studio, Beverly Hills, c. 1935
1. *Bob Holdeman, scenic designer;*
2. *My sister, Margaret (Peggy) Jones-Hammer, inker/teacher, who married Bill Hammer, sculptor;* 3. *Frank Tashlin, Terrytoon/Warner Bros./Columbia, live-action director of Jerry Lewis films;* 4. *Irv Spence, animator, later joined Tex Avery at MGM;* 5. *Steve Bosustow, head of UPA, sold out to Hank Saperstein;* 6. *Richard Bickenbach, animator, later at MGM with Hanna-Barbera;* 7. *Al Eugster, animator from the east coast;* 8. *Jimmie (Shamus) Culhane, animator;* 9. *Ub Iwerks, partner with Disney, animator (*STEAMBOAT WILLY, TREES AND FLOWERS, *etc.), formed own studio, failed, returned to Disney as master of all technical matters, had no sense of humor or story;* 10. *The great Grim Natwick;* 11. *Berny Wolf, animator, one of the New York group;* 12. *The greater Carl Stalling;* 13. *Mary Tebb, head of ink-and-paint for Ub Iwerks and Disney, and best friend of Dorothy, my first wife;* 14. *My first wife, Dorothy Webster Jones, Ub's private secretary, married to C.J. for 43 years (!), mother of Linda.*

ancient and hallowed artist of thirty-eight. I, his assistant, was a squirming piglet. All I could offer him was adoration, and that was not nearly enough. He needed competent help, when my sole talent was fawning subservience.

Suddenly realizing I was part of his tragic past, Ub Iwerks emulated Walt Lantz by firing me for the second time. But having a superb artist such as Grim was not going to save the Ub Iwerks studio. It was doomed to fail, and fail it did. The greatest of the early animators (Ub Iwerks) and the superb abilities of Grim Natwick, Shamus Culhane, Al Eugster, Berny Wolf, and others could not compensate for cartoons that were not funny. Tragedy is often sadly simple. Without good writing, the animator, like the actor, is helpless. So off went most of the artists and animators to Disney, where they belonged—and back went the brilliant Ub to his proper harbor at Disney, too.

We celebrated Grim Natwick's 100th birthday in 1990, attended by an antiquated mélange of juniors, ranging in age from sixty-nine to ninety-six. Anyone below fifty was admissible only when accompanied by their parents.

Grim called me a few weeks after this boisterous birthday. "Chuck," he said, "I don't see much reason to try for two hundred." A hundred and one didn't appeal to him either. He was never a man for small triumph, so at one-hundred-and-a-month-or-so he left the world, without an enemy.

6. Following my second firing by Ub Iwerks, I

71

Celebrating Grim Natwick's 100th birthday. Top row (from left): Wolfgang ("Woolie") Reitherman, Disney feature director; Bill Littlejohn, prime animator of Snoopy; Tee Bosustow, son of UPA head, Steve Bosustow; Chuck Jones; Charles Solomon, critic at the LOS ANGELES TIMES. Second row: Cal Howard, Warner Bros. writer/gagman. Front row: June Foray, Grim Natwick, Marc Davis.

A BUCK AND A HALF.

*My fee for a black-and-white charcoal portrait on
Olvera Street was one dollar. Here we have
a buck and a half.*

earned an unsteady living as a dollar-a-throw portrait artist and puppeteer on Olvera Street.

It was said that Christine Sterling, the "great and good friend" of Harry Chandler, owner and publisher of the *Los Angeles Times*, couldn't decide what she wanted for her birthday, so she decided on a street: Olvera Street, to be exact.

Olvera Street was an integral part of the beginnings of El Pueblo de Nuestra Señora la Reina de los Angeles de Porcíuncula, pronounced then as "Los" (as in "dose") "Ang-hay-lees" and more currently known as "Loss-an-juh-less," which was founded on September 4, 1781, to the dismay of the northeastern seaboard of the Lodges and the Cabots.

Now, by the year of the birthday of Harry Chandler's great and good friend, Olvera Street had degenerated into a small, squalid alley branching off the main square or plaza of the village. A street seemed a simple enough and reasonable request to Harry Chandler, so he bought it for Christine. They decreed that it should become again a Mexican paseo, attended in perpetuity by Mexican-Americans and their descendants, except for a few Anglos, including me for a few months before I joined Leon

Schlesinger. Grant Smith, a schoolmate and one of the Anglo exceptions, had established the small and esoteric Adobe Bookshop in the basement of one of the old buildings on the street, and he asked me to set up as a portrait artist at the entrance.

My fee for a black-and-white portrait was one dollar, an outrageous overcharge, considering my ability. The accuracy of John Singer Sargent's description of a portrait as "a picture in which something is wrong with the eyes" became quickly apparent. I couldn't draw eyes the way they appear in life—sparkling and

*My daughter, Linda, painted by her father.
Painting does what we cannot do—it brings a three-dimensional world into a two-dimensional plane.*

alive. Neither could Sargent, or any artist who ever lived. To avoid making a portrait stare like an enlarged photograph in an optometrist's window, Sargent never drew eyes precisely, giving the observer some choice in the matter.

It is amazing how little we can see in focus without moving our eyes. Hold your hand up in front of your face and spread your fingers. You will probably find you cannot focus on more than a small part of one finger. Our eyes quickly shift to focus where they are needed, working in little darts like a bird's head. An accurate painting of what we see at any moment would show everything but a tiny point out of focus. The missing element is Time. If I look at one finger, then the next, until I have formed a discernible whole, I have added Time to Height, Breadth, and Depth, and I am in the fourth dimension. What would a "natural" picture be? Certainly not one showing the world as seen by a one-eyed man with his head nailed to a fence. Any painting or photograph does what we cannot do—it brings a three-dimensional world into a two-dimensional plane. Our paintings are, of course, not natural at all—they are what we are conditioned to believe as fact.

He only in Bohemia dwells, who knows not he is there.

—*George Sterling (no relative of Christine's)*

When I was eighteen, I was briefly exposed to the craftsmanship of the Yale Puppeteers, who were masters of an arcane but close cousin to animation.

73

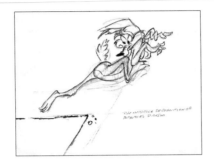

The Yale Puppeteers taught me that gravity is what believability is all about.

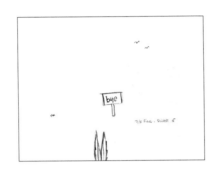

All by myself, I discovered the prime trick in portraiture: insist on drawing in profile. For one thing, nobody knows what they look like in profile (a possible exception was John Barrymore, who said, "I have one profile that is the envy of the gods; the other looks like a fried egg"), and with profiles the artist has only one eye to worry about. In addition—and this is important—you can make your subject very handsome or beautiful without complaint.

If, when making a sketch of Bugs or Daffy for a friend, I am asked, "Do you mind if I look over your shoulder?" I can respond with an unqualified "I don't mind," because during my days on Olvera Street everyone in the passing crowd who stopped to watch me work was an art critic—a negative art critic (is there another kind?). Also, the assembly routinely gorged on pine nuts and little green, pine-tree-shaped suckers, slurping the candies and cracking the pine nuts with their teeth while gazing at my artistry.

I also worked on Olvera Street with the Yale Puppeteers, who were masters of their craft. They later moved to the Turnabout Theatre on La Cienega Boulevard, where the audience sat on reversible streetcar seats and watched the puppets in the first half of the show, then reversed the seats during the intermission and watched Elsa Lanchester and her group perform at the other end of the theater.

The puppeteers taught me that *gravity* is what believability is all about. The animator's characters have no weight, but characters must appear to rest firmly on the ground to be convincing; marionette

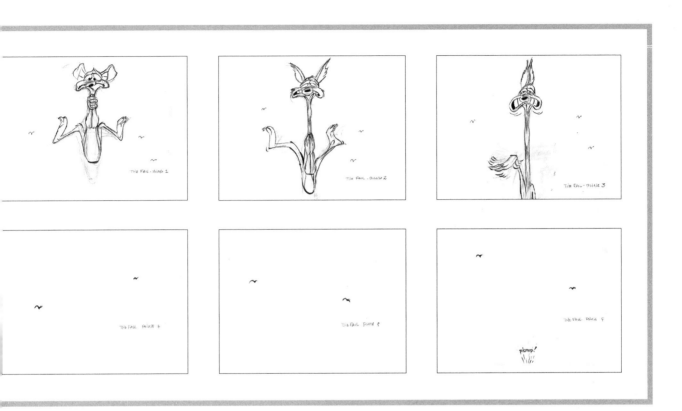

manipulators understand this, and the best achieve it. One of the Yale Puppeteers' most exciting acts opened on a little stage dotted with small palm trees and dominated by a gigantic golden Buddha, which was actually about the size of a man. Then a marionette moved out on stage, dancing lithely and lasciviously to the insistent sound of native drums, with tiny spotlights picking up her every action. She was manipulated by Bob Bromley, the Preston Blair of puppeteers. Socially he was probably the shyest man I have ever known, but when he operated this puppet from his position about ten feet above the stage, everything inside him came out. It was very sexy and so believable that the audience soon forgot she was a puppet; she began to appear life-size.

After some time, a glint appeared in Buddha's eye, then the giant statue's hand began to move. There was of course a man inside, but the audience was so convinced that the girl was about five feet tall that he appeared inhumanly huge. It took about a minute and a half for the ominous hand to come slowly around and suddenly grab the dancer. Her arms and legs thrashed around for a while, then she went limp, and the curtains closed. It was frightening. It takes a great manipulator to achieve an illusion like that.

Most marionettes appear to float when they move, as weightless as astronauts walking on the moon. Few people realize that the reason bad marionettes are unconvincing is that their feet don't stand firmly on the ground, but puppeteers know it, and if I am to be an animator I must know it too.

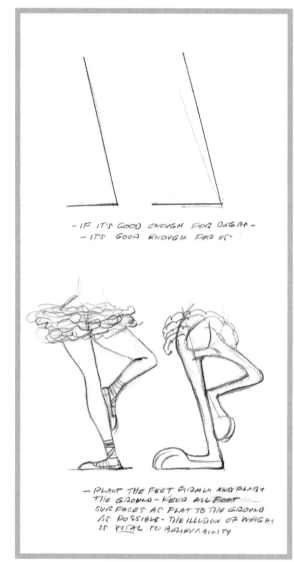

— IF IT'S GOOD ENOUGH FOR DEGAS —
— IT'S GOOD ENOUGH FOR US

— PLANT THE FEET FIRMLY AND FLATLY
THE GROUND - KEEP ALL FOOT
SURFACES AS FLAT TO THE GROUND
AS POSSIBLE - THE ILLUSION OF WEIGHT
IS VITAL TO ACHIEVABILITY

using a long, straight, vertical line, at right angles to the stage's horizontals, which is the most forceful statement that can be made about anything standing solidly on the ground. With one leg so securely grounded, the other could be in any position without suggesting instability. When Bugs comes to a stop, he often assumes a position like the Degas dancer, with his weight on one leg.

Degas could tell the entire story of a leg by the way he drew one side of it. The two sides of the dancer's leg are quite different, and each line has its own job to do. I seldom use parallel lines or draw the opposite sides in equal shapes, as I, too, believe that each line should say something unique.

Degas's drawings of the corps de ballet also show the power of implied action, such as a dancer wrapping her leg before a performance. Like many artists, Degas felt that the *preliminary* drawing, showing the moment before movement begins, has more vitality and mobility than a drawing of the action itself. The statue of the Discus Thrower, when the athlete is in anticipation of his move, illustrates the principle well.

When I began animating, I tried to tell the story completely through body movements, as if the characters were puppets. Then I discovered a technique D. W. Griffith had discovered many years before— the close-up. Early cartoons never went to a close-up, just as Sarah Bernhardt acted in her first film as if she were in front of a huge audience who couldn't read her face, and of course it looked absurd. The close-up allows subtle changes of facial expression—the raising of an eyebrow or the flicker of a smile—to become part of the action.

The faces of animal characters are open and available to the animator, all the more so because

When audiences see a character move with that sense of weight, they find it believable, although they don't necessarily think, "Gee, look how firmly his characters are grounded." Degas knew the necessity of this. He drew the back of a dancer's leg

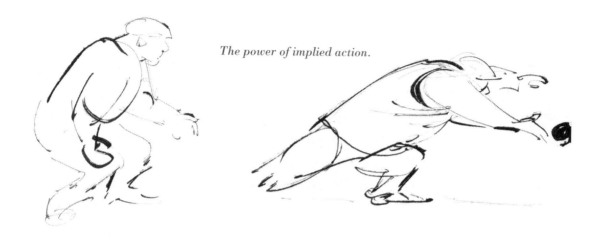

The power of implied action.

THE COYOTE IS LIMITED, AS BUGS IS LIMITED, BY HIS
ANATOMY. TO GIVE THE COYOTE A LOOK OF ANTICIPATORY
DELIGHT, I DRAW EVERYTHING *UP*—THE EYES ARE UP, THE
EARS ARE UP, AND EVEN THE NOSE IS UP. WHEN HE IS
DEFEATED, ON THE OTHER HAND, EVERYTHING TURNS
DOWN. YOU CAN'T DO THAT AS DRAMATICALLY WITH
HUMAN BEINGS, ALTHOUGH THE EMOTIONS EXPRESSED ARE
FULLY HUMAN.

77

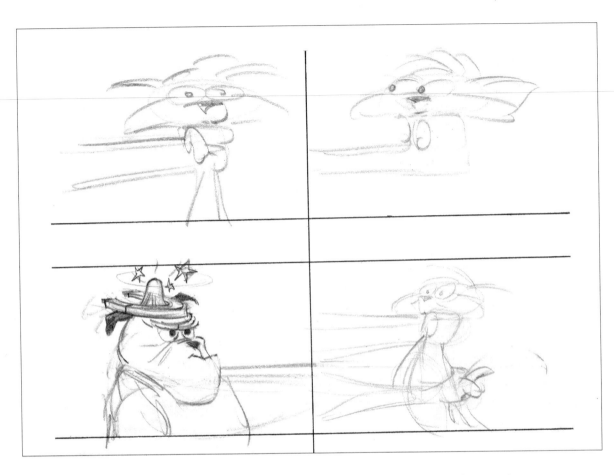

*The close-up, according to D. W. Griffith, allows subtle changes of facial expression—
the raising of an eyebrow or the flicker of a smile—to become part of the action.*

few animals have any facial expressions at all, and we usually misinterpret the few we do find. When monkeys look most ferocious, for example, they are probably *expressing* fear rather than trying to *inspire* it. And a dog who slobbers is not necessarily hungry. Dogs do develop mannerisms, but they are largely unfathomable to us.

Animals are also an inexhaustible source of inspiration. All you have to do is to look at the pop-eyes, the nervous mouth, and the strained neck veins of a camel to realize that here is someone with a shirt two sizes too tight. A photograph in *National Geographic* showed a dried-up, ragged camel who had just spent many days in the desert without water. As soon as he reached the oasis, he swallowed nearly half of his body weight in water. Unlike most mammals, the camel feeds water straight to his cells, and in the next picture, taken a little later, he had filled out completely and looked ready for another walk in the desert. That is an idea an animator can use. And camels have beautiful eyelashes too.

Life on Olvera Street was a pleasure and provided a lovely delusion that I was a Bohemian in the true Greenwich Village style. I wore a black smock, ate in small Chinese and Mexican restaurants for—literally—a few pennies, and relished my poverty.

When Leon Schlesinger opened his studio at the old Warner Bros. lot on Sunset Boulevard, I was reluctant to leave Olvera Street when another Chouinard comrade signed me on—an act, no doubt, he will have to answer for, come the Great Tribunal.

And so I found myself on Sunset Boulevard and Bronson Avenue, timidly introducing myself to Ray Katz, the blue-jowled business manager of Schlesinger's spin-off studio (spun off from the successful and highly talented studio of Hugh Harmon and Rudolf Ising: Harmon/Ising). Ray Katz, doubtless impressed by my past employment record, realized he could hire me for peanuts. He was ideally equipped to do this, since his previous employment had been to tend the peanut machines on the Warner Bros. lot, extracting pennies and refilling the machines.

Mr. Katz pursed his Edward G. Robinson-ish lips, the kind that look like they are smoking a cigar even when they are not, and offered me a five-year contract starting at $18.50 per week, with a $2.50 option/increase every six months, working eight to

If you want a midget to look like a baby, don't put a cigar in his mouth.

When monkeys look ferocious, they are probably expressing fear rather than trying to inspire it.

Warner Bros., 1937

1. Keith Darling, animator; 2. Fred ("The Beautiful") Jones; 3. Sid Sutherland, animator—he and Virgil Ross were the two animators who, with Bob Clampett and Chuck Jones, formed the first Termite Terrace animation team; 4. Volney White, red-haired animator; 5. Tubby Millar, early gagman; 6. Ace Gamer, effects animator; 7. Rich Hogan, storyman with Jones and Avery at MGM; 8. Virgil Ross (see 3.); 9. Phil Monroe, one of my grand old men, along with Ken Harris, Abe Levitow, and Ben Washam; 10. Gerry Chiniquy, Friz Freleng's ace animator; 11. Rod Scribner, ace animator for McKimson and Clampett; 12. Richard Thompson, animator; 13. Rudy Larriva, animator; 14. The great Smokey Garner.

five, six days a week, later modified to five-and-a-half days a week, provided I earned it by working four hours' overtime during the week. A week-long vacation could also be earned by accumulating overtime of forty-eight hours during the year.

On March 15, 1933, I leapt at this magnanimous offer. I was, on that date of infamy, not quite twenty-one, a two-year veteran in the art of *not* learning to animate, or at least not taking advantage of my opportunities to learn from masters like Iwerks and Natwick.

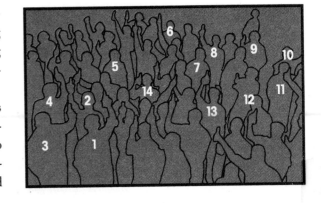

The first film I directed was THE NIGHT WATCHMAN *(1938). Its young star, Tommy the Cat, became Sniffles the Mouse* (right) *in later cartoons.*

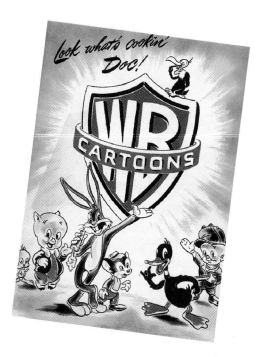

Full character animation is at the heart of Warner Bros. cartoons, but THE DOVER BOYS *(1942,* left and below) *is now considered a landmark film partly because of its innovative use of limited animation, a technique exploited by the cartoon factories supplying television's huge appetite twenty years later.*

Dan Backslide— coward, bully, cad, thief, and arch-enemy of the Dover Boys— abducts Dainty Dora Standpipe.

The heroic Dover Boys of Pimento University ("Good Old P.U.")— (from left) fun-loving Tom, serious Dick, and chubby Larry.

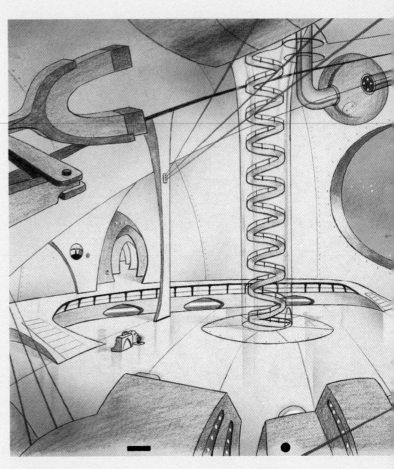

It has been my privilege to work with the great John McGrew. Among the many original backgrounds he created are those for BEDTIME FOR SNIFFLES (1940, above), THE UNBEARABLE BEAR (1943, top) and CONRAD THE SAILOR (1942, right), which was based on Eisenstein's BATTLESHIP POTEMKIN.

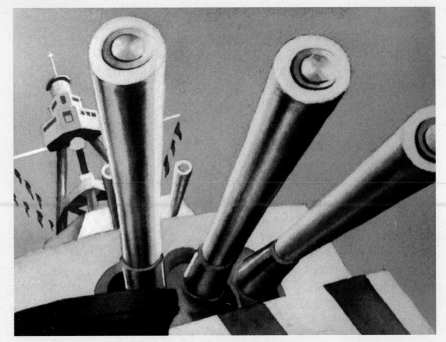

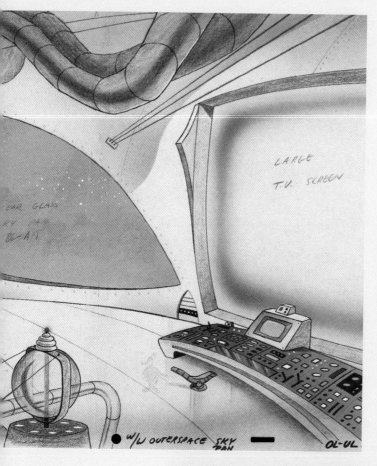

Maurice Noble is an artist of power, subtlety and imagination. The layouts for DUCK DODGERS AND THE RETURN OF THE 24½TH CENTURY (1980, left) are his, as are those of the original DUCK DODGERS IN THE 24½TH CENTURY (1953, below). NASA scientists must have borrowed ideas from Maurice's innovative launching pads and space stations.

The crisis begins for Duck Dodgers, as Marvin Martian disputes his claim to Planet X (above, right). As usual, Daffy throws himself wholeheartedly into his role, but Porky Pig, observer and space cadet (right), remains unconvinced by the heroics.

One more missed turn at Albuquerque, and Bugs and Daffy find themselves in a treasure cave guarded by the dim but beefy Hassan in ALI BABA BUNNY (1957). True to their natures, Bugs uses his wits to escape, whereas Daffy is overcome—and finally belittled (below)—by his greed.

Daffy's pearl of unwisdom— "It's mine! All mine! I'm rich! I'm wealthy! I'm comfortably well off!"

. . .

The Rape of the Lock

Leon Schlesinger would have been quite bald on top, but for a lock of hair that he had cultivated on the stern of his skull until it was three or four feet long.

Leon layered this prideful lock back and forth across the bald top to achieve a sort of lawn covering his bald spot. Occasionally, however, the lock—having a sense of humor of its own—would escape from under Leon's spiffy white Panama hat and trail its unraveled length three or four feet behind him like a bizarre pigtail, a joy to us and a puzzlement to passersby.

Leon Schlesinger's travels were unique travesties of good taste and good neighborliness. He spoke with slobbery nostalgia of the "Epicazootus" of his youth in vaudeville (read: "sexual intercourse"); he spoke fondly of the "Frog Hookers" (read: "French Prostitutes") along the "Champs Ulysses"; he once

came back from Mexico with "cucka rachos" on his fish-fat feet.

Having a producer who called huaraches "cucka rachos" and the Champs Elysees the "Champs (as in champion) Ulysses" helped while away the few dull hours we encountered in that wondrous termite-infested Oz where we were paid (lightly but miraculously) for doing what we enjoyed most: drawing and laughing.

During the hostilities of the 1940s, Phil DeLara took time out from animation to make a drawing of a smoldering, smashed Schlesinger cartoon studio. Overhead, in a circling Japanese bomber, an indignant pilot is calling to his bombardier: "I said *ammunition* dump, not *animation* dump!"

Away from the rich grandeur of the Disney studio, most of us worked in animation dumps, and few of the buildings needed help from the Japanese Air Force to achieve this status. Leon Schlesinger maintained a decent set of offices for himself at the prow

81

Daffy, accoutered à la Leon Schlesinger,
adopts his manner as well.

Leon Schlesinger's Christmas Party, 1933 or 1934

1. *Elmer Wait, the assistant animator who could not sleep; monitor of our early warning system;*
2. *Bugs Hardaway, writer;* 3. *Manuel ?, cameraman;* 4. & 5. *Tony and Lightning Pabian, animators;*
6. *Bob Clampett ;* 7. *C. Jones;* 8. & 8 1/2. *Bernie Brown and ?, our first music team;* 9. *Paul Smith, good animator for Friz Freleng;* 10. *The great Henry Binder, the secret weapon;* 11. *Friz Freleng, the child;* 12. *Ham Hamilton, the first fine animator I worked with;* 13. *Unknown by name, once head of Warner Bros. costume department;* 14. *The great Smokey Garner;* 15. *Don Williams, animator and associate in 1929 at KEM commercial art studio;* 16. *Earl Hurd, poor storyman from Disney, lousy director at Schlesinger;* 17. *Bob McKimson, key animator, then director;* 18. *A.C. ("Ace") Gamer, First World War pilot, fine special effects animator;* 19. *Leon Schlesinger.*

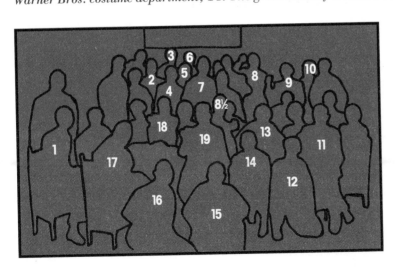

of our ancient building south of Sunset at Van Ness and Fernwood. It was similar to the bridge of the *Queen Mary* grafted onto a garbage scow, and he was always careful to wear gloves and overshoes when venturing inside the murky windings of his rabbit factory.

I am sure Leon never quite knew what was going on with the heterogeneous dwarfs who hacked out the dubious diamonds of animated wit that supported him, dwarfs named Friz, Tex, Mike, Cal, Tedd, and Smokey, rather than Dopey, Grumpy, etc.

If we saw Leon on our briar patch twice a week it was unusual. We saw his lackey Ray Katz (known fondly to us as "Old Catchfart") much more often, and this was a necessity for our growth, because it taught us that talent must be protected, that Philistines do not always come out of the hills but from the front office. In outwitting Ray Katz and his successor Eddie Selzer, I think that we learned how to teach others how to outwit Wile E. Coyote, Yosemite Sam, Sylvester, and the Tasmanian Devil.

If Leon knew not what his dwarfs wrought, he had nothing on the dwarfs. We were grotesquely young, our eyes wide and unembarrassed by knowledge, wisdom, or theory, and hopelessly uncluttered by tradition or precedent. We lived and worked in an atmosphere of no restriction. Anything was possible, everything probable.

The smallness of our universe was the essence of our creativity. We were just as unaware of the studio's business and day-to-day life as they were of ours, and we ignored in our humor all the facets of contemporary life outside our enclave. Our world was contained in a tiny shell bounded by Van Ness Avenue, Fernwood Avenue, Bronson Street, and Sunset Boulevard, and later in a building on the most extreme Siberiacal part of the Warner lot, on an ash heap at the foot of California Street and the Los Angeles River in Burbank. And in these Petri dishes of disparate DNA flourished the most diversified animated short subjects ever to exist.

I am sure Ray Katz, our gumshoed production chief, had no idea what was being produced, or why

Our view of a rabbit factory (1942).

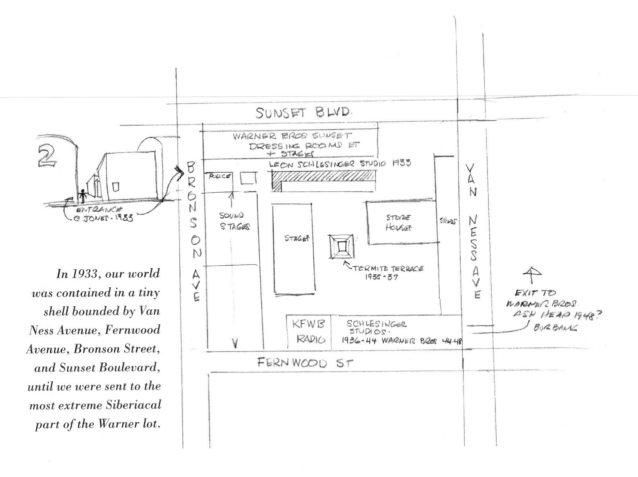

In 1933, our world was contained in a tiny shell bounded by Van Ness Avenue, Fernwood Avenue, Bronson Street, and Sunset Boulevard, until we were sent to the most extreme Siberiacal part of the Warner lot.

those wild-eyed minions of his sat around flipping telephone-book-like sheaves of paper. Without proper supervision, with only personal discipline, we had but two managerial demands: that the length of our pictures not exceed six minutes, and that our pictures make audiences laugh at least as much as we laughed making them.

The animators regularly slumped over their drawing boards, fast asleep until awakened by our internal alarm system warning them of a prowling Katz. As they sprang upright, two telltale pink indentations were visible on each sleepy forehead. These devilish impressions were made by the two pegs that held the animation paper on the drawing board (there were only two in those days). Somebody at MGM had told Ray to look out for these marks of guilt, and on entering a room he would scan foreheads for incriminating dents. It was unnerving.

Ray's odious successor, Eddie Selzer, loathed laughter. One day we heard him, rigid with rage, bawling, "What the hell has all this laughter to do with the making of animated cartoons?" He was at that moment not an appealing figure, standing in the doorway with his hands—or, rather, stubby fists—dug stiffly and fretfully in his coat pockets, and the tiny flaps that spanned the bridge of his bulbous nose aflame with anger. No one unfamiliar with Eddie Selzer would have known that he was happy.

Most of us, I think, are uncertain of the elements that will bring us happiness on every occasion. Liquor, love, triumph, filial or canine affection, satisfied conceits may all vary in making us as one with the cosmos.

Marc Anthony in CAT FEUD *(1958).*

Leon's uninspiring successor, Eddie Selzer, brought us new knowledge of the perfidy of fate. Here he is with the good and great production manager, Johnnie Burton, who, by his quickness, saved Eddie's neck every ten minutes.

But to Eddie, anger was ultimately satisfying, unvaryingly pleasant. Laughter he abhorred above all things, because he could not understand it. It was as the loon's call to the novice camper; he feared it and believed that it betokened danger to him.

Probably the only four-vowel word in the English language Eddie Selzer could spell correctly was "furious"; it fitted so aptly his permanent state of mind. He therefore felt justified in throwing out—or trying to throw out—the title of the first Coyote and Road Runner cartoon: *Fast and Furry-ous.*

The stunning Woods twins, Marilyn and Madilyn, all of nineteen years old, were among the first women to become part of our creative team, as assistant animators. Their appointment was not, sadly, because of any altruistic generosity or sense of duty on the part of management, who acted with severe reluctance, forced by the shortage of man (male) power during the war.

Typical peacetime employment for women and minorities was polishing the inked and painted cels (celluloids) before they went to camera.

The ink-and-paint division at full power. This small crew of perhaps forty girls completed thirty color films a year (6 minutes each, 4,000 to 5,000 drawings in each, 125,000 to 150,000 drawings a year).

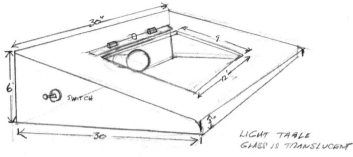

STANDARD ANIMATION
PAPER IS 10½ × 12½.

12½"

10½"

30"

9

6

12"

SWITCH

30

1

LIGHT TABLE
GLASS IS TRANSLUCENT

PEG BAR

12"
8½"

THIS BOARD SHOULD BE STANDARD EQUIPMENT
BOTH AT WARNER BROS AND LOA AND, IF PRACTICAL,
AT LICENSEES'— SUBMITTED DESIGN AND DRAWINGS COULD
ALWAYS BE SUBMITTED ON STANDARD SIZED PAPER- 10½ × 12½—
AND COULD EASILY BE CORRECTED ON THE LIGHT-BOARDS.
THIS DOES NOT LIMIT ANY COMPANY FROM DRAWING ANY
SIZE CONVENIENT TO THEM — DRAWINGS CAN BE EASILY
XEROXED TO THIS STANDARD SIZE PAPER.

Primitive but perfectly functional animation desk. Nearly all our films were produced on this model, inserted into a much wider drawing board. Today's animation tables are gadget-ridden, complete with everything from a bidet to a nail clipper and an elbow massager.

Bob McKimson at sweat-box session.

Cameraman at work.

Mike Maltese and I were in one of our dreamy reveries when the clatter of Eddie's dentures drew our attention to the stubby marplot of our stories standing a-tremble in a rage at our doorway.

"How," he demanded, shaking our dialogue sheets for *Fast and Furry-ous* in front of us, "do either of you ignoramuses spell 'few-ree-us'?"

"I don't know," Mike said. "How would you spell 'few-ree-us,' Chuck?"

"Ef-you-are-eye-oh-you-ess," I replied. Snap!

Eddie had the fascinating ability to foam at the eyes, which he did when he was happy about the faults of others. His eyes foamed redly now as he stabbed a hairy, cigar-stub-shaped index finger at the offending word: "Furry-ous."

"Then how come? *How* come?"—as though one "How come?" wasn't enough—"How come you spelled it 'ef-you-are-are-why-oh-us'?"

"I think I understand everything but the 'are-are,'" Mike said. To me: "Perhaps you can explain."

"The 'are-are' is part of 'furry,'" I said to Eddie. "Furry is what coyotes are. Coyotes are also fast, hence, 'Fast and Furry.'"

"The 'us,'" explained Mike, "is for Chuck and me."

"And for Mr. Jack Warner," I added. (If you were Eddie you always said "Mister.") "His secretary told us he loved the title."

"Well, I like it too!" said Eddie. "I mean, who wouldn't? It's a great title."

Eddie Selzer (second from left), wattles aflame, tries to ruin a script by his critique. John Burton, Chuck Jones, Friz Freleng, and Bob McKimson are awake.

An early (1948) Road Runner and Coyote model sheet. Note the oversized crest on the Road Runner, and the indeterminate length of the Coyote's legs—not a useful aid to the animator.

"We have another one," Mike said. "I know you'll like it. *Fierce and Fur-most.* And we also thought up a great slogan for Warner Bros. Pictures: 'If it's a Warner Bros. picture, you don't have to stand in line.'"

Eddie's wattles slapped joyously together. "Wonderful! Wonderful!!"

And off he went, buckety-buckety, to tell Jack Warner.

Our salvation, the vital saving factor, was that Leon and Eddie thought only of money; we thought only of the fun of our freedom. Although we were unaware that our atmosphere ("working conditions") was unique, life emerged out of that very uniqueness.

We had freedom, not because it was given to us, but because our overseers shared two qualities that provided that freedom: laziness and stupidity.

We were not brave, philosophic, or particularly brilliant, but what we lacked in intellect we made up for in opportunism. We knew a good thing when we saw it, so we went blithely ahead, knowing that if we didn't know what a theater audience wanted—in those deprived times there was no television—no one else seemed to know either. We sought and found our inspiration (we would have laughed at so pretentious a term) in each other, with occasional significant help from management. For example, one producer told us to use lots of purple. Purple, he said, was a funny color.

Drawing by Bill Scott
Back row (from left): *Tedd Pierce, Chuck Jones, Bob McKimson, Mike Maltese, Eddie Selzer, Bill Scott.*
Front row: *Warren Foster, Friz Freleng.*

February 14, 1936.

TO: CHARLES JONES

Your weekly animation average for 10 weeks ending February 7th was 30 ft. 2 fr.

Your average for the previous 10 week period was 27 ft. 5 fr. Therefore, your average has gone up ~~down~~ 2 ft. 13 fr.

RAY KATZ.

December 3, 1935.

TO: CHARLES JONES

Animation records are averaged over 10 week periods.

Your weekly animation average for 10 weeks ending November 30th was 27 ft. 5 fr.

A new 10 week period started on December 2nd.

RAY KATZ.

Ray Katz judged quality by speed. No other method need apply.

A music bar sheet from Ali Baba Bunny (1957). Note that there are four beats to the measure (32 frames). This is the picture as presented to Carl Stalling.

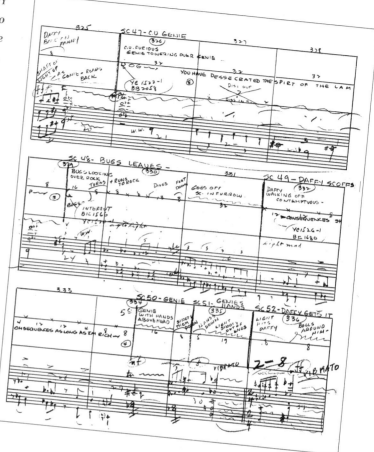

Golden Rule I: You must always trust management—in reverse.

At Warner Bros. nobody ever came to management for approval. The accidental, unplanned growth and flowering of animation in the thirties, forties, fifties, and sixties was due to a simple, unstated idea: put talented people in a room together and good ideas will emerge.

Management was creatively inept but implacable in seeking economies, and their greed imposed unusual creative disciplines on Termite Terrace. Form followed finance. At Disney they could animate *101 Dalmatians*, but if I had tried to make *One Dog Named Spot* for Leon Schlesinger, he would not have let me do it. Spots cost money.

The wealthy studios such as MGM and Disney could also overshoot scenes—even shoot a scene and leave it out of the picture entirely—but life at Warner Bros. was very different. Leon insisted that the cartoons had to be six minutes exactly, so the Warner Bros. directors had to learn to time a picture exactly to 540 feet—six minutes precisely. We might stray over by half a second, but no more.

To complicate matters, there was *no editing*. The editing was all done in the director's head and laid out on musical bar sheets or exposure sheets before the animators became involved. Some of my early films as a director, made when I was learning the art of timing, now seem sloppy and slow, but these films were not edited. Although we used the term "editor"

Treg Brown adds his perfect touch to the sound effects on the almost completed film.

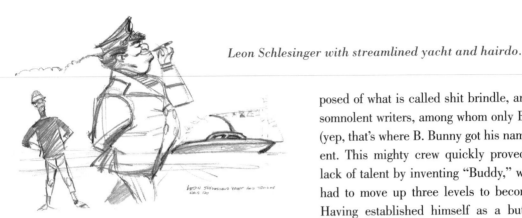

to describe Treg Brown on the credits, he did not edit the picture; he simply spliced it together and added his superb and incongruously funny sound effects.

I thought at the time that this was the normal way of making an animated cartoon, so I didn't complain. It's a terrible thing to be put upon and not know it.

The only time Leon Schlesinger ever invited us to his house was to say goodbye after he had sold the studio to Warner Bros. To mark the occasion he gave each director a gold pen and pencil. Although he often said that he didn't want any poor people on his yacht, he did once invite the animation directors aboard. When we reached Avalon on Catalina Island, Leon in his great vulgarity had the crew display all the flags in the locker. As they were doing this, a beautiful little sloop came sailing in. It was a racing vessel, a star boat, hard to rig, hard to sail, and very expensive. With great skill and delicacy, the sloop's crew threaded through the crowd of yachts, dropped sail, and came precisely up to the mooring. It was a fine sight, inspiring Leon to comment dismissively that "them sons-of-bitches don't even have a motor." That was Leon.

In the beginning, Leon Schlesinger never hired anyone unless they offered to save him money, and in this way he employed some very ordinary people, such as Earl Hurd and Jack King, who had been unsuccessful writers and directors at Disney. He also hired two remarkably untalented musicians, three background men who painted all backgrounds in a palette com-

posed of what is called shit brindle, and two or three somnolent writers, among whom only Bugs Hardaway (yep, that's where B. Bunny got his name) had any talent. This mighty crew quickly proved its grotesque lack of talent by inventing "Buddy," who would have had to move up three levels to become fifth string. Having established himself as a butcher of talent and a lover of the mediocre, and being incapable of distinguishing between the two, Leon looked like a man destined for death by drowning in the sea of his crudity, when greatness was thrust upon him in the persons of Friz Freleng and Tex Avery, two of the finest cartoon directors ever to live. Neither had yet directed a credible cartoon when they appeared at the Schlesinger studio, just as the gangplank of bankruptcy was being extended for Leon.

Bill Scott's drawing shows Chuck Jones indicating his displeasure with the quality of a Tedd Pierce story idea.

Sketch by Bill Scott of some forgotten occasion starring Friz Freleng.

Friz and his brilliant character layout man, Hawley Pratt.

• • •

Enter Friz Freleng

Leon employed Friz Freleng to be the senior director, and Friz was the key to the whole future and success, because his talent attracted other talents.

Friz always contended that he couldn't draw, but he drew beautifully. His timing has never been bettered, and he brought character to animation. In the 1920s, cartoons were drawn like comic strips that moved, which was startling enough in itself to appeal to audiences for a while, just as seeing what appeared to be a live actor was enough to make early talking pictures remarkable.

In the 1930s, animation came into its own as a necessary element in a cinema show. When the stars of the live-action shorts—Chaplin, Keaton, Laurel and Hardy, and the rest—went into features, cartoons dropped into the slot thus vacated. At first, Disney made just animation shorts; when his top animators moved up to features, Warner Bros. came in and dominated the field. The greatest Disney shorts were made against the background of the Great Depression, when audiences needed sweet, sympathetic films. Although we made films before World War II, the heart of our production is really post-war, when we felt a sudden sense of release, and Warner Bros. cartoons came charging out of the gate with an irreverence and exuberance that would have been unacceptable in the Depression. Similarly, *Brother Can You Spare a Dime?* or *Who's Afraid of the Big Bad Wolf?* would no longer serve after the war. Afraid of *what* wolf? We *killed* the wolf! During the war, there was a feeling of a very integral, violent, huge enemy, so you got into the habit of walking up and spitting in the enemy's

93

Friz Freleng not only drew beautifully—in spite of his protestations of incompetence—he drew "funny" (a compliment seldom given by one cartoonist to another).

eye. All we had to do to turn this feeling into cartoons was to modify it down to a point where the situation was similar but not quite so dramatic; then it became humorous.

Even though we didn't know it at the time, we learned from Disney. Character animation started in 1933 with one picture—Disney's *Three Little Pigs*, where we saw for the first time how characters who *looked* alike could be differentiated by the way they moved. I was an in-betweener when Disney made *The Three Little Pigs*, and I saw immediately that if I wanted to remain in this business, I would have to learn the art of character animation.

Walt Disney, along with many other producers, may have had the political acumen of a squid, but to me he is the patron saint of all animators. When I

94

In 1943 we were doing animated maps for the Fort Western branch of the U.S. Army, led by Colonel Frank Capra. Here Bernyce Polifka pleads her case.

IF YOU START WITH CHARACTER, YOU PROBABLY WILL END UP WITH GOOD DRAWINGS. THESE ARE ALL SKETCHES, NOT MODEL SHEETS OR DIRECTOR'S LAYOUTS, THAT FOUND THEIR WAY INTO WARNER CARTOONS.

saw *The Three Little Pigs,* I wrote him a letter to say how much I admired the picture, and to my surprise he replied, expressing the hope that I would continue to work in animation and that my work might one day stimulate the people at Disney. I was very proud of this piece of paper, and for years I always carried it in my back pocket and showed it to everyone until I wore it out.

Over the years I wrote perhaps four more letters to him, and he always wrote back. About six months before he died, I was at the hospital across the street from the Disney studio, and a nurse told me that Walt was a patient there and suggested I go and say hello to him. I found him alone, sitting up in his bed. Shading his eyes, he invited me in. I told him about the letters and thanked him for replying to every one. He said something peculiar: "It wasn't difficult. You are the only animator who ever wrote to me."

It is strange to think that he was adored by so many millions of people but apparently not by those he adored—his own animators, who could do something he could not do and whose talent he so admired.

Disney's animators were more likely to play practical jokes on their boss than write him fan letters. There were stables a short quarter-mile from the old Disney studio, and the hungry horseflies who lived there soon learned that there was food to be had from Disney employees lunching al fresco by the Los Angeles River. These horseflies were as big as bees, and they gave one alert animator an idea. He began by netting a few of these muscular insects. Knowing that Walt Disney and his family were solidly right-wing Republicans, he tore off some long strips of toilet paper, wrote "Vote for Roosevelt" on each one, and glued them to the rear end of the netted flies. Later that day, he released his miniature

The Disney Studio, c. 1935. Walt Disney holds Mickey's left hand, with Roy Disney on the mouse's right.

squadron in Walt Disney's quarters, where they flew around trailing their political message and driving Walt's brother Roy crazy.

Carefully crafted jokes were a feature of the animation studios. Leon Schlesinger was another occasional and prized victim. Leon equated all experience to the excrement of poultry ("I ask for chicken salad, and you give me chicken shit") or to the nether sections of the digestive tract (after seeing Disney's *Snow White:* "I need a feature cartoon like I need two assholes"). There was one somewhat unflattering and constantly repeated exception. "That," he would state regarding a story idea—or any idea, for that matter—"is flat as Kelsey's nuts." When he had time to kill, Leon would deliberately irritate us by making us all turn up at night for a story meeting.

John McGrew and Gene Fleury's enthusiasm at Tedd Pierce's presentation.

At one of these unwelcome meetings, Leon was greeting the jokes with his usual cry of "That's flat as Kelsey's nuts," when he suddenly halted in his anatomically negative criticism of our efforts, becoming aware of a strange face in our midst, actually a bartender friend of Edward Stacey Pierce III. Before he could fire the stranger (he often fired people who did not work there), Cal Howard introduced the alien. "Mr. Schlesinger," he said, "I would like you to meet Mr. Kelsey," adding sotto voce, "He's Jack Warner's uncle." At this point Mr. Schlesinger could, I am sure, have used two recta.

Some practical jokes had no victim. Four of six animators working in one studio were dedicated smokers, but the other two yearned for smoke-free air. The two non-smokers decided to invent a solution. They used two tubes for each offender. One end of

both tubes came through the smoker's drawing board, and the other went out through the wall, where a cigarette holder was inserted in the end of one tube and an ashtray hung underneath it. When the need for nicotine overcame somebody, a colleague would go into the corridor and hold a light to a cigarette fixed in the holder, while the smoker sat at his desk sucking on the other end of the tube. He exhaled the smoke into the corridor through the second tube. Somebody walking along the corridor who knew nothing of all this would be surprised by the sight of a wall puffing contentedly on several cigarettes.

Practical jokes were just a part of the young animator's life, and they contributed to our effectiveness as animators. I was only nineteen, and everybody was under twenty-five (Walt Disney was the Old Man

97

Eddie Selzer caught in a maelstrom of talent.

of Animation at twenty-nine). How many times in history has it been possible for a group of young people to enjoy working together and to find themselves in a happy hunting ground where that kind of behavior actually made them do their work better?

Termite Terrace was certainly a nuthouse, but it was a productive one. While we had fun, we were turning out thirty cartoons a year. Managers such as Leon Schlesinger, Ray Katz, and Eddie Selzer may have been ridiculous and stupid, but they were also cruel people. If you asked Ray Katz for a raise, he would say, "I could go down on Main Street and stumble over fifty better animators than you," and he had the power to say it. We shrank away from this stranger in a strange land like snails from salt, although much faster. The practical jokes were vital to our survival.

Tex Avery's arrival at the Schlesinger studio was in a sense a practical joke played on Leon. Confident that Leon was too lazy to check anything out, Tex told him that he was an experienced director, even though he had never directed a picture in his life. And, of course, Leon never called Walt Lantz to check out Tex's bogus claim. All he cared about was that Tex had promised to save him money.

Tex showed us that we could go beyond rationality. At a time when we were learning to animate and realizing that respect for anatomy is vital for believability, Tex showed us that a character can come out of that anatomy very briefly for a violent, distorted reaction. However, the distortion can't continue for long, or it becomes the way of drawing, and credibility is gone.

Look at Red Riding Hood's dance in Tex's *Red Hot Riding Hood.* It is the sexual spark that sends the ordinary wolf off into his star-struck paroxysm. Before the wolf's wild responses, in which his eyeballs fill the frame and his body flies apart, he is established as a solid and plausible character. Fifty years later, in *The Mask,* Jim Carrey is similarly established as a nice guy before he acquires the mask and begins to do things Tex Avery would do, and both Carrey and the wolf return to their normal shape when the effects of the mask or the woman wear off.

Roger Rabbit came into being as a result of Tex Avery's imagination, but unlike Tex's characters, Roger Rabbit was never at rest, only in visual and

Wit has truth in it; wisecracking is simply calisthenics with words.

—Dorothy Parker

auditory distortion. You can have fun with Silly Putty, but no one will ever love it or care what happens to it. A great problem with some Saturday morning television animation is that it is outrageous *all* the time, destroying believability. If the characters are walking around like Tex Avery extremes all the time, this creates a problem for the animators. When they want to add an accent, they can't, because there's nowhere left to go.

Not one of Tex Avery's characters survived as an individual in its original concept, except Droopy, who had a warm and quiet personality. However, nearly all of Tex's *pictures* survived as products of his wild imagination, of his ability to take a simple premise and celebrate it with pyrotechnics and a visual fire never before or since attempted.

For me, and Friz too, Bugs and Daffy had to be greatly modified and carefully crafted as more believable personalities in order for us to direct them to

become what they are today; that is, not just conveyors of wild action, not insane sky-rockets, but individuals, recognizable by their actions.

Noel Coward's admonition to a frenetic actor gave me a clue: "Don't just do something, stand there." That is directorial advice that applies to nearly every historically memorable animated character (and live action too).

The Termite Terrace years began with Tex's arrival, when Bob Clampett and I were assigned to work for him. Eventually, Tex managed to squeeze out of his contract with Leon and went to MGM, where he made some wonderful pictures, including the incomparable *Red Hot Riding Hood* series. No rotoscoping (tracing from live-action film onto animation paper) was used to animate the stunning performances by Red Hot Riding Hood or Cinderella. These sequences were all animated by Preston Blair, who was a great animator. The woman's movements and expressions are genuinely sexy, and nothing was traced from live action.

Tex himself was gallant, funny, and shy. Many years later, when he was dying—and he knew he was dying—he said, "I don't know where animators go when they die. They probably don't need another animator." He thought a minute and added ". . . but I bet they could use a good director."

On rare occasions I would employ Tex Avery distortion—of the eyes in this case— but only on my birthday.

Right and below:
*Tex Avery and friends at
Big Bear Lake, 1944.*

Fred ("Tex") Avery was a genius. As one of his group of animators at Warner Bros. in the late 1930s, I was ignorant of his genius, yet I learned from him the most essential of all truths about animation: Animation is the art of timing. Tex was impossible to imitate, and he was never known to pontificate, but he did teach by example. He showed me that the director must trust and implement the impulsive thought, the unexpected flash of inspiration; that you must not mock what you caricature (unless it is as absurdly pompous as the live-action travelogues he satirized); that you must always respect the single frame of film; and that character is all-important in making a great comedian. All of us in animation, all of us who have laughed with him, owe so much to Tex Avery, artist and genius.

From left: *Our receptionist Ginger Morgan's husband (also called "Ginger"), A.C. Gamer and his wife Jane, Katy Vallejo, Richard Hogan, Dorothy Jones, Chuck Jones, unknown, Bob Givens (writer), Ada Ruinello (Leon Schlesinger's secretary), Henry Binder.*

Tex Avery, Friz Freleng, Lilian Freleng, unknown, unknown.

Dr. Frank Baxter and the Clown Prince, Jack Warner. It seems appropriate that the biggest mouth in Hollywood should pose in front of the biggest mouth in the world.

In 1937 Leon Schlesinger decided he could use another director—me. Fifteen years later, when Jack Warner, seeking a director for Warner Bros.' first three-dimensional film, *The House of Wax,* chose Andre de Toth, who only had the use of one eye, I at last was able to understand the kind of logic that had made *me* a director of animation. If Jack Warner felt that a one-eyed man was a logical and appropriate choice to direct a three-dimensional film (de Toth never saw it dimensionally—the red-and-green glasses didn't help him any), then for Leon Schlesinger to select out of so many brilliant animators a talent-pallid, pale, and wan twenty-four-year-old as a director, was a true, if minuscule, example of the Warner Bros. logic of that time and era.

In all fairness to Mr. Warner—and it takes a ponderous pile of fairness to make remote sense out of his thinking—he was probably unaware of my promotion, but the de Toth wisdom would by illogical osmosis have filtered down to the mossy brain of Leon

Schlesinger. And so I became a director. The dreaded deed occurred, and all of animation shuddered.

My shudder was perhaps the most shuddery of all as news of this whimsical idiocy seeped into my artistically unplowed brain. I could think of no one in animation less equipped than I to handle the intricacies (not to mention the vicissitudes) of directing ten six-minute animated cartoons per year.

Mark Twain, while dictating his autobiography, said that as he got older it became much simpler to remember things that didn't happen than those that did. I appreciate the value of his point of view as I do of every opinion, paragraph, verb, adverb, period, comma, and semicolon he ever magically wrote, and in recalling the days at our home in Termite Terrace on the old Warner lot in Hollywood, I find it increas-

Two sketches by the great cartoonist/mousekeeper, Roy Williams, drawn during my short voyage to Disney. Right: *Back view of Roy Williams with Chuck Jones and Ward Kimball.*

ingly difficult to bring logic or even credible reasoning to bear on the ofttimes bizarre happenings in those sacred, dusty, laughing halls. How, for instance (among many, many for instances), to make believable our test cameraman, the redoubtable Henry ("Smokey," "Swamp-Rabbit") Garner, who once traveled through the mossy vaudeville circuit of the lesser bayous with a seal named Eunice? How can one embellish or sharpen the image of writer Tedd (Edward Stacey III) Pierce, who abandoned his wealthy Back Bay family at nine years old for the perfectly logical reason that his patrician-jawed, hawk-nosed mother insisted that he eat lobster?

The members of the Chuck Jones unit at Termite Terrace arrived by curious routes, none odder than that of animator Ben Washam. In the early 1930s, Ben ran a small hamburger stand with Bob Wyant in Glendale, California, about ten miles outside of

Animator Bobe Cannon, planning a new studio with layout man Art Heinemann, unaware of a ponderous Jones looking overhead.

Drawing by artist John McLeish of Tedd (Edward Stacey III) Pierce, who abandoned his wealthy Back Bay family at nine years old because his mother insisted that he eat lobster.

Los Angeles. It was an Ernest Hemingway kind of place; if you want a description of it, read *The Killers*. Ben and Bob were partners. Bob ran the counter, and Ben was the cook. One day Bob had an idea: take the same amount of hamburger meat and make *two* patties out of it rather than one, make two cuts in the bun so that there are two levels, and everyone will think they are getting MORE. That's how Bob's Big Boy Hamburger was invented. Ben drew the original Big Boy logo, which Bob used for about twenty-five years, long after Ben had decided that he didn't want to flip hamburgers—single or double patties—for the rest of his life and found a job at Schlesinger's. He spent the last few years of his life teaching animation to anyone who wanted to learn, and he didn't charge a penny. As he would say, "I was worth it, too."

Drawing by animator Phil DeLara of a philosophical discussion between Ben Washam, brother Dick Jones, and myself. Shortly after this, Lieutenant Richard Jones found himself on Okinawa as an army combat photographer.

Lethargic group: Ben Washam on the left, Rudy Larriva and Sue Gee in the center.

The Return of Alex Masianoff

The last thing I expected that brisk October day several years after World War II was to hear from across Sunset Boulevard this clarion call from the past: "The Chuck Jones! Great Animator! I have two potash mines; you shall have one of them!"

I had no hesitation in identifying this unique member of genus homo sapiens. If I was *the* Chuck Jones to him, he was *the* Alex Masianoff to me. Alex the unique, Alex the true one-of-a-kind, Alex the author of *The Poosie Ring the Bell* of sacred memory. Alex Masianoff was one of Leon Schlesinger's peccadilloes, and Leon, who tried to obstruct creativity wherever it attempted valiantly to flourish, swung a mean peccadillo.

Seeing Alex through

the thrashing traffic on Sunset Boulevard was, I suppose, similar to an ornithologist spotting a whooping crane on Times Square, and I felt the same anxiety the bird-lover would feel as Alex, turning smartly on his cavalryman's heel, strolled out into the five o'clock rush-hour traffic.

Alex lifted an imperious, elegantly gloved hand, and from both directions cars, trucks, and taxis slid, shuddered, and vibrated noisily to a stop, forming a clear lane for Alex's passage. It was the right of kings—or czars—at its most impressive.

"I am so pleased to compliment you, to at long lasting to compliment myself for writing the beginnings of so fonny characters.

So known everywhere,

even in Dinsk,

105

> "*I am so pleased to compliment you, to at long lasting to compliment myself for writing the beginnings of so fonny characters.*"—Alex Masianoff

even along the Kurfürstendamm. I was so pleased! So honored! So delighted! Upon your breast I pin medal decoration the first order of Nicholas, the cross of Peter Nov Gorod. You took my little song, my little idea, my sperm and my ozoa and made great stars out of them! The essence of them was there! You brought them to life! Listen: *The Poosie Ring the Bell*. The poosie, ha, ha, the great Sylvester! Up jumped the little doggie: Pluto!"

I tried to protest. I would love to take credit for Pluto, but . . .

Alex would not have it. "My next excruciatingly fonny line, 'Where is Mister Hen?'—Daffy Duck! Artist's license! Both poultry! Next historical line: 'She's out with the raccoon.' Poopie La Poo! Genius!

Sheer genius! My little creatures! On all screens all over the world! I am so proud!"

We crossed Bronson Avenue, against the red light, and Alex's disdainful magic prevailed again amid the screeching smoke of Goodyears and Dunlops.

Alex patted my craven shoulder. "You shall come to my house at Lake Arrowhead. We shall have Lamb Keebooboob, kasha blinis [and something that sounded like 'palminos']. We shall have soup if necessary! But no ice! I hate ice!" At this point the great Masianoff fades temporarily from my memory, the only person in the galaxy of strange people that decorate my life who hated ice—but would, if necessary, serve soup.

Early sketches of the villainous rat for
THE NIGHT WATCHMAN *(1938). The drawing on the left is
mine, the other two are by storyman Tedd Pierce.*

* * *

The first cartoon I directed was *The Night Watchman,* in which Sniffles the Mouse first appeared on-screen, as Tommy the Cat. It is strange that in his first incarnation Sniffles was a cat, although perhaps not as odd as Mickey Mouse having a dog and a kitten as pets. Mickey's kitten could serve as a flea. Tommy and Sniffles are similar personalities, but they are structurally very different. Tommy belongs to the primitive dumbbell period, in which characters were constructed like the early Mickey Mouse, but Sniffles's body is pear-shaped.

Sniffles the Mouse was timid and sweet, reflecting the man who was drawing him. The broader humor did not break through in my films until I directed *Super Rabbit.* I was only twenty-six years old at the time of Sniffles's debut, so you have to forgive me.

One vital directorial talent I am sure I had and have today is the ability to surround myself with talent, and the members of my unit at Termite Terrace were all extraordinarily talented. I didn't and don't care whether an animator has a sense of humor or not, but I wouldn't hire an animator who couldn't do the work better than I could myself. Everyone working on a film should do their job better than the director, but in the end the director is responsible for the whole picture.

I timed my films to the frame (one twenty-fourth of a second), and I knew exactly what they would look like in action before they went to the animators. I knew, for example, how many frames it took for the Coyote to disappear after he fell off the cliff, and how many frames later we would hear him hit the

Famished rat after gobbling pretzel.

C. Jones and two of the talented people
who made him possible: animators Ken Harris
(center) and Ben Washam.

Harry Love and assistant checking scenes
for errors.

Rats in THE NIGHT WATCHMAN *harmonize on a swinging Benny Goodmanish version of "The Shade of the Old Apple Tree."*

ground. When I gave my animators the layout drawings, I wanted them to live by that timing and follow it exactly. Not a frame must change.

At Warner Bros. no writer was even allowed to begin a story without the director's approval. If a writer had a story idea, he would make a couple of sketches and try to sell it to the director, but he would *never* complete the story without first discussing it with the director.

I worked closely with writer Mike Maltese. Mike made the storyboards, but we created the story together, and every line of dialogue was carefully crafted before Mel Blanc saw a script. I always took great trouble with the dialogue, because I didn't want any fat in it.

The dialogue in Warner Bros. cartoons will forever be associated with Mel Blanc. Friz Freleng was responsible for Mel joining the Schlesinger studio. Friz was directing *I Haven't Got a Hat,* with the stuttering pig (an early Porky) trying to recite "The Midnight Ride of Paul Revere" at his kindergarten graduation ceremony, as he fights an obvious and urgent need to go to the bathroom. For the pig's voice, Friz had hired an actor who stuttered naturally. In those days we recorded the voices on film, which could only be used once before being destroyed. The uncontrollably stammering actor just kept using up expensive and un-recoverable film. At that opportune moment, Mel came to see Friz, who asked him if he could stammer. "Oh yes," Mel said, "I can sta-sta-stutter." "Can you stop stuttering?" asked the concerned Friz. Mel could stop, and he got the job.

Mel could handle Porky's stutter with ease, but Bugs's eating habits presented a serious problem: Mel was allergic to carrots. If ever he swallowed carrot, he broke out in a nasty rash. Being more humane than Leon, the directors tried to overcome Mel's plight by substituting apples, celery, and other edibles for the famous carrot, but none of them crunched quite right. In the end, we stood by him with a wastepaper basket while he bit the carrot,

Notes from Eddie Selzer's nighttime story session on the completed storyboard of ROBIN HOOD DAFFY (1958). Few of these notes were usable. They all sound as if they came from Eddie's steeltrap mind—it would snap shut on any usable idea.

chomped it a little, recorded the words, and spat out the vegetable-chew before the symptoms began. It seemed ironic that the only man in the world who had to chew raw carrots for a living was perhaps the only man in the world allergic to them. He suffered for his art.

A thoughtful critic once said of Mel Blanc that he was indeed a man of a thousand voices—all the same. No great actor need change the pitch or texture of his voice to play a part, from that of an idiot or a lover (is that redundant?) to a pathological killer. Edmund Gwenn did play

MALTESE * JONES

#1470 – ROBIN HOOD DAFFY

Have staff hit Daffy on nose on word "Parry", not on word "Thrust." Indent staff over beak so that when staff is removed it shows imprint of Daffy's beak.

Have Friar tap Daffy with small, light club, rather than twig or branch.

Instead of aiming catapult at tunnel, have it fastened directly to mouth of catapult so that it can't miss going straight into it.

Change Porky's line to "I'm still not convinced that you're Robin Hood."

Have sign indicating "King's Deer Reserve." Porky asks Daffy where his merry men are if he is Robin Hood. Daffy blows horn – hunters come up and fire arrows at Daffy. .... or

Daffy to lead into deer episode remarks "I'll use stealth." Then he gets into deer outfit, goes into woods. We hear from distance baying of hounds, twang-twang of arrows, Daffy staggers out of woods full of arrows, but still in deer costume, gasping, "Those woods are full of poachers."

Daffy spins morning star and it takes him up like a helicopter. Tnen it falls, taking Daffy with it and wraps itself around him like a cocoon. .One ball is still spinning slowly above Daffy. He tries to draw himself into cocoon with "What a stupid place to put a duck", before ball hits him on head.
...   then slowly descents to Bop Daffy on head.

just such a killer in *Foreign Correspondent*, to reappear without change of voice or tonality as Santa Claus in *Miracle on 34th Street*.

It is hard to overstate how good Mel Blanc was. He was one of the most brilliant actors I have ever known. He was extraordinarily quick, able to transfer his personality instantly into a character. He would come in about an hour before a recording, without having seen my story layouts, and not really knowing how he was going to play the character. I would go carefully over the layouts with him, then I would read the lines to show him what intonation I wanted, where the accents should fall, and where I needed hesitates. And that was all he needed.

Some of Mel's voices were speeded-up versions

Mel Blanc and Bob McKimson at a
recording session.

of others. Daffy's voice, for instance, is the same as Sylvester's, but speeded up. The big problem with speed changes came when Mel had to sing, particularly if he was singing a duet at different speeds. But Mel *could* sing a duet between Daffy and Sylvester. He would sing Sylvester's part at normal speed, then change both key and speed for Daffy. I don't know how he did it—I just stood there in amazement.

Mel never tried to be comic. Bugs and Elmer singing opera in *What's Opera, Doc?* and trying to get it right is sufficiently funny in itself. Both Mel Blanc and Arthur Q. Bryan (the voice of Elmer Fudd) were musicians. Mel played the violin, while Arthur had actually been a singer. He also played a character called Doc Gamble on a popular radio show called *Fibber McGee and Molly,* and Doc Gamble helped us understand Daffy. The more Doc Gamble talked, the angrier he would become, until he was about to explode. Mel also started in radio, where, if you worked hard enough, you could eventually get to do it for nothing.

Mel Blanc did not provide the voices in all my cartoons. In *The Dover Boys,* for example, the narration was supplied by John McLeish, who also narrated the opening of *Dumbo. The Dover Boys* was considered a revolutionary cartoon when it appeared in 1942, but in many ways it looked back to older melodramas such as *The Drunkard,* in which actors would strike exaggerated poses. The hero would lean forward like a destroyer heading out to sea, villains would cow and sweep dark cloaks over their faces, and no character could announce an intention of going upstairs without pointing very positively in the general direction of the staircase.

The Dover Boys was one of the first animated parodies, and of course the distributors in New York hated it, because they had never seen anything like

it before. They would have refused to release the picture, but they had paid for it, so they tried to have me fired instead. They would have succeeded, but they could find no acceptable replacement. This loathing of originality continues to some extent in television today: when something original does successfully appear, everyone imitates it, but most are afraid to do something genuinely new.

• • •

Here's Fudd in Your Eye

As Mark Twain said, waiting to be punished is one of the most uninteresting times of a boy's life, but for sheer horror nothing could equal the completion of my first film as a director. I had forgotten that there was such a thing as an audience connected with film, and I was afraid that my first cartoon, *The Night Watchman,* would be so bad that the audience would hiss at the ushers.

Fortunately for me, audiences were kinder and gentler then, and I survived—and I have seldom had cause to regret it. I did not have the guts to go see my first film in the theater, and to this day I go to a

Left: *The Dover Boys appeared on August 29, 1942.*

Below: *Story sketches from The Night Watchman.*

screening only with a kind of keening trepidation similar to the anticipation of the rack or the bastinado. I cannot believe that anyone will laugh.

Jackie Gleason said that comedy is the most exacting form of dramatic art because it has an instant critic: laughter. And the making of film comedy adds what to the performing comedian must seem an almost unbearable discipline: the film must be complete in its naked entirety *before* it is exposed to an audience.

With tragedy it's a bit more difficult. What do you do—go down into the audience and count the number of tears, or collect them to measure later? ("Gee . . . two quarts tonight!") We didn't do audience tests with our cartoons either; we just went

111

ahead and made pictures we thought would be funny.

The interpretation of tests is not a simple art. When *Snow White and the Seven Dwarfs* came out, for example, there was a lot of criticism of the witch, so tests were made. Child experts ran the picture for kids, with paddy wagons standing by to carry the audience away when they went mad with fear of the witch. In fact, they stayed sane, but—and this is very scientific—there was evidence of a mass wetting of pants. The experts pointed and pontificated: "Ah-ha! When that witch showed up, those kids started wetting their trousers, and no wonder. By God, this film should be taken out of circulation!"

But then a wise child behaviorist—something you don't expect to find—came along and made a suggestion. "Why," he asked, "don't we get some chairs carrying a light electric current, so they will respond when each child wets, and we'll see at precisely what moment in the film it happens?"

The little kids agreed (practically unanimously) that it was time to pee when they heard the dwarfs going off to work singing their signature song. Well, how could they resist? How else could they express their delight?

All of a sudden, the child behaviorists (with the exception of one) were hiding behind bushes.

Feature-film directors routinely test their films by taking them out to preview. And if their film fails to receive the response they want, they will go to another theater and another theater, until they find someone who *does* like it.

I always tried to avoid seeing my cartoons with an audience, and refused all invitations to attend theatrical showings. It was just too frightening. But most artists eventually find out that we must face the crowd if we are to survive. It does the matador little good to make beautiful passes alone with a bull in a moonlit pasture. By selecting the bullfight as his profession, he must some day face the bull and the crowd.

Eventually I was tricked by my first wife, Dorothy, into going to the Warner theater on Hollywood Boulevard. I didn't know that a cartoon of mine was playing, and when the title appeared I immediately went under my seat and into the fetal position in abject terror. Then I heard the dearest words ever spoken in the English language. Behind me, a small eight-year-old

How else could they express their delight?

112

girl's voice piped up, joyous and delighted: "Mommy," she said, "I *knew* we should have come here."

I have always had a sneaking feeling that producing comedy is somehow rather trivial, and that my life would have been more meaningful and significant if I had built a bridge or discovered a toilet freshener or something equally rewarding, but once you have heard a strange audience burst into laughter at a film you directed, you realize what the word *joy* is all about.

Writers Dave Monahan, Rich Hogan, and Bob Givens.

Once you have heard a strange audience burst into laughter at a film you directed, you realize what the word joy is all about.

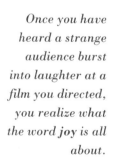

113

A QUESTION OF CHARACTERS

115

The last quarter of a century of my life has been pretty constantly and faithfully devoted to the study of the human race—that is to say, the study of myself, for in my individual person I am the entire human race compacted together. I have found that there is no ingredient of the race which I do not possess in either a small way or a large way. When it is small, as compared with the same ingredient in somebody else, there is still enough of it for all the purposes of examination. In my contacts with the species I find no one who possesses a quality which I do not possess. The shades of difference between other people and me serve to make variety and prevent monotony, but that is all; broadly speaking, we are all alike; and so by studying myself carefully and comparing myself with other people and noting the divergences, I have been enabled to acquire a knowledge of the human race which I perceive is more accurate and more comprehensive than that which has been acquired and revealed by any other member of our species. As a result, my private and concealed opinion of myself is not of a complimentary sort. It follows that my estimate of the human race is the duplicate of my estimate of myself.

—from The Autobiography of Mark Twain

$\mathscr{H}$e does not draw Bugs Bunny; he draws pictures of Bugs Bunny." That small boy's response to his father's introduction of me as "a man who draws Bugs Bunny" identified with perfect clarity what we were trying to accomplish at Termite Terrace.

We drew pictures of Bugs and Daffy and Wile E. and Pepé and the rest. All of them existed in three-dimensional reality in our minds and drawings. And each was individual and unique in movement, mannerisms, expressions, joys, mistakes, stumblings, and triumphs. "*Of.*" The perfect word.

Bugs Bunny and Daffy and Elmer and Porky were all characters whose personalities had to be carefully developed from their crude beginnings to their successful realization as Warner Bros. stars. Each of the characters has certain ways of standing, of running, of

Marc Anthony (top left) *will hopefully never have to protect his pet kitten from an invading Martian.*
Papa Bear (left), *with Mama Bear and Junyer, many years before Archie Bunker and* **his** *family.*

smiling, of frowning. It is what makes each the special personality he is. Bugs Bunny is always graceful, always under control. If he makes a gigantic reaction, he is kidding, in the same sense that Daffy Duck in the same circumstance is not kidding.

At Warner Bros., characters weren't simply assigned a personality; personalities developed over a period of time under the director's hand. The director therefore had to find out not only *what* his characters were, and *where* they were in the film, but most of all *who* they were: the personality traits, the peculiarities, the meaningless movements (sometimes called "displacement activities") that decide the unique individuality in each of us.

Developing animated characters is very like meeting people—you start with an exterior and work your way inside to discover who the person is.

116

The "what" of the character is what they look like or how they are drawn. (Send me a photograph of yourself and I won't know who you are; I might think you look like a nice person, but you might be a murderer.) The "who" of a character is who they really are, and you have to get close and talk with

somebody to discover that. It is this search that brings a character to life. As you become acquainted with a character you are creating, you add parts of yourself that are pertinent to that character. Individuality is revealed in the timing, the hesitations, the body mechanics, and it all must come from the director.

Different people bring out different sides of us, and the behavior of the Warner Bros. characters changed with each director. Bob McKimson's style of acting, for example, was very different from mine, or from Friz Freleng's. Far from being a follower of Stanislavsky, Bob preferred early American melodrama, in which speech was backed up by broad movements and gestures. This is partly why his Foghorn Leghorn pictures are so good, because Foghorn Leghorn is a character who naturally acts that way. I don't believe in doing anything twice: if acting it, don't say it; if doing it with color, don't repeat it with line.

BATON BUNNY (1959).

If a character such as Daffy Duck or Bugs Bunny is clearly established and understood by several directors, then that character will be reasonably consistent from film to film, even though the drawings or timing may vary. In fact, such details as the length of Daffy's bill or Bugs's ears and/or legs differed so much that I or any director can usually identify the director even from an individual drawing.

Animation enabled us to evoke emotion, response, and life where none existed before. It was not an imitation of comic strips—it was not our style of drawing but the way our characters moved that made them who they were and are. Nor was our animation an imitation of motion pictures—it was an extension of motion pictures into an area live action could not believably reach.

The animation director works with his animators in much the same way that a live-action director

DAFFY DUCK
© WARNER BROS
ANIMATION INC. 1991

This material is the property of Warner Bros.
Animation, Inc. It is unpublished and must
not be taken from the studio, duplicated, or
used in any manner except for production,
without written permission from an authorized
officer of the company.

2/14/91

works with actors. The difference—and it is a big one—is that the animation director not only demonstrates what he wants to see on the screen, he makes drawings of it.

The basic tools of the animator were then and are now quite simple: a stack of paper, a pencil, a light board, and an inquisitive mind directing a trained hand. With these tools the animation group—for group it was—could evoke life *before* the camera started shooting.

The animator was to animation what the actor is to the living stage. His art lived without color, background, or camera. The animator, in the purest sense (and I have known many impure animators), had a complete art form from the moment he finished a set of action. He could hold the stack of paper in his hands and by flipping it achieve all the basic life it would ever know. If he wanted to enlarge his audience or embellish the action, he could have the drawings inked, painted, and set under a camera

against a background; he could add sound and music; but he would not change the essential form.

If, as a child, you drew stick figures on the edge of a notebook, then flipped the pages to watch a spastic and funny little dance, you were animating. Even today those dancing sticks are the ultimate in character animation. Norman McLaren's laughing squiggles and strokes brought universal and deserved praise, and I believe that their joyous *life* was the cause of it. Each of us will draw our own conclusions about the meaning of the films, but they touch an area of response in all of us that has very little to do with rationality.

Animation was then an extension of live action, the art of the impossible—or the inconvenient. In those days—and to a certain extent today—if you wanted film of an elephant walking or a centipede strolling, you had to hire yourself an elephant or a centipede and shoot the necessary footage with a motion-picture camera. You could save money this

118

If you wanted film of an elephant walking, it was less expensive to hire a live-action camera than an animator. But if you wanted to see Horton the elephant (right) coming to a sudden stop, there was no substitute for animation, which could do what could not be conveniently done by any other method.

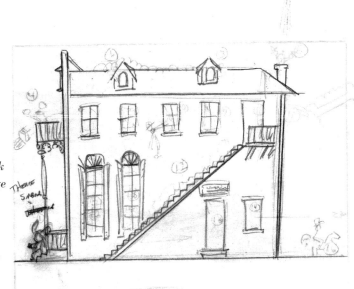

Any child who draws simple stick figures on the edge of a notebook, then flips the pages to watch a jerky little dance, is animating.

FOLLOW FIST FIGHT THRU ENTIRE BUILDING — JUMP FROM SPOT TO SPOT — VERY ZIPPY, FIGHT TO END ALL FIGHTS

AT END SHOT OF CONTENDERS SLICK & NO EVIDENCE OF DRASTIC STRUGGLE

way, because it would take a good animator two hours to do what a camera could do in a second. But if you wanted to see a pterodactyl flying, that is where the unique quality of animation came in. It could do what could not be conveniently done by any other method then known.

Today we have the wonderful technology of George Lucas's Special Effects Division at Industrial Light and Magic, and others. But personal, individ-ual animation must still be done by the skilled hand of the traditional animator.

Designing a character does involve drawing, but as soon as the character is animated, it is the *animation* that makes the character, not the drawing. When you are engaged in full animation, the character pushes you aside and takes over. Drawing becomes as unconscious a necessity to you as body mechanics are to the dancer during a performance. You are the

*Daffy Duck plays
Robin Hood.*

*Opposite and below:
We would all like to yell and
bellow at every frustration like
Daffy Duck or Yosemite Sam.*

interpreter of actions that surprise both you and the character you vitalize. You and the character become that series of surprises that is comedy.

"Animation is not a series of drawings that move, it is drawings of movement," said Norman McLaren.

In other words, we must have a clear idea of what our character is doing before we start to draw him. For instance, when Daffy Duck plays Robin Hood, we must be thoroughly familiar not only with Daffy himself but with how he would approach the role of Robin Hood. If Bugs Bunny played Robin Hood, it would be with a different manner, attitude, and body movement. Why? Because Bugs is an entirely different individual and must be approached—as we must approach every

one of our characters—as an individual, not only in appearance but in personality.

There is no such thing in animation or live action as a lasting and beloved character who could not be correlated to human experience, human failure, and human triumph. Being funny doesn't mean anything unless there is an underlying human note.

All of the original Warner Bros. characters were written subjectively, as were (and are) *all* great comedic characters in all media. In short, we were talking about ourselves, revealing ourselves, examining ourselves. For myself—and, I believe, equally for the other directors—each character represented a multiplication of some trait that resides in me and (I suspect) in everyone else. Within us all dwells the capability of being Daffy Duck, Yosemite Sam, Wile E. Coyote, Torquemada, Lucretia Borgia, or Elmer Fudd.

The great comic characters usually reveal foibles rather than heroic strengths. If we look at the history of comedy from Chaplin and Keaton to Richard Pryor and Robin Williams, we find the same sad little per-

Each character represented a trait that resides in me.

sonality traits we all know, recognize, and understand, but purified and emphasized to an extent we would all like to imitate if we only dared. Who of us would not like to bellow at the top of our voice at every frustration, like Yosemite Sam? Justify to our audience every dethspicable act, like Daffy Duck?

With weak characters, the animation director looks for the points where they are strong; with strong ones, we look for where they are weak. That is how we came to make Daffy Duck and Bugs Bunny believable.

Daffy's weaknesses are that he is avaricious and demanding, and he believes that the world owes him a living. Rather than trying to hide these characteristics—as most of us would try to hide our failings—we expand and stress them in the animation.

Balancing this classic company of losers and wimps is a much, much smaller, more select group: the comic heroes, best exemplified by Bugs Bunny, but accompanied by Speedy Gonzales, Tweety Bird, and Pepé le Pew, to mention a few of the very few comic heroes at Warner Bros., or anyplace else.

Pepé would be in the first group, except he does not know or recognize his failings, as do the characters in our cartoons who run off cliffs but do not obey the law of gravity and fall until they realize they are in midair. Pepé represents without apology the kind of graceful acceptance of his own desirability that most of us would give our eyeteeth if not our right arms for. Speedy is a hero not because of his speed but because he always uses it unselfishly for the benefit of the rodent community of Mexico. An admirable mouse indeed. Tweety is also a hero, simply because he triumphs. And, above all, there is Bugs Bunny.

These few represent our dreams and ideals, and if they are to be successful, they must be handled with the best kid gloves or they will become unmotivated bullies like Heckle and Jeckle, or Woody Woodpecker at his worst. The woodpecker would tease somebody without provocation, just like bullies I suffered from as a child.

121

The comic heroes: Pepé represents graceful acceptance of his desirability, Speedy is a hero because he uses his speed so unselfishly, and Tweety is a hero simply because he wins.

I-JIM SORRY. BUT I CAN'T JOIN YOU
I'M CONVINCED YOU'RE JUST
NOT ROBIN HOOD

Between the heroes and the wimps we have a very small marginal group who don't really qualify either way.

Porky Pig in earlier films was a stolid, rather uninteresting, sometimes vapid, and usually infantile fool. But in later pictures—at least for me—he became a more complicated figure, as in *Robin Hood*

122

Daffy, Duck Dodgers in the 24½th Century, Rocket Squad, and *Dripalong Daffy.* The dog Marc Anthony, too, simply doesn't make it as wimp or hero. He is so human he becomes an almost perfect dog. And the Road Runner remains in a kind of limbo, peculiar only to himself/herself. (In France, the Road Runner is known and appears on the title as "Mi-Mi." Perhaps the French can't understand any kind of chase unless there is a sexual need.) Whatever its sex, the Road Runner is simply a kind of endearing nonentity, existing only as a very fast dish of caviar to the Coyote.

But basically, and aside from a few oddities, the litmus test for all lasting characters must be the ability to see and laugh with characteristics recognized with regret in ourselves. Without that recognition there is no hope of achieving the surprising kind of immortality the world found in the characters we blundered into over those thirty years at Warner Bros. We are not observers. We are all participants.

Porky Pig became a more complicated figure in later films.

CHRONOLOGY OF THE FIRST APPEARANCE OF WARNER BROS. ANIMATION STARS, 1935 TO 1967

Note: Early directors were called "supervisors" for some Schlesingerian whim.

YEAR	STAR	PICTURE TITLE	CREDITS
1935	**Porky Pig** (& Beans)	*I Haven't Got a Hat*	Supervised: Isadore Freleng Animated: Rollin Hamilton Animated: Jack King
1936	**Porky Pig** (starring)	*The Blow Out*	Supervised: Fred Avery Animated: Charles Jones Animated: Sid Sutherland
1937	**Daffy Duck** (embryonic; not yet named Daffy; with what later became Woody Woodpecker's voice)	*Porky's Duck Hunt*	Supervised: Fred Avery Animated: Virgil Ross Animated: Robert Cannon
1937	**Elmer Fudd** (embryonic)	*Egghead Rides Again*	Supervised: Fred Avery Animated: Irvin Spence Animated: Paul Smith
1937	**Petunia Pig**	*Porky's Romance*	Supervised: Frank Tashlin Animated: Don Williams Animated: Volney White
1938	**Daffy Duck** (formative)	*Daffy Duck and Egghead*	Supervised: Fred Avery Story: Ben Hardaway Animated: Virgil Ross
1938	**Bugs Bunny** (embryonic)	*Porky's Hare Hunt*	Supervised: Ben Hardaway Story: Howard Baldwin Animated: Volney White

123

YEAR	STAR	PICTURE TITLE	CREDITS
1938	**Egghead** (identified as Elmer Fudd)	A Feud There Was	Supervised: Fred Avery Story: Melvin Millar Animated: Sid Sutherland
1939	**Sniffles**	Naughty but Mice	Supervised: Charles M. Jones Story: Rich Hogan Animated: Phil Monroe
1939	**Elmer Fudd** (formative; first use of "Elmer" voice by Arthur Q. Bryan)	Dangerous Dan McFoo	Supervised: Fred Avery Story: Richard Hogan Animated: Paul Smith
1939	**Bugs Bunny** (the link between the rabbit and the name is made)	Hare-um Scare-Um	Supervised: Ben "Bugs" Hardaway Supervised: Cal Dalton Story: Melvin Millar Animated: Gil Turner
1939	**Inki**	Little Lion Hunter	Supervised: Charles M. Jones Story: Robert Givens Animated: Philip Monroe

YEAR	STAR	PICTURE TITLE	CREDITS
1940	**Elmer Fudd** (mature; Bugs Bunny formative)	Elmer's Candid Camera	Supervised: Charles M. Jones Story: Rich Hogan Animated: Bob McKimson
1940	**Daffy Duck** (mature; with Daffy's voice)	You Oughta Be in Pictures	Supervised: I. Freleng Story: Jack Miller Animated: Herman Cohen

YEAR	STAR	PICTURE TITLE	CREDITS
1940	**Bugs Bunny** (*mature;* *"classic" Bugs*)	*A Wild Hare*	Supervised: Fred Avery Story: Rich Hogan Animated: Virgil Ross
1942	**Tweety Bird**	*A Tale of Two Kitties*	Supervised: Robert Clampett Story: Warren Foster Animated: Rod Scribner
1942	**Henery Hawk**	*The Squawkin' Hawk*	Supervised: Charles M. Jones
1943	**Hubie & Bertie**	*The Aristo-Cat*	Supervised: Charles M. Jones Story: Tedd Pierce Animated: Rudy Larriva
1943	**Granny**	*Hiss and Make Up*	Supervised: I. Freleng Story: Michael Maltese Animated: Gerry Chiniquy
1944	**The Three Bears** (*early*)	*Bugs Bunny and the Three Bears*	Supervised: Charles M. Jones Story: Tedd Pierce Animated: Robert Cannon
1945	**Pepé le Pew** (*embryonic*)	*Odor-Able Kitty*	Supervised: Charles M. Jones Story: Tedd Pierce Animated: Robert Cannon
1945	**Sylvester**	*Life with Feathers*	Supervised: I. Freleng Story: Tedd Pierce Animated: Virgil Ross

125

*Note: Up to this point, animators and storymen were credited in rotation, one at a time.
Leon Schlesinger felt that more than one credit involved needless payments to a lettering man.*

| 1945 | **Yosemite Sam** | *Hare Trigger* | Directed: I. Freleng
Story: Michael Maltese
Animated: Manuel Perez
Animated: Ken Champin
Animated: Virgil Ross
Animated: Gerry Chiniquy |

| 1946 | **Gossamer** | *Hair-Raising Hare* | Directed: Charles M. Jones
Story: Tedd Pierce
Animated: Ben Washam
Animated: Ken Harris
Animated: Basil Davidovich
Animated: Lloyd Vaughan |

| 1946 | **Foghorn Leghorn** | *Walky Talky Hawky* | Directed: Robert McKimson
Story: Warren Foster
Animated: Richard Bickenback
Animated: Cal Dalton
Animated: Don Williams |

126

| 1947 | **The Goofy Gophers** | *The Goofy Gophers* | Directed: Arthur Davis
Animated: Don Williams
Animated: Manny Gould
Animated: J. C. Melendez
Animated: Cal Dalton |

| 1947 | **Charlie Dog** | *Little Orphan Airedale* | Directed: Charles M. Jones
Story: Tedd Pierce
Story: Michael Maltese
Animated: Lloyd Vaughan
Animated: Ben Washam
Animated: Ken Harris
Animated: Phil Monroe |

YEAR	STAR	PICTURE TITLE	CREDITS
1948	**Hippity Hopper**	*Hop, Look and Listen*	Directed: Robert McKimson Story: Warren Foster Animated: Charles McKimson Animated: Manny Gould Animated: I. Ellis
1948	**Marvin Martian**	*Haredevil Hare*	Directed: Charles M. Jones Story: Michael Maltese Animated: Ben Washam Animated: Lloyd Vaughan Animated: Ken Harris Animated: Phil Monroe
1949	**Claude Cat**	*Mouse Wreckers*	Directed: Charles M. Jones Story: Michael Maltese Animated: Lloyd Vaughan Animated: Ken Harris Animated: Phil Monroe Animated: Ben Washam
1949	**Coyote & Road Runner**	*Fast and Furry-ous*	Directed: Charles M. Jones Story: Michael Maltese Animated: Ken Harris Animated: Phil Monroe Animated: Lloyd Vaughan Animated: Ben Washam
1949	**Pepé le Pew** *(mature)*	*For Scent-imental Reasons*	Directed: Charles M. Jones Story: Michael Maltese Animated: Ben Washam Animated: Lloyd Vaughan Animated: Ken Harris Animated: Phil Monroe

YEAR	STAR	PICTURE TITLE	CREDITS
1949	**The Three Bears** *(mature)*	*Bear Feat*	Directed: Charles M. Jones Story: Michael Maltese Animated: Ben Washam Animated: Lloyd Vaughan Animated: Ken Harris Animated: Phil Monroe
1950	**Sylvester Jr.**	*Pop 'Im Pop*	Directed: Bob McKimson Story: Warren Foster Animated: Charles McKimson Animated: Rod Scribner Animated: Phil DeLara Animated: Manuel Perez Animated: J. C. Melendez
1952	**Wile E. Coyote** *(talking)*	*Operation: Rabbit*	Directed: Charles M. Jones Story: Michael Maltese Animated: Ken Harris Animated: Phil Monroe Animated: Lloyd Vaughan Animated: Ben Washam
1952	**Marc Anthony & Pussyfoot**	*Feed the Kitty*	Directed: Charles M. Jones Story: Michael Maltese Animated: Robert Gribbroek
1953	**Ralph Wolf & Sam Sheepdog**	*Don't Give up the Sheep*	Directed: Charles M. Jones Story: Michael Maltese Animated: Ken Harris Animated: Lloyd Vaughan Animated: Ben Washam
1953	**Speedy Gonzales**	*Cat-Tails for Two*	Directed: Robert McKimson Story: Tedd Pierce Animated: Rod Scribner Animated: Phil DeLara Animated: Charles McKimson Animated: Herman Cohen

YEAR	STAR	PICTURE TITLE	CREDITS
1954	**Tasmanian Devil**	*Devil May Hare*	Directed: Robert McKimson Story: Sid Marcus Animated: Herman Cohen Animated: Rod Scribner Animated: Phil DeLara Animated: Charles McKimson
1954	**Witch Hazel**	*Bewitched Bunny*	Directed: Charles M. Jones Story: Michael Maltese Animated: Lloyd Vaughan Animated: Ken Harris Animated: Ben Washam
1954	**Ralph Phillips**	*From A to Z-Z-Z-Z*	Directed: Charles M. Jones Story: Michael Maltese Animated: Ken Harris Animated: Ben Washam Animated: Lloyd Vaughan
1955	**Michigan J. Frog**	*One Froggy Evening*	Directed: Charles M. Jones Story: Michael Maltese Animated: Abe Levitow Animated: Richard Thompson Animated: Ken Harris Animated: Ben Washam
1967	**Cool Cat***	*Cool Cat*	Directed: Alex Lovy Story: Bob Kurtz Animated: Ted Bonnicksen Animated: Ed Solomon Animated: Volus Jones Animated: LaVerne Harding
1967	**Merlin the Magic Mouse***	*Merlin the Magic Mouse*	Directed: Alex Lovy Story: Cal Howard Animated: Ted Bonnicksen Animated: LaVerne Harding Animated: Volus Jones Animated: Ed Solomon

(*These two characters were conceived after the "good-folks" were tossed out.)

Balls and pears are convenient drawing aids for the animator, fixed elements that set up the composition of a character working in space, but they are not the only way of drawing. The artists at United Productions of America (UPA) drew without using balls and pears, and other studios' human characters, such as Snow White or Superman, have to be drawn differently.

NO MATTER HOW DIFFERENT THE BUGS BUNNY OF 1939 IS COMPARED TO THE BUGS BUNNY OF TODAY, THE TWO *DO* HAVE SOMETHING IN COMMON.

EACH OF THEM HAS A PEAR-SHAPED BODY, AND EACH OF THEM HAS A ROUND OR OVAL HEAD. THESE ARE THE BASIC ELEMENTS THAT ALL THE WARNER BROS. CHARACTERS HAVE IN COMMON—AND MOST OF THE DISNEY CHARACTERS TOO, FROM DONALD DUCK AND THE MATURE MICKEY MOUSE TO THE SEVEN DWARFS. THE SEVEN DWARFS ARE—WITHIN LIMITS— SEVEN DIFFERENT CHARACTERS, ALTHOUGH THEY ARE IN A WAY LIKE SEVEN GRINCHES, EACH WITH A SINGLE PECULIARITY COMPARABLE TO THE GRINCH'S LOATHING OF CHRISTMAS: GRUMPY IS GRUMPY *ALL* THE TIME, DOPEY IS *ALWAYS* DOPEY, AND SNEEZY . . . NOT MUCH BASIS FOR A PERSONALITY PERHAPS, BUT IT'S ENOUGH TO DISTINGUISH HIM FROM THE OTHERS.

There are no circles and pears in Michigan J. Frog's body because the frog has no defined head. Frogs and toads don't really have necks, and an interesting oddity about Michigan J. Frog is that his mouth is part of his body. These are rough preliminary sketches trying to establish who he is.

131

IN THE EARLIEST ANIMATED CARTOONS, CHARACTERS' BODIES APPEARED TO BE BUILT OF TWO CIRCLES—ONE FOR THE HEAD AND ONE FOR THE THORAX—LINKED BY TWO LINES, TO FORM A SHAPE LIKE A STRONGMAN'S DUMBBELL WITH ARMS AND LEGS. MICKEY MOUSE BEGAN LIFE THIS WAY, BEFORE HE EVOLVED INTO A BALL-AND-PEAR SHAPE. FOR SOME CURIOUS REASON, THE EARLY ANIMATED CHARACTERS ALSO STOOD BOW-LEGGED.

WE ARE DEALING IN SHAPES, SHAPES WITH INDIVIDUAL CHARACTERISTICS, VARIATIONS ON A COMMON ANATOMICAL STRUCTURE, INDIVIDUAL COLORS, VOICES, AND—MOST IMPORTANT—INDIVIDUAL PERSONALITIES, SO THAT IN THE SAME CIRCUMSTANCE THEY REACT IN DIFFERENT WAYS. PUT ALL THESE ELEMENTS TOGETHER AND THEY SPELL ANIMATION. WARNER BROS. ANIMATION, THAT IS.

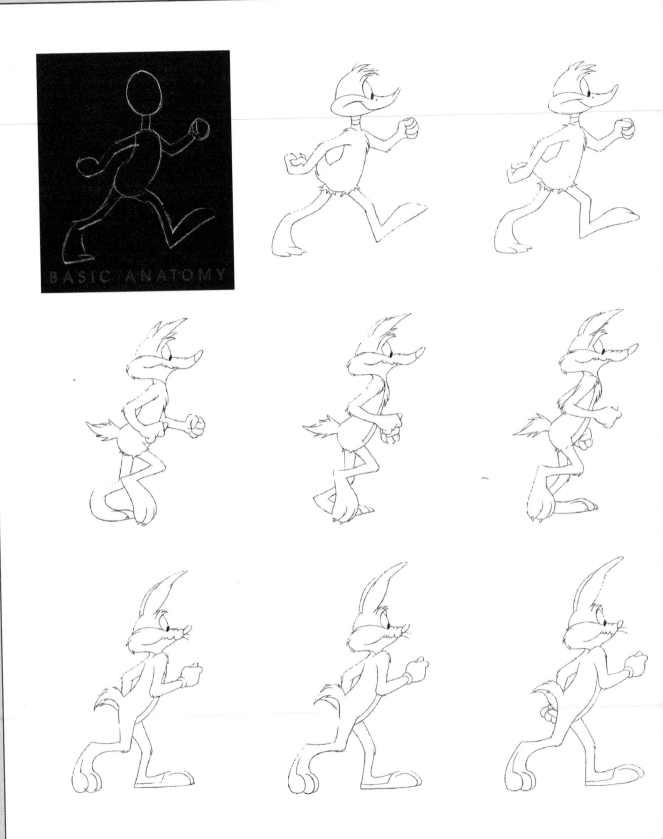

Daffy Duck becomes Wile E. Coyote becomes Bugs Bunny in seventeen easy moves,

showing that it is the surface that counts as well as the basic anatomy in all living things.

Above: *Stubby, early rabbit drawn by the author.*
Right: *Later rabbit, re-designed by several artists
—but primarily by Robert Givens and
Robert McKimson (bottom).*

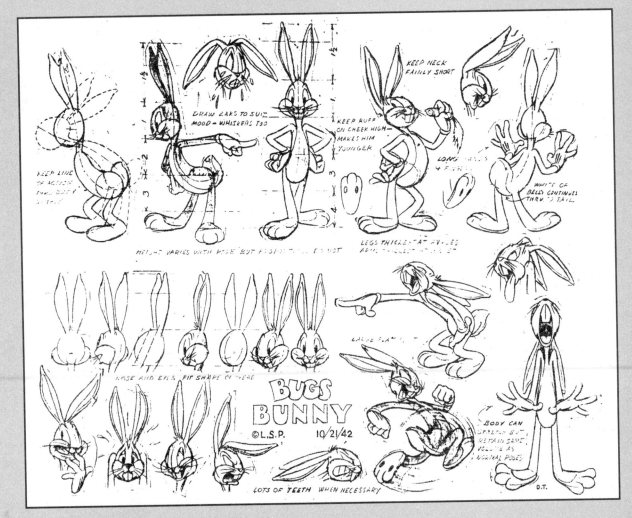

BUGS BUNNY

"Bugs Bunny is wonderful," said Warner writer Bill Scott, who later wrote the "Rocky and Bullwinkle" cartoons. "All you have to do is put him in front of a camera and you've got a hit."

I have come to know Bugs so well that I no longer have to *think* about what he is doing in any situation. I let the part of me that is Bugs come to the surface, knowing, with regret, that I can never match his marvelous confidence.

Bugs Bunny is a comic hero, a very rare bird indeed. Nearly all great comedians represent the small people of the world, the losers, the accident-prone, the put-upon, the persistently unsuccessful, and at Warner Bros. we found that few of our most successful characters were triumphant even in the pursuit of such trivial aims as catching a Road Runner or a ca-

nary. The Disney short subjects bear out this tradition: Donald Duck, Goofy, and Pluto were all more notable for their mistakes than their triumphs. Even Mickey Mouse succeeded in spite of himself. But Bugs Bunny is a winner.

A comic hero can be a tough character to work with. Bugs is such a strong character that he can easily seem to be a bully unless he receives some serious knocks in the course of a story. His adversary must be worthy of him, for there is nothing heroic about beating an opponent who is in no position to beat *you*. Bugs must not appear to be Super Rabbit per se.

Like all heroes and heroines, Bugs Bunny grew strong when strong villains began confronting him, just as Dorothy became strong against the Wicked Witch of the West, and just as Snow White's witch

Above: *HAIR RAISING HARE (1946)*.

gave *her* spine, too. Even Charlie Brown has his Lucy, one of the great non-motivated villainesses of literature. Her sole purpose, it seems, is to remove every vestige of dignity from Charlie.

Bugs is in many ways an unusual rabbit. Whereas most rabbits have hundreds of offspring, Bugs had several fathers—Tex Avery, Friz Freleng, Bob McKimson, Bob Clampett, and me. Just as people behave differently in different company, so Bugs's behavior varied according to the director. Bob Clampett's Bugs was funny, but a lot wilder and more physical than Friz's or mine, as was Robert McKimson's rabbit, who would plant a very combative kiss on an adversary's face rather in the style of Tex's earliest Bugs.

There is a real difference between Bugs Bunny as I interpreted him and the way he was animated in his

Top: *Bugs's dream mansion—after all, who could resist a carrot-shaped swimming pool? Bugs is not a penny-pincher, even though he started life* (above) *as a nose-pincher.*

first couple of appearances. The early Bugs is truly crazy. My Bugs *pretends* to be crazy, which is, I believe, arguably far funnier.

All the directors who worked with Bugs at Warner Bros. followed certain rules, the first of which was that Bugs must always be provoked rather than being the aggressor. Bugs has been described as mischievous, cunning, impudent, a rascally heckler, a trickster. He even describes himself as "a stinker." Not so. If left alone, he would be the mild-mannered Rex Harrison of rabbits. Bugs never engages any opponent without reason. He is a rebel *with* a cause. Our occasional deviations from the rule usually misfired. For example, Bugs's unprovoked heckling of Elmer Fudd in one of their earliest confrontations—*The Wacky Wabbit*—seemed simply malicious, while audiences were somewhat unhappy about the tortoise's regular outwitting of Bugs in the replays of the old *Tortoise and Hare* fable.

Bugs Bunny can lose a skirmish, but never a battle, much less a war. Once his battle cry has been heard—"Of course, you realize *this* means war"—there will be no separating him from the conflict. It is now war to the finish as he protects his rights. Bugs emerges into the battle zone as a sort of cross between Groucho Marx, Dorothy Parker, James Bond, and Errol Flynn. Bugs loves the fun of the chase. Once engaged, he is the most enthusiastic of participants: saucy, impudent, and very quick with words in circumstances that would confound most of us. This is the second rule: his wits are his basic weapon; he tries to avoid physical conflict when possible, believing that almost all contretemps can be solved with intelligence and humor. He despises the use of any Rambo-like destructive device. Why do we have wits if not to use them?

All of us would love to have the courage and quickness to take on an adversary who outguns us and who is much higher in the pecking order. Bugs is, in short, the very model of a modern comic hero. We would all love to be Bugs Bunnies—most of all, we who breathed life into him. Without Bugs, where would all of us closet cowards be?

137

SCAREDY CAT (1948) Sylvester's better self wrote this admonishment of his fear of horrid mice!

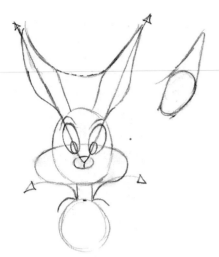

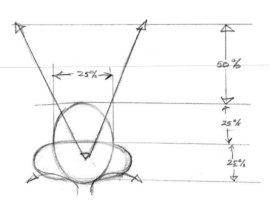

My Bugs doesn't look like a rabbit; he looks like Bugs Bunny. I have often told eager students that the easiest way to draw him is probably to draw a carrot and then hook a rabbit onto it. However, I usually begin a drawing of Bugs with the tiny triangle that passes as the nose. The ears and eyes are located on imaginary lines leading out from the angles of the nose. Bugs is actually a bit cross-eyed, but we never made a point of that. If I am in a generous mood, I allow him three whiskers, in spite of Leon Schlesinger, who thought we could save money by using only two.

The first few times I worked on Bugs Bunny I realized that he has something in common with Sonja Henie, the ice skater who became an extremely popular movie star. Sonja had chubby cheeks,

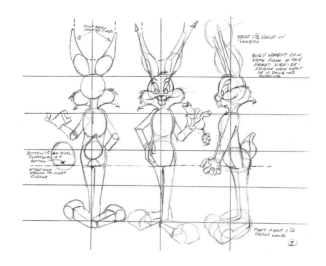

LIKE A BABY'S, AND WHEN SHE SMILED, THE CHEEKS OBSCURED THE CORNERS
OF HER MOUTH. PLUMP CHEEKS ALSO FORCED HER EYES UP, GIVING THEM AN
ELFIN SLANT. BUGS, TOO, HAS VERY HEAVY CHEEKS, WHICH COVER A LOT OF
HIS MOUTH, AND THAT LEAVES ME VERY LITTLE OF THE MOUTH TO WORK
WITH, EVEN THOUGH THE SMALL VISIBLE SECTION OF HIS MOUTH IS VITAL TO
AN UNDERSTANDING OF HIS CHARACTER. WHEN HE IS HAPPY, THE INFERENCE
IS THAT THE SMILE GOES WAY UP UNDER THE CHEEKS. WHEN HE IS SAD, THE
LITTLE VISIBLE PART SAGS AND THE CHEEKS DROOP. TO GIVE HIM A SARDONIC
LOOK, I DRAW ONE SIDE UP AND THE OTHER DOWN.

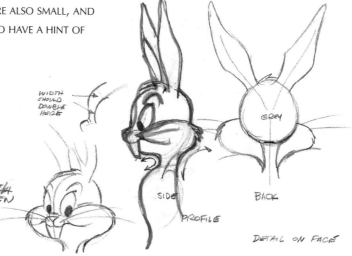

IN SPITE OF THE PLUMP CHEEKS, I WAS NOT TRYING TO MAKE BUGS LOOK
LIKE A BABY. ON YOUNG CREATURES, THE LOWER PART OF THE SKULL IS
NOT FULLY DEVELOPED, AND THE FACIAL FEATURES ARE SQUASHED
INTO THE LOWER THIRD OF THE FACE, RATHER THAN THE LOWER
HALF AS IN THE ADULT ANIMAL. THE TEETH ARE ALSO SMALL, AND
THE NOSE IS CLOSER TO THE EYES. BABIES ALSO HAVE A HINT OF
CONNIE CHUNG AROUND THE CORNERS OF
THE MOUTH. WHATEVER THE SPECIES,
DROPPING THE EYES, NOSE, AND MOUTH
INTO THE LOWER PART OF THE FACE MAKES
AN ANIMAL LOOK YOUNG AND CUTE.

CERTAIN GESTURES ARE
CHARACTERISTIC OF BUGS. FOR
EXAMPLE, HIS PINKIE IS RAISED AS
HE CHEWS ON HIS CARROT. IT'S
AN ELEGANT KIND OF THING.

Saga Of Bugs Bunny

It would be amusing, even though incorrect, to report that Bugs Bunny, America's favorite cartoon character who is currently on the Strand screen in the hilarious Technicolor cartoon in a bottle of ink. Actually, he lives, yes, even in the hearts of the 200 men and women of Warner Bros. Cartoons, Inc., who make him cavort across the screens of the nation.

Our hero was created, by pencil sketch, sometime in 1936 as an "extra" appearing in a cartoon featuring Elmer Fudd, another comical fellow, who went hunting the unnamed rabbit. Bug was not an immediate hit. In fact, he had so little screen appeal at the time that he was practically forgotten for nearly two years.

Then, early in 1938, the cartoon studio was called upon to make an extra picture in the shortest possible time. Some of the men involved in the task recall it as a "quickie."

It, too, was to be a hunting cartoon, Director Isadore Freleng fondly recalls, and that may have brought to mind the rabbit character which had appeared so briefly two years before. They decided to revamp the rabbit; "streamline" him in both character and proportions, and give him a voice and characteristics similar to "Daffy Duck," whose impudence was already famous.

Artists Recall Beginning

At this point, the three directors largely responsible for Bugs: I. Freleng, Charles M. Jones and Robert McKimson, together with the writers Michael Maltese and Tedd Pierce, gathered around on one of the floors of the studio's consultation room and interrupted each other with recollections..

"We gave him a Brooklyn accent," recalled Michael Maltese. "We made him use his wits," said Tedd Pierce.

"He was full of mischief," added Freleng, "but he always started out minding his own business. We made a mistake once. We started out with Bugs going hunting for trouble. That wasn't successful because it wasn't true to type. He never starts the scrapes he gets into any more!"

Bugs Bunny's first hit was made in the hunting comedy released in 1938. The "streamlined" rabbit, intended victim of a cartoon hunter, came up out of his hole chewing a carrot and asked another rabbit, "What's up, Doc?"

"When we saw him on the screen we knew we had a hit character," explains Freleng. "He was the most timid of animals, yet he had courage!"

Gradually, through the process of planning and drawing from six to eight Bugs Bunny cartoons each year, the full character and appeal of Bugs Bunny was developed. He has been kept in the wild state, never given houses to live in, or clothes to wear. He has no steady girl friend, although he can have occasional romances.

Mel Blanc, who supplies the voice, accent and all, for Bugs Bunny, is allergic to carrots, which he must chew, for the sake of realism, while speaking the rabbit's lines. "He doesn't swallow a piece of the carrot," it is reported, "because they make him sick."

Creators Explain Success

The artists responsible for the adventures of the wacky rabbit are amused and yet deadly serious in their explanations of the character who is, after all, bread, butter and shelter for themselves and their families.

Based fundamentally on the idea that the public enjoys watching an underdog get the better of his oppressors, these men constantly try to think of situations in which Bugs could become involved through no fault of his own, and then turn the tables on the trouble makers. It is one of the simplest of all comedy routines, but Bugs is guarded as carefully as any living actor might be!

The men and women who plan, direct and draw the adventures of the rabbit feel about him almost exactly as other directors or producers might feel about the discovery of a Bette Davis or an Errol Flynn. From Edward Selzer, who heads the Warner Bros. Cartoon Studios, on down, Bugs is a top favorite. Says Selzer, "Bugs is the most popular cartoon character on the screen today." Some confirmation of this claim reached Selzer's office only recently. He was told by a rescued man on the carrier Lexington that when that ship went down, it carried with it at least two Bugs Bunny pictures!

The creators of Mr. Bunny also are proud of the service record supplied for him by the U. S. Marine Corps. In addition, his impertinent likeness serves as the mascot insignia for many branches of our armed services, including the new hospital ship, the U. S. S. Comfort. Also, Bugs and his carrot adorned the lead Liberator bomber that made the first attack on Davao which started this country's march back to the Philippines.

All in all, no one could be blamed for calling our hero "an American institution"—and we don't mean the "Bug House," either!

Some character combinations work well on screen, while other pairings prove to be as incompatible as mismatched guests at a bad dinner party. Most dull or disastrous combinations died on the storyboard at Termite Terrace, but after I left Warner Bros., Daffy Duck and Speedy Gonzales appeared together in several cartoons, and I saw no virtue in that. My own poorest piece of casting came in *Rabbit Rampage* (the follow-up to *Duck Amuck*), in which Bugs Bunny is the victim of the vicious animator—Elmer Fudd. It didn't work, because Bugs is a comic hero, and to demean him is like making a bride look bad on her wedding day.

On the other hand, some unexpected combinations were a success. I liked Bugs and Wile E. Coyote working together, particularly in *Hare-Breadth Hurry*, in which Bugs is standing in for the Road Runner, who has "sprained a giblet" cornering too fast. Porky and Sylvester were another happy pairing in a series of films in which I used Sylvester as a *cat* rather than the anthropomorphized animal who was so often Tweety's antagonist. My Sylvester walks on four legs in these cartoons, and he doesn't speak; in other words, he is Porky's pet.

• • •

When playing or animating the part of someone extra-large or overweight, go for grace—not awkwardness. Heavy people tend to underplay their actions gracefully; the bumpkin, the oaf, the angularly awkward are the ones who throw themselves about in an agony of elbows, knees, ankles, and wrists. Oliver Hardy, Zero Mostel, W. C. Fields—all moved with great conservation of physical activity. The finest rotund comedians are comfortable in their bodies. Where Errol Flynn or Douglas Fairbanks would execute a beautiful parabolic arc when entering a scene, Mostel would slide in gently, look enquiringly over his shoulder, and delicately point a toe in an understated and implied leap. When Topol in *Fiddler on the Roof* lifts his arms in his conversation with God, they come up reluctantly, with the elbows close to the rib cage. Never do they attain a Danny Kaye–like thrust to the heavens.

Even W. C. Fields's sudden stops, almost leading to the loss of his hat, are very limited in scope. Think of a small child stuffed in winter clothes; his arms become like the flippers of a penguin. So Fields's arms at rest have only a slight space to cover to catch his hat. As his shoulders hunch forward, his head moves forward also to close the gap even more. It is a fat man's version of a thin man's chasing a hat down a windy street.

Oliver Hardy's delicate twiddling of his tie is to show

141

In the 1930s a lady with the not really odd name of Bunny Warner found herself listed in the Burbank telephone book—right after Warner Bros.—as "Warner Bunny."

DAFFY "CALL ME A BOY.."

BUGS BUNNY WAS MOST AT HOME WITH THE CHALLENGE OF GIGANTIC VILLAINS, SUCH AS HASSAN, THE GUARDIAN OF THE CAVE *(ABOVE AND LEFT)*, THE MUSCLE-BOUND CRUSHER *(BELOW, LEFT)*, OR NASTY CANASTA, HIS LONG-TIME ADVERSARY *(BELOW)*.

I NEVER CONSIDER THE RELATIVE SIZE OF CHARACTERS WHO ARE NOT GOING TO WORK TOGETHER. JUST FOR THE FUN OF IT, I OCCASIONALLY PUT THEM ALONGSIDE EACH OTHER IN A LINE-UP, BUT THAT HAS NOTHING TO DO WITH PICTURE MAKING.

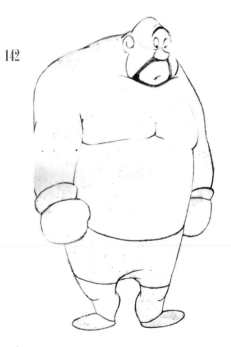

Porky and his trembling cowardly cat enter a haunted hotel in SCAREDY CAT *(1948).*

frustration and displeasure in their most minute detail of expression. But think how effective it is. Where only violently broad expression is needed, such as Hardy losing a round to Edgar Kennedy, the response is passed to Stan Laurel who can—and does—burst into tears, something that the restrictions vital to the Hardy character will not permit him to do.

I often put Bugs up against large adversaries, whereas Friz Freleng's prime villain was the diminutive Yosemite Sam. Friz's star characters were often small, as was Friz himself. Perhaps he just drew small characters better than I did, but I suspect that what we are really talking about when I make Bugs face a giant opponent is my belief that adults are the average child's adversaries. A child is surrounded by six-foot bureaucrats who have control over its life. They tower overhead, and they still look big even when the child has grown to adult height.

The psychological explanation for my interest in oversized opponents probably involves my father worship or penis envy or some such thing. It could go back to the time I first saw my father naked. "Jeez,"

I thought at the time, "have I got to grow one of those things?" Or as Daffy might say, "This looks like a job for Super Freud!"

When Bugs faced the huge bull in *Bully for Bugs*, I was sorry in a way that I could not include the big beast's genitalia in the picture, as that impressive bag is so characteristic of the animal.

I had never thought of making a film about bullfights until Eddie Selzer raised the possibility. I still don't know why he mentioned the subject. Mike Maltese and I were just standing in the studio laughing when we noticed Eddie with the flashing eyes, standing in the doorway and bawling, "There's nothing funny about bullfights." We decided the subject must be worth investigating.

We set about researching bullfighting, not only because it seemed unwise to work in ignorance, but also because it is a lot more fun to parody something the way it is intended to be. We read Ernest Hemingway's *Death in the Afternoon* and *The Brave Bulls*, by Tom Lea, and I even went to a bullfight in Mexico City to see what it was all about.

*If Ernest Hemingway could
view a real bullfight, so could I.
He loved it; I tried to escape.*

The matador at the beginning of *Bully for Bugs* is a caricature of the great Spanish bullfighter Juan Belmonte (drawn from photographs in *Death in the Afternoon*), but the person inside him is *me*. Before I went to the Mexico City bullfight, my sympathies were with the bull, but then I saw a slender little man saunter out into the ring, and the door smashed open, powered by a savage animal weighing about 3,000 pounds, with enormous horns outthrust. It scared the hell out of me. I immediately changed my opinion and traded my seat for one higher up in the stadium.

My education in bullfighting was completed in California by Bob Gribbroek. Bob was one of my first background designers, and he had strange hobbies. He built his own adobe house in Taos, but because he had used green hay in its construction, the whole house sprouted every spring, and he had to go over it with manicure scissors. He loved the flaming desert colors of New Mexico, but he once traveled north, lured by descriptions of the region's beauty, to spend two weeks painting in the Pacific Northwest; he returned two days later, wild-eyed and complaining that "it's like living inside an old mossy bucket; everything's so goddam green."

Before joining Termite Terrace, Bob had undergone training as a bullfighter. In his first lesson, he discovered that splints are strapped back and front to the legs of trainee bullfighters to stop them from bending their knees. This helps them achieve that beautiful straight-legged pose and stand erect as the bull charges. But it also makes it impossible for the bullfighter to flee from an approaching bull. At his first sight of a charging heifer, Bob realized he was immobilized, damped his pants, fell down in shame, saw that his dream was over, and decided on a career change.

144

*Bugs's casual and typical
posture before a snorting,
oversized adversary.*

Junyer pursues his panicky father with a blunt and jagged razor, as the dysfunctional Bear family celebrates Father's Day (above) in A Bear for Punishment *(1951). This cartoon—and the more blissful moments of parenthood (left)—were inspired by my own experiences.*

If you can't do it yourself, animate someone who can. The characters we created at Warner Bros. all reveal aspects of the directors, for we were all talking about ourselves, examining ourselves. As I became acquainted with each individual character, I would add parts of myself which were pertinent to that personality.

In FROM A TO Z-Z-Z-Z, *Ralph Phillips crosses swords with numbers during a daydream (above, left), swims to the bottom of the sea to rescue a submarine in distress (left), and delivers the mail to the fort (below). Below, left:* one of Maurice Noble's pencil sketches and *(below, right)* Phil DeGuard's finished background painting. *The film was nominated for an Academy Award.*

Bugs's bull does not move its massive body up and down as it charges the rabbit. Rumbling forward like a steamroller, its horns aligned with its body, it stays very close to the ground. This is because all action is *conservative*, and all animals move efficiently, using minimum effort (unless they are young). And if you know that, you are way ahead in animation. Only the young waste energy, because they have not yet learned to conserve it. An adult elephant who bounced along like Pepé le Pew would wear himself out the first time he wandered across the road, so he raises his feet just high enough to stop them scraping along the ground.

In his Monday drawing classes, Don Graham taught us that if we wanted to make something *look* big, we should make the limbs small, and the bull bears this out—his huge body is supported on little bitty legs. This principle also applies to caricature, which is not only the art of over-exaggeration but of under-

exaggeration as well. Jimmy Durante, for instance, had a famously prominent but not enormous nose. However, if you draw his face with those remarkably small, mischievous eyes and the small, lopsided mouth, you can make even a normal nose look oversized.

Caricature is a broad visual example of all art, because all art is dramatization, overstatement and understatement in shades so delicate that we mistake it for actuality.

Don Graham also taught that drawing a sumo wrestler is very different from drawing a body-builder on Muscle Beach. Muscle Beach Man prides himself on his tiny hips, and his arms are so developed that his body doesn't look large in comparison. He is big in detail but not en masse, big in particular places but not in silhouette. Ray Katz, our business manager, was fat in detail rather than in silhouette. From

The matador at the beginning of BULLY FOR BUGS is a caricature of the great Spanish bullfighter Juan Belmonte, but the person trembling inside is me.

In order to make believable the enormous weight and power of the bull, we kept him close to the ground. After all, there is very little up-and-down to a locomotive.

a distance he looked bulky, but you would not know he was fat. As he came closer, his fat nose, his fat eyes, and his fat ears became visible. He was the only person I have ever met who had fat fingernails.

A sumo wrestler, on the other hand, has flab fitting into his silhouette, around the breasts, back, and stomach. His arms are quite unlike the muscle man's; they look rather small compared to the bulk of the man. The legs are fat but not large, and tucked in there is a tiny butt, a sort of *buttius minimus*. And no matter how fat the man's back may become, he will usually keep that tiny dice butt.

When a heavyweight character sits down, the butt loses its roundness, just as when you press the fingers of two hands together, the line between them becomes straighter the harder you press. To show that a person on a chair is heavy or fat, the body is therefore flattened where it meets the seat. Bugs Bunny's bull is all muscle, as if he was made of cement, and if he came to a stop and sat down, it would be clear that he carries no fat in his tiny butt.

There is something strange about the edge of the frame in animated films. Characters often reach off-scene to grab whatever they need without having to explain. When Bugs leaves the frame during the dance in *Bully for Bugs*, the bull looks around and can no longer see him. Why not? We are in a world that is not the way it seems.

146

  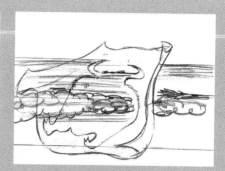

* * *

How I Met Yosemite Sam Before Friz Created Him

In order to understand the event that occurred at 115 Wadsworth Avenue that one autumn night in 1924, it is necessary to see the downstairs floor plan of our house.

Uncle J. was my father's younger brother. He had been a Texas Ranger, a captain of infantry in World War I (his father embarrassed him by showing up in Uncle J.'s company as a buck private), a U.S. marshal, a bounty hunter. He was a man who would not think twice if offered the choice between walking down a street without his pants or without a sidearm. He had a permanent starboard list, and his clothing draped to the right side, responding to the pull of gravity of a gigantic .45 Colt revolver. He was the only man I ever encountered who wore artillery strapped to his bathing suit. When he appeared thus caparisoned on our beach, father accused him of wanting to shoot barracuda. Uncle J., who would shoot anything that moved and some things that didn't, had never met a barracuda but was willing to shoot one anyway, but Father said that he had to have a barracuda shooting license. (My ears

were working; see *Duck! Rabbit, Duck!* of later years.)

Uncle J., coming from Texas, had never heard that you needed a license to shoot anything, but was nevertheless persuaded by my father to disarm before entering the water.

Uncle J., even without his revolver, almost missed his appointment with Father's orange wine. I think he'd forgotten that he didn't know how to swim, and he'd probably never before encountered a problem that couldn't be solved by gunfire.

I don't think Uncle J. really believed that first eight-foot wave. He probably thought of it as a sort of vertical Rio Grande, big but surely not more than two inches thick. He didn't walk into it with courage. He approached it with abysmal ignorance and self-assurance, a risky attitude when playing with an ocean holding all the cards.

Uncle J.'s red bathing suit disappeared like a jellybean dropped into a cement-mixer. While all of us were trying to figure out what to do, we caught fascinating glimpses of Uncle J.—mainly of Uncle J.'s feet—in the foam, froth, bubbles, and spume. He seemed to have more feet than normal for a thirty-six-year-old Texan.

It took the combined visual efforts of all the enthralled audience on the beach to find out where Uncle

J. was in all the turmoil of several succeeding waves, each vying with its predecessor in maniacal turmoil and size. My sister finally spotted him sailing majestically out to sea on a foaming riptide, feet up treading the air, a swimming stroke unknown to all of us. It must have been efficient—he was moving at close to thirty miles an hour. I have no doubt that using this interesting stroke he would have kicked his way to Catalina Island if he hadn't run into a seagoing dory rowed by a local Portuguese fisherman called Tom Delinquent. Tom fished Uncle J. from the sea, more out of curiosity than compassion, and delivered him ashore, Uncle J. sputtering all the while that he had been bushwhacked while unarmed.

148   During the afternoon and evening, Mother tried to calm him down with periodic dosages of Father's orange wine, considered by one and all as a superb palliative for half-drowned Texans.

I suppose it was around twelve o'clock that night when the house finally settled down, our family asleep in the upper bedrooms, Uncle J. in the den downstairs. This was a pleasant, fragrant little room: study, den, guest bedroom, and—of course—brewery. In the long, astringent years of Prohibition it was here that Father brewed his famous orange wine, a mysterious witch's potion of oranges, raisins, stick sugar, cloves, and other secret ingredients. He usually kept six or seven five-gallon bottles fermenting at different aging stages, secured by canting corks lightly holding muslin screens in their necks to keep the flies away. It was important that the bottles be kept lightly corked to allow the gases generated by the brewing process to escape into the air. If the cork was pressed into the neck too tightly, gas pressure would build up to the point where the bottle would literally blow its cork; there would follow a series of ricochets, momentarily arousing but never alarming our sleeping household.

This fateful night there were to be somewhat different results. At two o'clock in the morning (we were able to determine the time exactly, since Uncle J.'s pocket watch died at 2:00 A.M. with a bullet through its face), all of us were sleeping peacefully except Uncle J., whose slumber was fitfully interrupted as he had it out with that unfair ocean once again. It is possible that in his thrashing he may have landed on one of the corks.

At any rate, one of the bottles impatiently decided to blow its cork. The difference between the sound of an orange-wine cork popping and that of a pistol firing is, no doubt, academic. At any rate, Uncle J. came out of bed, pistol in hand, firing at the unseen enemy. It was a highly creditable performance for one shooting in the dark. He not only killed all the wine bottles and his watch, but put a bullet through the dining room wall and hit Colonel Terhune's moosehead trophy in the ear.

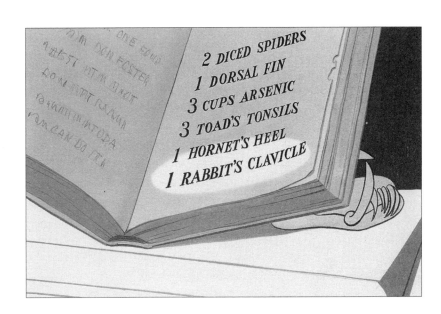

Witch Hazel's favorite recipe for stupefying a wayward rabbit.

Daffy, however, (below) found solace in champagne.

Our family trooped tentatively down in the wake of this artillery barrage, and we distributed ourselves carefully along the short stairs leading down into the murky den. As the light flicked on, there stood Uncle J., blinking in the glare and fanning the room with his empty revolver, blue smoke curling around his head, calf-deep in orange wine. He had hit every one of those demijohns dead center, and each of them gave up its redolent alcoholic ghosts and sent them curling up and entwining Uncle J., who, as he disappeared, shouted, "That'll teach 'em!"

We were never able to remove the memory of the orange wine from that room, and for months afterward all one needed to forget one's cares was to take a nap in the den. Many years later, my four-year-old daughter, given a teaspoonful of champagne and sugar on New Year's Eve, was asked how she liked it. "I like it," she replied. "It's full of jokes." That den on Wadsworth Avenue in Ocean Park was full of dreamy jokes for years.

149

ANIMATION: MOVEMENT

THE MECHANICS OF PLAYING OR BEING A DRUNK

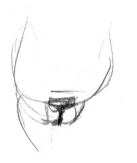

WE TEND TO THINK OF THE ULTIMATE DRUNK AS A SLOBBERING, INARTICULATE, WOOZY, DROOLING BUM. THERE OBVIOUSLY ARE SOME SUCH, BUT OUR EARLY EXPERIENCE WITH INEBRIATION IS MOST LIKELY TO OCCUR AT A COCKTAIL OR DINNER PARTY OF OUR PEERS, AND WE MUST THEREFORE TRY TO MAINTAIN A KIND OF BEHAVIORAL CONTROL, FORCED UPON US BY FEAR OF SOCIAL REPRISALS. INSTEAD OF SPEAKING WITH SLURRING SYLLABLES, OUR YOUNG INEBRIATE IS MORE LIKELY TO SPEAK WITH WHAT HE PERCEIVES TO BE GREAT DISTINCTION, SUCH AS PRONOUNCING ALL HIS G'S: "I HAVE *NOT* BEEN DRINK-KING TOO MUCH. I HAVE HAD PRECISELY TW-THREE MART-EENIES." ("MUCH" MAY COME OUT AS "MUSH" AND "PRECISELY" AS "PREESE-ICE-UHLY," BUT THE EVIDENCE OF THE DEGREE OF OUR INDULGENCE IS IN THIS VERY PRECISION.) DICK VAN DYKE, WHO SHOULD KNOW, HAD AN ACT WHEREIN A SLOBBERING DRUNK AT A PARTY SNAPS INTO PERFECT POSTURE AND SPEECH WHENEVER HIS WIFE PASSES—A PERFECT EXAMPLE OF FEAR TRIUMPHING OVER INDULGENCE.

OVER-INDULGENCE IS ALSO BETRAYED BY BODILY MOVEMENT. THE ANIMATOR AND THE ACTOR KNOW THAT ANY NATURAL MOVEMENT OCCURS IN STAGES: IF WE TURN FROM A STANDING POSITION, THE EYES MOVE FIRST, THE HEAD CATCHES UP DURING THE TURN, THE SHOULDERS FOLLOW, AND THE BODY MOVES INTO THE FALLING POSITION THAT IS THE ESSENCE OF ANY WALK—OR RUN, FOR THAT MATTER—IN WHICH THE BODY, CARRIED ALONG BY THE MOVEMENT OF OUR LEGS, IS ACTUALLY FALLING OVER; WE ALWAYS HAVE THE ASSISTANCE OF GRAVITY. TRY WALKING WITH YOUR BODY THRUST BACK, OR DIRECTLY UPRIGHT, AND THE EXPENDITURE OF ENERGY INVOLVED WILL SURELY CONVINCE YOU THAT GRAVITY IS NOT A BAD ALLY.

OUR INEBRIATED FRIEND, HOWEVER, IS NOT RELAXED. HIS UNORTHODOX PRECISION OF SPEECH HAS SO DEMONSTRATED. JUST AS IN HIS RIGID SPEECH PATTERN, SO HIS PHYSICAL ACTIVITY IS OVERLY PRECISE, AND HE MOVES MORE LIKE A MANIKIN THAN A MAN. HEAD, EYES, AND BODY TEND TO MOVE AS ONE; HE HAS A RATHER UNSTABLE SKELETON, AND HE MUST BE VERY CAREFUL TO BALANCE EVERY BONE WITH PAINFUL DETERMINATION.

150

TO SQUEEZE THE WORDS HARE, RABBIT, BUNNY, WABBIT, AND DOC INTO A CARTOON TITLE

1. THE ABOMINABLE SNOW RABBIT
2. ACROBATTY BUNNY
3. ALI BABA BUNNY
4. ALL THIS AND RABBIT STEW
5. BABY BUGGY BUNNY
6. BACKWOODS BUNNY
7. BALLOT BOX BUNNY
8. BARBARY COAST BUNNY
9. BASEBALL BUGS
10. BATON BUNNY
11. BEANSTALK BUNNY
12. BEDEVILLED RABBIT
13. BEWITCHED BUNNY
14. BIG HOUSE BUNNY
15. BIG TOP BUNNY
16. BILL OF HARE
17. BONANZA BUNNY
18. BOWERY BUGS
19. BROOMSTICK BUNNY
20. BUCCANEER BUNNY
21. BUCKAROO BUGS
22. BUGS AND THUGS
23. BUGS BONNETS
24. BUGS BUNNY AND THE THREE BEARS
25. BUGS BUNNY GETS THE BOID
26. BUGS BUNNY NIPS THE NIPS
27. BUGS BUNNY RIDES AGAIN
28. BUGSY AND MUGSY
29. BULLY FOR BUGS
30. BUNKER HILL BUNNY
31. BUNNY AND CLAUDE
32. BUNNY HUGGED
33. BUSHY HARE
34. CAPTAIN HAREBLOWER
35. CASE OF THE MISSING HARE
36. COMPRESSED HARE
37. DEVIL MAY HARE
38. DOCTOR DEVIL AND MISTER HARE
39. DUCK! RABBIT, DUCK!
40. 8 BALL BUNNY
41. ELMER'S PET RABBIT
42. THE FAIR HAIRED HARE
43. FALLING HARE
44. FALSE HARE
45. A FEATHER IN HIS HARE
46. 14 CARROT RABBIT
47. FORWARD MARCH HARE
48. FRESH HARE
49. FRIGID HARE
50. FROM HARE TO HEIR

51. THE GREY HOUNDED HARE
52. HAIR-RAISING HARE
53. HALF FARE HARE
54. HARE-ABIAN NIGHTS
55. THE HARE-BRAINED HYPNOTIST
56. HARE-BREADTH HURRY
57. HARE BRUSH
58. HARE CONDITIONED
59. HAREDEVIL HARE
60. HARE DO
61. HARE FORCE
62. A HARE GROWS IN MANHATTAN
63. HARE-LESS WOLF
64. HARE LIFT
65. HARE REMOVER
66. HARE RIBBIN'
67. HARE SPLITTER
68. HARE TONIC
69. HARE TRIGGER
70. HARE TRIMMED
71. HARE-UM SCARE-UM
72. HARE-WAY TO THE STARS
73. HARE WE GO
74. THE HASTY HARE
75. THE HECKLING HARE
76. HERR MEETS HARE
77. HIAWATHA'S RABBIT HUNT
78. HIGH DIVING HARE
79. HILLBILLY HARE
80. HIS HARE RAISING TALE
81. HOMELESS HARE
82. HORSE HARE
83. HOT CROSS BUNNY
84. HURDY GURDY HARE
85. HYDE AND HARE
86. JACK-WABBIT AND THE BEANSTALK
87. KNIGHT-MARE HARE
88. KNIGHTY KNIGHT BUGS
89. LIGHTER THAN HARE
90. LITTLE RED RIDING RABBIT
91. LONG-HAIRED HARE
92. LUMBERJACK RABBIT
93. MAD AS A MARS HARE
94. THE MILLION HARE
95. MISSISSIPPI HARE
96. MUTINY ON THE BUNNY
97. MY BUNNY LIES OVER THE SEA
98. NAPOLEON BUNNY-PART
99. NO PARKING HARE
100. NOW HARE THIS

101. OILY HARE
102. THE OLD GREY HARE
103. OPERATION: RABBIT
104. PEOPLE ARE BUNNY
105. PERSON TO BUNNY
106. PORKY'S HARE HUNT
107. PRE-HYSTERICAL HARE
108. RABBIT EVERY MONDAY
109. RABBIT FIRE
110. RABBIT HOOD
111. THE RABBIT OF SEVILLE
112. RABBIT PUNCH
113. RABBIT RAMPAGE
114. RABBIT ROMEO
115. RABBIT SEASONING
116. RABBIT'S FEAT
117. RABBIT'S KIN
118. RABBITSON CRUSOE
119. RABBIT STEW AND RABBITS TOO
120. RABBIT TRANSIT
121. RACKETEER RABBIT
122. REBEL RABBIT
123. RHAPSODY RABBIT
124. ROBOT RABBIT
125. ROMAN LEGION HARE
126. SAHARA HARE
127. SHOW BIZ BUGS
128. SLICK HARE
129. SOUTHERN FRIED RABBIT
130. SUPER RABBIT
131. TO HARE IS HUMAN
132. TORTOISE BEATS HARE
133. TORTOISE WINS BY A HARE
134. THE UNRULY HARE
135. UNSWEPT HARE
136. WABBIT TWOUBLE
137. THE WABBIT WHO CAME TO SUPPER
138. WACKIKI WABBIT
139. THE WACKY WABBIT
140. WATER, WATER EVERY HARE
141. WET HARE
142. WHAT'S COOKIN' DOC?
143. WHAT'S OPERA, DOC?
144. WHAT'S UP, DOC?
145. WIDEO WABBIT
146. WILD AND WOOLY HARE
147. A WILD HARE
148. THE WINDBLOWN HARE
149. A WITCH'S TANGLED HARE
150. YANKEE DOODLE BUGS

ELMER FUDD

SLIMEOUS ELMEREMIRGIOUS

NEANDERFUDDIUS ERECTUS

SIR ELMER OF FUDD, EARL OF CLOVES

400,000 B.C.　　　　**15,000 B.C.**　　　　**circa 847**

152 Elmer Fudd is smaller than many of Bugs's adversaries, but he carries a big gun, which makes even the saddest of wimps dangerous. When I was growing up, it was considered quite natural to buy a boy his first BB gun at an early age, soon to be followed by a more lethal .22 rifle. It was—and is—a classic practice for a man to dress up like Elmer Fudd and go out to shoot something in the woods. I am, in fact, one of the few men of my age I know who has never done so. This makes it hard for me to identify with Elmer, but the part of Elmer Fudd that is Chuck Jones comes out when he defends his motive: "I'm a vegetawian. I just hunt for the sport of it." In a way, I am excusing him for what he is.

In many cartoons Elmer was just a hunter tracking Bugs, and in these films the limit of his personality seemed to be his claim to be a sportsman. But Elmer will play whatever part is assigned to him, whether it's the *Beanstalk Bunny* giant or the innkeeper in *The Scarlet Pumpernickel*, who greets Daffy with the words, "Oh, Mr. Nobleman, you honor my humble wodgings." (If you insult yourself, Daffy will go along with your insult; "Yes, they are humble, aren't they?")

Although I don't believe Elmer's character runs deep, he had more personality for me than for some other directors who worked with him, because I put him in situations where he *had* to have a personality, such as his appearance as the giant in *Beanstalk Bunny*. I didn't draw Elmer very differently when he was a giant (the body was a little longer and the face a little less childlike), but like any actor he will change

EGG-HEADIUS FREDAVERII

FUDDIUS FATIUS CLAMPETERIUS

FUDDII EMBRYONICUS JONESI

ELMER FUDDIUS
DELIGHTII RABBITRACTIUS

circa 1937   **circa 1941**   **circa 1949**   **circa 1957**

his make-up to suit the demands of the role. Note: never confuse the words "childlike" and "childish."

Elmer is more widely known for his voice than for his personality. He generally

sounds as if he is about to cry, a mannerism that is an expression of his constant anxiety. The famous nervous laugh—he is really neither laughing nor crying—represents his attempt to buy time as he assesses a situation. Occasionally the little "ha, ha, ha" is delivered as if he expects his audience to laugh with him, but of course nobody responds. And what could be more terrifying than to say something you feel is funny, only to be met by silence? The laugh is Elmer's version of "er," a meaningless verbal gesture that falls into the category of displacement activities.

A rabbit talking back to a hunter is itself a joke, but "What's up, Doc?" is probably the most incongruous question imaginable from the hunter's intended victim. The same question asked of the manager of a guillotine by a French duke would be equally incon-

153

Bugs Bunny and Daffy Duck confront a giant Elmer in BEANSTALK BUNNY (1955)—an opponent can be too big!

"HOW DARE YOU"

DISBELIEF

gruous, and if the executioner replied, "I'm cutting the heads off aristocrats," it would be very close to "I'm hunting rabbits." Elmer's reply is odd and almost funny in itself, but it loses all claim to rationality when the hunter pronounces the word "wabbits." Hunters simply do not say, "I'm hunting wabbits." Nor do they turn to the audience to say, "Shh. Be vewy, vewy quiet—" How can the audience possibly disturb Elmer's lethal hobby? It cannot, and logic therefore takes a beating, as the whole situation turns wonderfully absurd.

Incongruity! Without it where would comedy be? Webster defines "incongruous" as: "Not consistent with what is logical, customary, or expected." The essence of Bugs Bunny stories is not how to catch, shoot, dispose of, or defoot a rabbit. It is how, in a believable way, *not* to catch, shoot, dispose of, or defoot a rabbit.

In order to survive, we must be aware of incongruities, of things that deviate oddly from the norm.

154

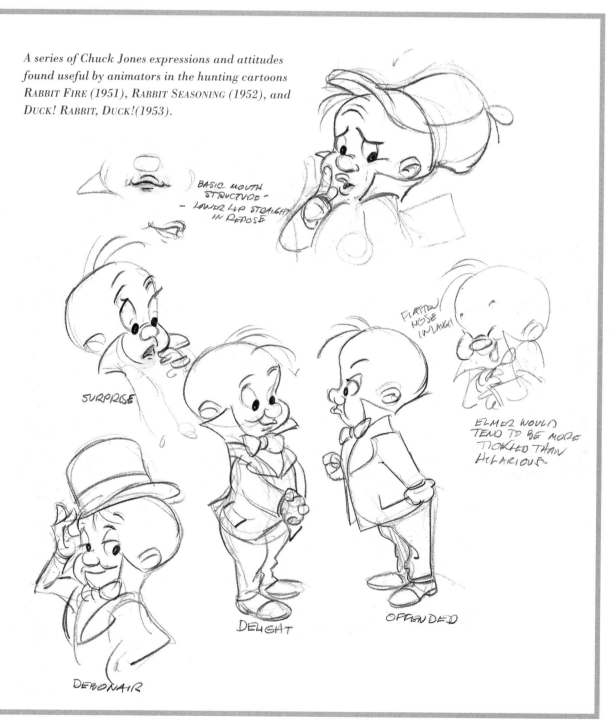

A series of Chuck Jones expressions and attitudes found useful by animators in the hunting cartoons RABBIT FIRE *(1951),* RABBIT SEASONING *(1952), and* DUCK! RABBIT, DUCK! *(1953).*

BASIC MOUTH
STRUCTURE –
– LOWER LIP STRAIGHT
IN REPOSE

SURPRISE

FLATTEN
NOSE
IN LAUGH

ELMER WOULD
TEND TO BE MORE
TICKLED THAN
HILARIOUS.

DELIGHT

OFFENDED

DEBONAIR

155

Top: *An inspirational sketch by Maurice Noble for* What's Opera, Doc? *(1957). Above and right: Elmer sings opera music by Richard Wagner and lyrics by Mike Maltese. Could anything be grander?*

WHAT'S OPERA, DOC?

A CASE HISTORY

I first heard Wagner's music as a child, when my father brought home a phonograph. Although I knew nothing about music at the time, I had soon heard enough to decide that Wagner was gratingly hideous. I was therefore stimulated beyond conception when I read a line by Mark Twain, who had lovely opinions about everything. "Wagner's music," he wrote, "is better than it sounds." When we needed BIG music for *What's Opera, Doc?*, I knew Wagner was the right choice.

Many cartoons using classical music have failed because they don't take the music seriously enough. I always felt that Bugs and Elmer were trying to do the opera right. Even though we squashed the entire *Ring of the Nibelungen*, which runs about fourteen hours, down to six minutes for *What's Opera, Doc?*, the music was played properly and respectfully. To keep Wagner-

ian opera's sense of grandeur, we used a huge eighty-piece orchestra. It would have been lese majesty to do anything unfair to the music. Although when I visited Wagner's grave, I did hear a whirring sound.

There are *no gags* in the film. We believed that a rabbit and a hunter working with that grand music in a fully Wagnerian environment would be funny enough in itself. But with the humor coming from personality rather than from gags, the need to play the music properly and to make the action logical became more emphatic.

Once the idea for a film was fixed, Mike Maltese and I worked closely together on the story. Incongruous play was an important element in these story sessions. We would speak as the characters, and often, for good exercise, we would act out scenes that

WAGNER PEICES - (IN ORDER-)

1. THE FLYING DUTCHMAN OVERTURE -
2. - THE RIDE OF THE VALKYRIES -
3. - SMALL BIT OF THE FLYING DUTCHMAN -
4. (CHASE STUFF) -
5. (ELMER AT TREE STUMP -) -
6. (BUGS GETS MAGIC HELMET.) -
7. - (BUGS CUTE STUFF WITH HELMET.) -
8. (ELMER SNEAKING IN TO GET HELMET.) -
9. - TANNHAUSER OVERTURE + VENUSBERG MUSIC -
10. - TANNHAUSER OVERTURE - (SINGING.) -
11. - ELMER ANGRY - "SIEGFRED'S FUNERAL -
12. - STORM - THE FLYING DUTCHMAN - #2 -
13. - SIEGFRIED IDYLL -
     - TANNHAUSER OVERTURE -

Left: *Mike Maltese's notes
to Richard Wagner.*

this aerial routine in *Super Rabbit*, when the cowboy and his horse take to the air in pursuit of Bugs.

Because of such working practices, it is impossible to say which of us wrote which lines of dialogue, but the director invariably had to decide which words would eventually be used, making the director ultimately responsible for *all* the dialogue in the picture. None of the Warner Bros. directors took their final words from the writer, because the meaning of a film invariably altered to a greater or lesser degree as the director developed it from the storyboard.

In principle, we usually tried to tell our stories through action rather than words. My first films as director were too wordy, but I learned not to use dialogue when actions would suffice. Decisions on

158 had no necessary link to the film we were working on. We might, for instance, decide to play World War I aviators. We would place our two chairs one behind the other, and we were instantly in a Sopwith Camel on dawn patrol, airborne and gallant. It was a great way to clear our minds.

As we flew over the ravaged plain, one of us would tap the other on the shoulder and point to an enemy plane sighted below. The pilot in our twin-chaired fighter would angle the plane down, and the chairs would tip accordingly as we went into the attack, but—disaster—we would sustain a hit, sending our chairs (the plane) spinning out of control with the pilot dying in the cockpit. A crash landing was our only hope. Lifting our chairs up, we would bring them down hard on the floor. The pilot slumped dead over his companion, who rose slowly and, lifting a bugle, sounded taps. It was a tragic story, and one that Ray Katz and Eddie Selzer would have considered a criminal waste of time, but in fact we used

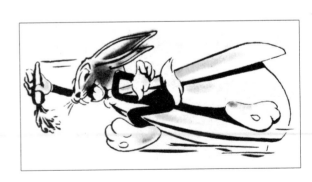

*Super Rabbit en flight
with Super (what else?) Carrots.*

dialogue then usually came down to the discipline of fitting everything into a six-minute cartoon.

Mike Maltese's storyboards for *What's Opera, Doc?* tell the story we created. Mike was a fine writer with an odd twist to his mind, and some of his work at this stage was inspirational. Bugs's delicate reply to Elmer's complimentary "You're so wuvvwy"— "Yes, I know it. I can't help it"—sounds like Mike's work, and I think it rings true because it is what many live-action screen stars of the time thought about themselves.

But it is noticeable that the thoughtfulness of the cartoon's final poses is lacking in the storyboards. Not only had the entire ballet scene still to be choreographed, I still had to work out what the characters would actually be doing in every scene. This is something the average writer cannot come to grips with. If he could, he would doubtless be a director—

if he could draw very well indeed and had been an animator long enough to understand timing.

The choreography in *What's Opera, Doc?* is almost as authentic as the music. When we were making the film, Titania Riabachinska and David Lichine of the Ballet Russe de Monte Carlo were working on the Warner Bros. lot, and we went to the studio where they were rehearsing to sketch them before creating the *What's Opera, Doc?* scene. Or so I remember it.

When a dancer pirouettes, she doesn't spin at constant speed; she comes to a stop each time around, and those slight hesitations are important to believable animation. The stop may last only six or eight frames, but it must be there.

159

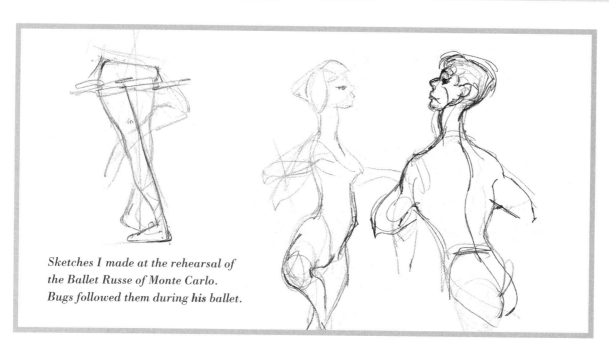

*Sketches I made at the rehearsal of the Ballet Russe of Monte Carlo. Bugs followed them during **his** ballet.*

Mike Maltese's storyboard for What's Opera, Doc? *It was then my job to bring them to life.*

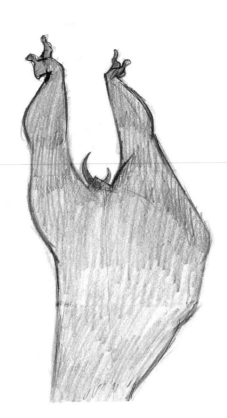

(Note: I add that last remark because historians of animation are constantly describing what they consider to be my faulty dating. That's fine with me—it's how they make their living. If they weren't doing that, they could always take up hemstitching.)

There are, of course, elements of parody in the film. The opening of *What's Opera, Doc?* was a tribute—a very sweet and loving tribute—to "Night on Bald Mountain" in *Fantasia*, which is a powerful, beautiful, strong scene animated by Bill Tytla, the Michelangelo of animation. *What's Opera, Doc?* opens with the huge, dark shadow directing the

storm to the sound of Wagner's marvelous, ponderous music. When you bear down and discover it is Elmer Fudd casting the shadow, I think the film gets off to a solid start. I loved laying that scene out. Abe Levitow animated it, and he, like Tytla, had a remarkably powerful way of drawing.

The cartoon continues with Elmer's really ridiculous attempt to kill the rabbit by stabbing at the hole with his spear, as if Bugs was right there. There's something about the idea that works, but I don't know what it is. There's also something about it that *doesn't*

work for me, and it is something I see every time I watch the film. Elmer's skirt is made of short metal slats, and when he is jabbing the hole, his head is at one point lower than his feet, causing the skirt to turn over one slat at a time. I envisaged the slats making a metallic musical scale as they flipped over, slat by slat—do, re, mi, fa, so, la—but we never recorded it, and I miss that sound every time.

If you can look at anything you do and be satisfied with it, you are in the wrong trade. Frustration and anxiety are the handmaidens of creative work, and in this sense every animator should be a *failed* animator. When you see the blank piece of paper staring at you, anxiety is a vital and necessary response. But when you start to draw, you become one with the gods, and anxiety disappears until you stop drawing. No work of art is ever completed; it is only abandoned by the artist.

We took longer to abandon *What's Opera, Doc?* than any other film we made. A typical cartoon was in production for five weeks, but *What's Opera, Doc?* required seven. It was an unusual production in many ways. Most cartoons were discussed at storyboard stage by all the directors at "Yes" sessions, when anyone could say anything at all about the project as long as it was positive. But we held no "Yes" sessions on *What's Opera, Doc?*, as I felt that mockery might harm it, and I couldn't risk exposing it to the dead mind of Eddie Selzer, who often tried to sit in on these meetings.

For a typical cartoon I would supply the animators with perhaps 300 key drawings, but I made almost 500 for *What's Opera, Doc?* as well as a further 1,500 unused roughs. While I was making the layout drawings, Maurice Noble worked on what we called "inspirational color sketches," and then we pulled in the musicians and went over the whole story with them.

We could not let management know that we were devoting two additional weeks to this one cartoon. To make up the time, we stole a week each from two Road Runner cartoons, which we all knew well enough to do fast, so the work sheet indicated the usual five weeks. The studio never understood why the film cost so much, as it came in at the standard length.

In fact, management didn't seem to understand the film at all. Eddie Selzer declined to submit it to the Academy, even though it qualified, declaring it unworthy of consideration.

Eventually the film became the first animated short subject to be honored by selection for the National Archives.

Without Maurice Noble's beautiful sets, *What's Opera, Doc?* could not have worked so well. Maurice Noble lives in a very mysterious world, shifting gear between locales the way I move among my characters. Between us we could assemble the elements that Mark Twain said were necessary to the writer about to begin a novel: some people in mind, an incident or two, and a locality. Mike Maltese and I would provide the story, then I would take off with the characters, Maurice would work on the environment, and we would bounce.

Drawing characters has never been Maurice's strength, and I have never been good at stagecraft. When I made the environmental layouts for a scene—perhaps twelve drawings—I would simply

View of C. Jones from Abe Levitow's 6'3".

Maurice's staging never mistook the prime purpose of the design—
to show the actor off to the greatest advantage.

Since we didn't have a
voluptuous soprano at hand,
I designed a voluptuous
horse as a stand-in.
Below: *Bugs's slide to
Wagnerian glory.*

*Like all great divas, Bugs was not
without self-confidence about his beauty.*

indicate where the characters should be and where things such as tables, windows, and doors were located, without knowing what they were going to look like. The *intent* of a scene would be clear from my drawings, but there would be little or no scenery. Maurice would trace all the character drawings onto one sheet of paper, then play with the spaces open to him to design background. In a way, my drawings fulfilled a similar function to the chalk marks on a stage during rehearsals, showing the actors where they should stand and where they must move.

Maurice was unlike the many stage designers who think that design is more important than the characters, but on occasion the environment he created *was* the story. This was the case with the opening

*Elmer, star-stricken
by Bug-Hilda's beauty.*

scenes of *Hare-Way to the Stars*, for which he created the first space station, in a simple age when people still believed that gravity continued clear out into space. I know of nobody who had visualized those beautiful clear panels before Maurice created them for that film, and now NASA works with them. Maurice is a master.

There are more cuts in *What's Opera, Doc?* (104, I believe) than in the typical Warner Bros. cartoon, and there is a reason for every cut.

A motivated camera is the most important of all things. In both animation and live action I believe that cutting—that is, moving the picture from one point of view to another—must be reasonable and must be motivated by the needs of the story:

1. To accent and isolate a story point (the purloined letter).
2. To obtain a point of view (a child's view of a policeman; a coyote's view of the Grand Canyon).
3. To change tempo. To excite the audience by staccato cutting (of a drummer; vicious angles of a Hitler), or by intercutting what is being seen with contrasting views of those watching.
4. To make a dramatic point.
5. Or it can be just the viewpoint—dramatic or comedic—of the director.

Cutting should not be noticeable to the audience except as it affects them.

Enraptured Elmer's approach as seen from Bugs's elevated viewpoint.

Upshots are often abused. In a scene showing an adult and a child talking together, it is perfectly legitimate and desirable to have a downshot on the child and an upshot on the adult to establish point of view. In that case, the attitude of the camera ensures that their relationship is understood by the audience, but for directors to put in upshots simply to satisfy their own ego is absurd. A few years ago, student films regularly started with somebody walking down a railroad track—a harmonica would usually be involved—and within a minute there would be an unprovoked upshot or downshot. Film is a tool, and that's all it is.

DAFFY DUCK

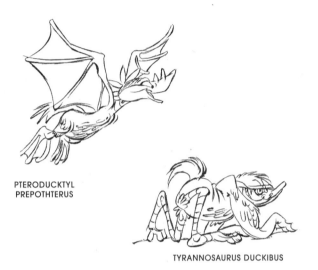

PTERODUCKTYL
PREPOTHTERUS

TYRANNOSAURUS DUCKIBUS

DUCKPTERYX FRUSTRATORUM

DUCK-BILLED OSTRICH
EXTINCTUS PECULIARIUM

| 1,936,500 B.C. | 193,000 B.C. | 19,360 B.C. | 1,936 B.C. |

168 "Bugs talks, and Daffy talks too much," said film teacher Richard Thompson. Most of us know when we should stop, and so does Daffy, but *his* where to stop is way beyond ours, and he repeatedly lands himself in trouble by going too far.

Bugs is a much more contained character than Daffy, who is usually out there expressing himself like a baby. Subtle ranges of expression do not exist for either Daffy or the baby. (The baby has two expressions—cute and outraged—and little in between.) Daffy is constantly scowling, even when his mouth is grinning, because he thinks he might have to scowl *soon*—it is there in case of need.

Like the Coyote, and to some extent Elmer Fudd, Daffy has an ongoing need to succeed. Bugs succeeds because he is successful, but Daffy needs

Lobby card for ALI BABA BUNNY *(1957).*

DUCKIBUS IDIOTICUS TEXAVERII

DUCKIBUS ALMOST-THERIUM

CONFIDENTIUS DUCKIBUS ABSURDUS

*Duck's progress
from primal slime
to prime time.*

A.D. 1936　　　　**A.D. 1947**　　　　**1990 adinfinitum**

great determination in the fight to win the recognition he knows he deserves. The whole plot of *Robin Hood Daffy* is built on his determination to prove, against all odds, that he *is* Robin Hood. A public loss of dignity will all but destroy him. He needs to be successful in the eyes of the public, and he is always afraid somebody is going to get the better of him. To some extent, of course, he does succeed, starting his career as a bit player in cartoons and ending up a star—a classic Hollywood success story.

George Orwell, when saying "I never met a man worse than I am," might have had Daffy Duck in mind. He *is* what we are afraid to admit. In *Ali Baba Bunny,* when he and Bugs Bunny dig a tunnel into a cave full of a treasure so enormous that fifty ducks could swim in it, Daffy's first reaction is, "It's mine!

All mine! I'm rich! I'm wealthy! I'm comfortably well off!" as he tries to jam Bugs back into the tunnel. It is never a struggle for him to determine his priorities. Daffy does what *we* would like to do if we had the guts.

Good comedy arises from the ability to bring to the surface, without shame, parts of yourself you would rather keep hidden. A character such as Daffy can act out things that you are not particularly interested in having anyone associate with you, but that you are perfectly willing to associate with someone you draw.

He is so honest that it hurts. Underlying his avariciousness, sneakiness, and selfishness is an admirable will to survive. As he announced in *Duck! Rabbit, Duck!,* "I am a duck bent on self-preservation!" He will marry for money *(His Bitter Half),* fight a losing battle with a drunken stork to

plays the Errol Flynn role up to the hilt. "Perchance, foppish that I am, *I* might be the Scarlet Pumpernickel," he suggests suavely to Porky and the villainous Sylvester. But just as in *Robin Hood Daffy,* when he fails to convince Porky that he is Robin Hood, Sylvester and Porky collapse in laughter at the idea of Daffy as the Pumpernickel, even though they are actively looking for him.

Daffy's character—his acceptance of the idea that he really is what we say he is—drives the whole picture. He thinks of himself as Errol Flynn and complains because he has to suffer indignities unknown to Errol. Mike Maltese and I wrote the narration perfectly straight, not basing it on a specific Errol Flynn film but on the entire action genre, in which a line about a "daring outlaw, as slippery as an eel" might

keep an egg from being delivered to his home *(Stork Naked)*, or fight a losing battle with an implacable animator *(Duck Amuck)*. But there is incredible energy always, and good humor too. When he plants "Rabbit Season" signs during duck season *(Rabbit Seasoning)* he points out to the audience, quite logically, that it is a matter of "survival of the fittest," and then adds as a happy afterthought ". . . and besides, it's fun!"

 Sixty years after his creation, Daffy Duck, like other Warner Bros. cartoon stars, is far more recognizable than most of the live-action stars who dominated the Hollywood studios in the 1930s and 1940s. Our animated stars had no more choice about their roles than did Warner Bros. live-action actors: they, too, had contracts, and they had to appear in the films assigned to them by the studio. *The Scarlet Pumpernickel,* for example, is a dark, spectacular, and star-studded picture, in which the actions echo an Errol Flynn film and the animated characters fill their roles like live-action stars.

Porky Pig is the film's Claude Rains, Sylvester plays a Basil Rathbone role, and even Mama Bear appears as a lady-in-waiting—she was the only character I had who would fit the part. Daffy, of course,

With avariciousness, sneakiness, and selfishness, how could this marriage fail?

Our animated stars had no more choice about their roles than did Warner Bros. live-action actors: they had to appear in the films assigned to them by the director. That great Gothic romance THE SCARLET PUMPERNICKEL (1950) is a sterling example.

well have been spoken. In fact, it was probably used repeatedly in "B" pictures, which were routinely written in all seriousness by people who didn't know how to write. What made the dialogue in *The Scarlet Pumpernickel* funny was that the lines were being spoken by these particular animals.

A comedian like Daffy delivers a circumstance of which the line is part—usually a very small part. Witness Bugs Bunny's "What's up, Doc?" or Jack Benny's "Well." Both depend on careful definition of character, of circumstance, and of the condition preceding the occurrence to make them funny.

"You're dethspicable" is not a funny line in itself—Daffy is not a stand-up comedian, whose lines can be repeated by someone else and still draw a laugh. And if anyone had told me that I would write a line that would get a laugh out

The artist in any field must be accident-prone—he or she must stumble, then get up afterward and not walk away, for that is when it all happens. Stumbling is the untoward, unexpected event that corresponds to a mutation in genetics. It is the mutation of creativity. Without it, we would continue to do only those expected things the experts so adore. Without stumbling, we wouldn't have gotten into the Stone Age—much less out of it. And we would have missed a lot of laughs.

of Daffy's "pronoun trouble"—well, it's absurd! Even when I put it in the film *Rabbit Seasoning*, I thought it was nothing more than a quirky little moment.

Above all, Daffy is a rationalist. He will explain to the audience his reason for an act that might be considered less than honorable. "After all," he claims in *The Abominable Snow Rabbit*, "it's better that it should happen to him than to me. I'm not like other people. I can't stand pain—it hurts me!" And he admits: "I know I'm a louse, but I'm a live louse."

I have more than once used his assertion that he's different from other people because pain hurts him when I have found myself sitting in the dentist's chair. One dentist took me seriously and explained earnestly that there is indeed no such thing as a universal pain threshold. Some people I know have their dental work done without anaesthetic, but when a dentist asks me if I want novocaine, I say, "Yes, I do! What was it ever invented for!"

Daffy looked—and behaved—like a completely different character when he first appeared in *Porky's Duck Hunt.* In that picture, he was drawn rather like a pot, with a mallard-like band across his long neck and a long, unbroken bill. He may even have had gloves. Bob Clampett, who animated *Porky's Duck Hunt* for Tex Avery, kept Daffy cross-eyed and crazy, quite a bit broader than my duck.

Daffy Duck's looks and personality changed over the years, his character developing, just like anyone else's, a little bit at a time. He began as the wild and unrestrained "screwy duck" encountered by Porky in *My Favorite Duck.* When I made *Daffy Dilly* in 1948, he was still a wild character, but now only in order to earn a fortune by making a cheerless old millionaire laugh. Eventually he stopped bedeviling people for

no reason at all, and as he moderated, his shape changed a little. He stopped performing as a duck in a duck environment and became more of a human being, a person who just happened to be a duck. A story about a man is not important because he is a man but because of what kind of man he is, and it is the same with ducks. The more you know Daffy, the better you like him, because you are going to recognize yourself. To me, he is Daffy, that is all.

Daffy has no teeth except when needed: in broad, guilty, caught-in-the-act or embarrassing situations.
Left: *Just one of many mysterious honors—well, I do have all my original teeth at age 84.*

172

University of Southern California
School of Dentistry
Human Factors Research Division

This Certifies That

CHUCK JONES

was a participant in the first
National Conference on Programmed
Audio-Visual Instruction in Medical
and Dental Education
April 28-30, 1963
Los Angeles, California

Co-Chairman

Co-Chairman

Co-Chairman

Co-Chairman

The right angle is the strongest of all angles. In one of his characteristic stances, Daffy stands rigid, shoulders high, pointing accusingly at the Shropshire Slasher (whose occupation is also "Shropshire Slasher"). A series of right angles contributes to the strength of Daffy's position, with straight lines backing up straight lines.

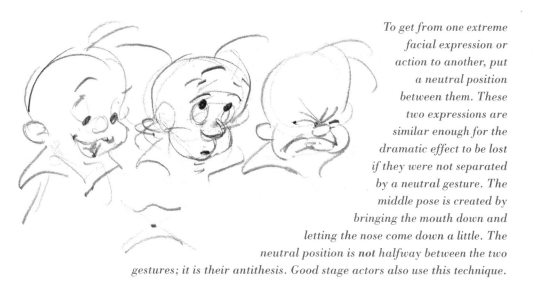

To get from one extreme facial expression or action to another, put a neutral position between them. These two expressions are similar enough for the dramatic effect to be lost if they were not separated by a neutral gesture. The middle pose is created by bringing the mouth down and letting the nose come down a little. The neutral position is **not** halfway between the two gestures; it is their antithesis. Good stage actors also use this technique.

Daffy's upper bill always maintains its original relationship with his skull, just as his (and Bugs's) upper teeth do not bend or stretch.

IN A HUMAN HEAD, THE UPPER TEETH ARE ANCHORED TO THE SKULL (UNTIL THE DENTIST HAS HIS WAY WITH THEM), WHILE THE LOWER JAW— COMPLETE WITH TEETH—CAN MOVE INDEPENDENTLY. DAFFY'S UPPER BILL, LIKE THAT OF THE ROAD RUNNER OR ANY OTHER BIRD, IS IN EFFECT HIS UPPER JAW, BUILT RIGHT ONTO THE SKULL AND AN IMMOVABLE PART OF THE STRUCTURE. HIS LOWER BILL IS HINGED TO THE SKULL AND CAN MOVE FREELY UP AND DOWN.

WHEN HE SPEAKS, THE UPPER BILL DOES NOT MOVE. IT CAN'T. THE SKULL IS SOLID, AND THERE'S NOTHING HE OR I CAN DO ABOUT IT. IN PRACTICE, I WORK ON THE SUPPOSITION THAT THE SKULL HAS A LITTLE GIVE IN IT, ALTHOUGH ITS *VOLUME* MUST REMAIN CONSTANT. THIS GIVES ME A CERTAIN DRAMATIC LEEWAY WHEN I WANT, FOR EXAMPLE, TO EXPRESS DAFFY'S SURPRISE BY ELONGATING THE SKULL, OR TO FLATTEN HIS HEAD IN ANGER. IF HE WAS ABOUT TO REGISTER SURPRISE, I WOULD MAKE HIS HEAD COME DOWN, THE HAIR WOULD FLATTEN, AND THE SHOULDERS WOULD COME UP. THIS MAKES THE EFFECT FAR MORE DRAMATIC WHEN THE SHOULDERS GO BACK AND THE FACE OPENS UP IN AMAZEMENT. BUT THE VOLUME MUST REMAIN THE SAME, IF YOU WANT BELIEVABILITY.

174

When Daffy laughs, he laughs.

Draw feather breaks only at the shoulders, wrists, and elbows.

Feet—think swim fins.

Daffy does not wear gloves. His hands are a cross between fingers and feathers.

To draw Daffy, get out your old swim fins, draw them, and hang a duck on the drawing. When necessary, he can look like a human being, but I like him to be bird-like. I might draw tiny breaks where the feathers show at his shoulders and elbows, but the breaks are less noticeable than on the Coyote, as feathers cling more tightly to the body than fur. This detail is not strictly necessary; I break Daffy's feathers because I want to and because it gives character to the animal. Also, unlike so many animated characters, Daffy doesn't wear gloves. His hands have a thumb like a human thumb and pointy fingers that are a cross between human fingers and a bunch of feathers.

*To draw Daffy,
get out your old swim fins.*

175

Daffy on his dignity.

Disgust

If this happens to Daffy, it's comedy; if it happens to me, it's tragedy.

176

LOWER BILL AT SLIGHT ANGLE TO HEAD

FLATTEN BODY SHAPE A LITTLE AT BASE

THE FUN OF PIE IN THE FACE IS THE INCONGRUITY OF THE MATTER. PIES WERE INDEED MEANT FOR FACES, BUT IN SMALLER PORTIONS AND AT THE WILL OF THE PIE-EATER. ONLY BABIES AND COMEDIANS RIGHTLY BELIEVE THAT THROWING FOOD AT OTHER PEOPLE'S FACES ADDS SOMETHING TO OUR CULTURAL HERITAGE.

LAUGHTER IS THE PROCESS BY WHICH WE INDICATE OUR RESPONSE TO ANOTHER PERSON'S TRIVIAL MISFORTUNE—LIKE SLIPPING ON TAMARIND RIND (I'M TIRED OF BANANA PEELS) OR RECEIVING GENEROUS PORTIONS OF DOUGH-ENCRUSTED CUSTARD IN THE FACE.

IF A PERSON WHO SLIPS ON A FRUIT RIND BREAKS HIS BACK, COMEDY QUICKLY BECOMES TRAGEDY. AND IT IS THAT IMPLICIT POSSIBILITY THAT GIVES DEPTH TO HUMOR.

CHAPLIN, KEATON, LLOYD, AND TODAY'S GREAT RICHARD PRYOR AND ROBIN WILLIAMS ARE ALL DEAR EVIDENCE OF THE NECESSARY ASSOCIATION OF COMEDY AND TRAGEDY. WHEN WOODY ALLEN'S IMPLIED FAILURES MIRRORED TRUE FAILURES AND TRUE HUMILIATION, ALL OF US FOUND HOW CLOSE TO TEARS HE HAD ALWAYS BEEN.

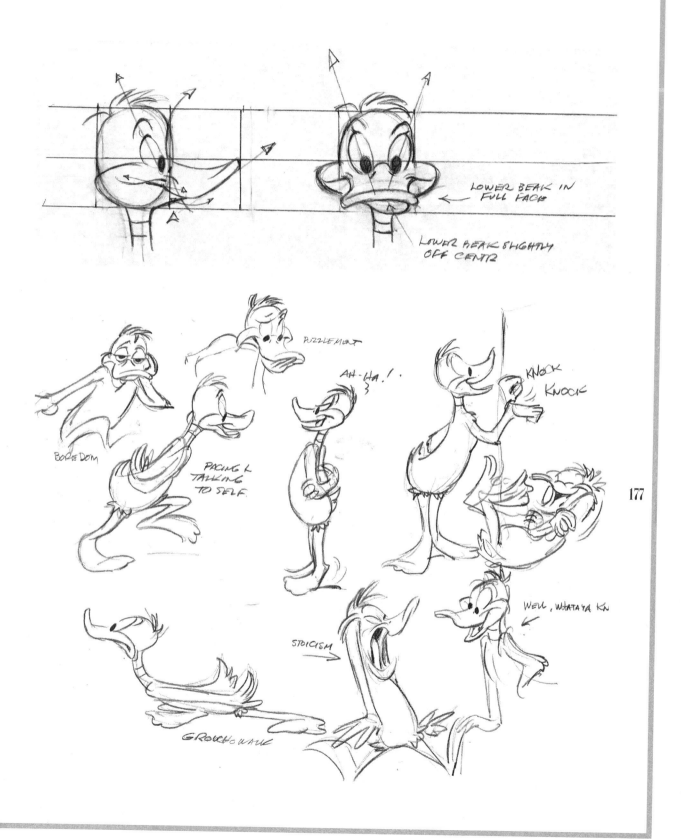

LOWER BEAK IN
FULL FACE

LOWER BEAK SLIGHTLY
OFF CENTR

PUZZLEMENT

AH-HA!

BOREDOM

PACING &
TALKING
TO SELF

KNOCK
KNOCK

WELL, WHATAYA KN

STOICISM

GROUCHO WALK

177

My character sheet (details, above) became the standard for Porky Pig in 1947. We didn't know what the early Porky was, so he could hardly know who he was. I began to discover Porky's unique character only when I gave him more sophisticated parts to play, and then he began to develop characteristics of his own.

PORKY PIG

Porky Pig was originally part of a Tubby Millar/Friz Freleng vaudeville-like team of "Porky and Beans." Beans can probably be found today, a toothless, out-of-work (since 1935) cat, sleeping fitfully on park benches, cursing the William Morris agency while his ertswhile partner, Porky, enjoys worldwide fame, acclaim, and pâté de foie gras galore.

Porky Pig is structured almost identically to Elmer Fudd except for his nose, but the pair's personalities are quite different. The early Porky had about as much personality as a can of Crisco. *We* didn't know what he was, so *he* could hardly know who he was, and he just walked through his roles. I began to discover Porky's unique character only when I gave him more sophisticated parts, and then he developed characteristics of his own.

As the space cadet in *Duck Dodgers in the 24½th Century* or Friar Tuck in *Robin Hood Daffy*, Porky is the observer, stating what the audience is thinking and only incidentally playing an active part in the plot. Porky the observer was a type of character I had not met before. The role became significant in *Duck Dodgers*, in which he acts as Daffy's assistant. The film's leading man could not appear heroic unless he had somebody to bounce off of, and a character such as Daffy required someone relatively meek for the role. Porky, responding on behalf of the audience, makes us realize the true craziness of what we are seeing.

Most of the great comedy directors (Billy Wilder and Frank Capra among them) found it useful to have a character in the film who represented the audience's

Daffy in the shadow of a falling boulder, which quickly becomes reality, in Robin Hood Daffy *(1958). Porky always innocently manages to avoid any situation that might be bruising.*

viewpoint, who could look at the situation and ratio-nalize it or be astonished by it. Some great comedians could also share the viewpoint of the audience as well as participating in the action. Groucho Marx would even step outside his part from time to time, and Tex Avery was very adroit at this technique. Porky played this role for me.

Humor always involves our knowledge of the way things ought to be. In his observer role Porky represents sanity, and that, I like to think, is the part of myself that I put in him. Even in me there is a small core of sanity.

I can understand Porky the observer, and I can find the *me* in him. It is particularly nice when he can perform duties for me that I cannot perform for myself: as a space cadet to Daffy's Duck Dodgers he maintains equilibrium, good sense, and, I think, a kind of dignified charm in situations in which I would lose my patience and my temper, thereby los-ing control of the picture too. To find this Porky (who also played Friar Tuck perfectly in *Robin Hood Daffy)* lurking in that infantile, gibbering piglet of the 1930s is as surprising as it would be to find your maiden aunt Daisy successfully playing Maggie Thatcher or Lucretia Borgia.

I like Porky, and I appreciate his willingness to cheerfully and competently bring believability and humor to roles that at the outset would seem to be puerile at best. He is, in short, a first-rate actor in supporting roles—supporting me, that is—and for that I am grateful.

⁂   ⁂   ⁂

For over seventy years I have carried the name of a pig around in the snap-purse of my mind where small ideas are stored, waiting for the improper char-acter to come along.

When I discovered that Cousin John Cone had stolen and eaten *all* the date bars in the kitchen be-fore honest me had had a fair shot at this pleasant felony, a Curie-like revelation spun forth: John Cone was not John Cone at all; he was actually and forever-more "Pig Newton"!

This sort of thing is catching, and although I have never found a character that would fit under the name Pig Newton, he will sometime, somewhere, somehow find himself under the candid animation camera.

Benny Washam, a one-time resident of Possum Foot Bridge, Arkansas, assured me that the following is a true anecdote concerning one of the porcine resi-dents of the Possum Foot Bridge metropolis.

It seems, according to Ben—honest animator, honest man, and chef extraordinaire of squirrel ragout—that the notorious oversized and under-brained Johnson brothers of nearby Cotton Mouth Farm, Arkansas, were out on foot this day in pursuit of their profession: the lifting of restless, unsupervised, and/or dissatisfied pigs. By fortuitous chance, the two Johnsons found just such a candidate for their chari-table attentions in an anxious-looking pinkish sow named Agatha, who might well have been a distant parboiled relative of the mature Orson Welles.

Levering the purloined lady into the battered back of their Chevy pick-up is but a matter of a half-hour for the nimble brothers, Frobe and Frank, and off they go, secure in the knowledge of a kindly deed well done. Accompanying their self-approval is the radio voice of Lavinny Crouch, "The Ozarks' Own Silver-Tongued Songbird of the Piney Ridge," singing "Ah cain't go on with you, without you, or under you, no matter what your druthers are."

*"Comedy Relief" and "Western-type
Hero" in* DRIPALONG DAFFY *(1951).*

This plaintive ditty is rudely interrupted by the harsh voice of the state police, warning all motorists that they are to be subject to a careful search of all vehicles for expropriated livestock, including pigs and especially pigs, and that roadblocks have been established on all major and minor roads, highways, byways, lumber roads, and goat and turkey tracks.

Although the Johnsons' vocabulary does not encompass the word *expropriate,* they properly assume from long practice that anything they do for pleasure is probably illegal. Therefore, they promptly put into action plan B (there is no plan A). Quickly turning the truck bed into a boudoir, they dress the unwilling Agatha in a tattered red hickory cloth shirt and the faded overalls of a Johnson grandma, who smothered the scales at nearly a quarter ton, just like Agatha. A battered straw hat discarded by a disgruntled scarecrow completes this stunning outfit, and with Agatha comfortably squeezed upright between the two brothers in the front seat of the pick-up, the entourage proceeds to the first roadblock. Two state troopers approach and peer suspiciously into the murky interior of the cab.

"What's yer name?" one asks Frobe.

"Frobe Johnson," grunts Frobe. If his reply sounds forced, it is probably because this is only the second time in his life he has spoken the truth.

"And your name?" the other trooper asks Frank.

"Newt Johnson." Frank sounds a little more believable, allowing that one truth does not a summer make.

"How about you? What's *your* name, Mr. Johnson?" the first trooper sarcastically asks Agatha.

"Oink," promptly grunts Agatha.

"OK, go ahead." The lead officer signals them on.

As the pick-up disappears in the distance, one officer turns to the other.

"Have you ever in your born life seen anybody as ugly as that Oink Johnson?"

And that is how "Oink Johnson" became the only synonym we ever needed around the studio for sheer unadulterated ugliness. Such pale nouns as "dog," "dragon," and "witch" were discarded as trash. O. Henry once described a man as "about the same size as a real estate agent," which leaves one an enormous amount of imaginary acreage to move around in. One man's Oink Johnson is not necessarily or aptly that of another, just as Medusa's idea of ugliness might be slightly different from that of Pollyanna.

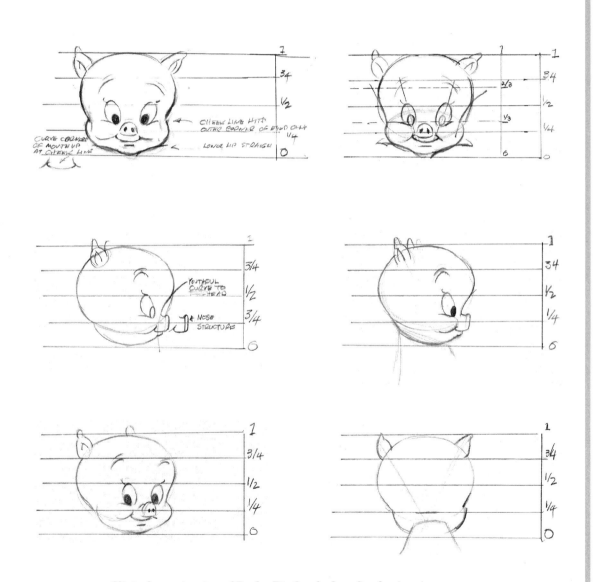

Clinical examination of Porky Pig for the benefit of animation crew,
hopefully encouraging consistency in drawing.

183

*Various poses
of Charlie Dog,
master self-salesman,
plying his trade.*

CHARLIE DOG

YOU AIN'T GOT NO DOG!
—I AIN'T GOT NO MASTER---
SO I'LL MAKE YOU
A PREPOSITION!"

Charlie Dog is one of my favorite characters. I don't understand him, but I do like him. He is so unquestionably a dog. Charlie is merely trying to find a master and a home, which are perfectly natural ambitions for any dog. Comedy is always concerned with simple matters such as this.

Charlie Dog is in many ways Daffy Duck on four legs. He never doubts his desirability as a pet dog ("You ain't got no dog; I ain't got no master. So I'll make you a preposition"), and he is openly obnoxious to anybody who appears unwilling to accept what is to him a very desirable proposition.

Unlike Daffy, however, Charlie does not believe that the world owes him a living. He does believe everybody needs a dog to call their own, and he therefore becomes the ultimate salesman, attempting to get what he deserves by selling himself.

Animated characters must show recognizable— not necessarily admirable—human attributes, and Charlie the salesman is a character we all know. Indeed, we have probably played the part in our own lives, for we all have to sell ourselves at times, and that involves presenting our best attributes to those we hope to impress. He differs from the majority in his complete confidence and his understanding of the mechanics of selling. He prances out with a big smile of good fellowship on his face and his tail up in the air (an important indicator of his personality), whether he is going to find something to eat or to prove to a potential master that he is the most wonderful of dogs.

When he spots a likely master, he begins his "big soulful eyes routine." Making the eyes look soulful is basically a matter of making them bigger, and the bigger the eyes, the more appealing they appear. To complete the effect, I would draw little highlights in Charlie's eyes, and perhaps add a couple of eyelashes; his ears would hang down, and he would wear the faker's smile. And since dogs smile with their tail, Charlie's tail would be wagging brightly.

Curiously enough, I would often make him a little pigeontoed in these scenes, or put one leg across the other. I have noticed that the models in magazines designed for young girls stand this way, with their toes pointing inward to suggest youth and cuteness. Models in the adult fashion magazines are less likely to point their toes at each other, and less likely to smile, as a smile and knock-knees are reliable ways of suggesting a character is young. Charlie understands this—being cute is his business.

He is the epitome of all dogs, who will do anything to be recognized. A dog will play any role you give him. If you decide he's a lapdog, he will leap onto your lap, even if he's a Great Dane. (Teaching a cat

to "heel" is a much tougher, in fact impossible, task.)

Every teenage boy with a pick-up truck used to have a dog roving around loose in the back, and just because he was back there, he became in his own eyes a guard dog, protecting whatever cargo happened to be on the truck, which was usually something nobody in the world would want, such as four pieces of smashed-up cement or an old garbage can. He would sit there, tail up, and he would manage to get his ears flattened back, even though the truck was heading in the opposite direction.

Charlie's essential nature can be captured in a drawing, but animation adds the typical little trot and makes the tail a much stronger feature as it sways back and forth. Music reinforces the effect, and Charlie's music is reminiscent of Pepé le Pew's, suggesting a carefree attitude that few of us can emulate as we go out to sell ourselves to the world.

Every teenage boy with a pick-up truck used to have
a dog roving around loose in the back.

I rescued Charlie from the Warner Bros. character pound, where he had been abandoned. He had appeared in Bob Clampett's *Porky's Pooch*, but he had grown into a different dog by the time he appeared in my pictures. In a similar way, Friz Freleng recreated Tweety Bird after Bob's departure. The Clampett Tweety, with big feet and a hydrocephalic head, was hardly a pretty little thing, but Friz reduced him in size and made him an altogether cuter and more loveable character.

Porky Pig is the unfortunate target of Charlie's sales pitch. Porky acts as an honorable straight man, failing to realize he has become half of a comedy duo. Charlie gives poor Porky a cruelly hard time. When Porky challenges his claim to be a Labrador retriever, Charlie is incensed. ("Get me a Labrador, and I'll retrieve it for you." "N-no." "That's fair, isn't it?" "N-no. N-no." "Have you got a Labrador?" "N-no. N-no." "Know where you can get a Labrador?" "N-no." "Then SHAT-UP!") You don't have to be a dog owner to know that a Labrador retriever is not a retriever of Labradors, but logic has been reversed, Porky has lost the initiative, and he finds himself defending a position he never wanted to adopt in the first place. I have frequently seen this dismaying strategy used by bullying Representatives in the United States Congress.

Porky and Charlie also provide a perfect illustration of a technique often employed by animators. Although few people notice it, characters frequently change their size within a cartoon, and this is quite acceptable as long as the character's looks remain the same and the change in size does not occur within a scene. Porky and Charlie start out exactly the same size, but when Porky has to carry the dog, I cut to a different viewpoint, and Charlie becomes smaller without destroying believability. A more dramatic example of this ploy occurs in *Pinocchio*. When Stromboli imprisons Pinocchio in the canary cage, Jiminy Cricket shrinks over a period of several scenes in relation to Pinocchio, this change of size enabling him to walk into the cage's padlock, where he succeeds in prying it open. Such changes in size must be subtle and appear natural.

187

Teaching a cat to "heel" is a sadly frustrating,
indeed impossible, task.

*Maurice Noble's
dramatic design for
Marc Anthony's home
in CAT FEUD (1958).*

*The kitten's model sheet.
Actually, she never had a
permanent name—
call her "Everykitten."*

pussyfoot.

© WARNER BROS. 1951
CARTOONS INC.

*Marc Anthony
in deep study.*

MARC ANTHONY

Marc Anthony is your basic big bulldog, but in *Feed the Kitty* he falls in parental love with a little kitten, in the way that any of us might fall for a cat or another small animal.

We all have visual patterns and expectations of things, and cartoon bulldogs are almost invariably big, powerful bullies. Marc Anthony is behaving true to this stereotype when we first see him. He is chasing a kitten, who is supposed to run away, but this one walks right across his gaping mouth and teeth in the middle of a growl—the most dangerous place of all, it would seem—and climbs blithely up on his back, curls up, and purrs himself to sleep, provoking Marc Anthony's surprise and, curiously, tenderness.

This smitten dog sweetly accepts the unusual role of the defenseless kitten's protector. He is so touching in that role that I fell in love with him. Toward the end of the picture he believes that his kitten has been baked as a cookie and almost collapses with grief. His mistress, misunderstanding his sorrow, hands him a cookie to cheer him up. Marc Anthony takes it and puts it carefully on his back where the kitten used to sleep. We *knew* the kitten wasn't gone, but the dog didn't, and that was what the scene—and the direction—were all about. Fool that I am, I feel tears slipping into my eyes every time I see that scene, or even just think about it. I didn't intend the scene to work that way at all; I thought the situation was comic, but I found that I shared a true sense of sorrow with the dog.

And I am not alone. This is one of the few occasions when I have seen audiences cry in what is

SECONDARY ACTION IS ESSENTIAL FOR BELIEVABLE ANIMATION. SECONDARY ACTION IS ANY ACTION THAT HAS NO MOTIVE POWER OF ITS OWN, LIKE LONG HAIR SWEEPING ROUND WHEN YOU TURN YOUR HEAD. HAIR HAS NO LIFE OF ITS OWN; IT IS NOT GOING TO SWIRL UNLESS IT IS MOVED BY THE WIND (MOTIVE POWER FROM THE OUTSIDE) OR BY A MOVEMENT OF THE HEAD (MOTIVE POWER FROM THE INSIDE). THE SAME PRINCIPLE APPLIES TO CLOTHES: HATS BLOW OFF IN THE WIND, AND WHEN CHARACTERS COME TO A STOP, THEIR CLOTHES TEND TO CARRY ON MOVING FORWARD.

THE LOOSE SKIN ON OUR BULLDOG'S BACK IS SECONDARY. WHEN HE COMES TO A SCREECHING STOP, NOT ONLY DO HIS EARS AND DEWLAPS SWING FORWARD, THE LOOSE SKIN ON HIS BACK CONTINUES FORWARD, CLIMBS HIS NECK, AND SETTLES BACK INTO ITS ORIGINAL POSITION WHEN THE ORIGINAL IMPETUS CEASES—THAT IS, WHEN THE DOG STOPS.

My rough sketch of Marc Anthony's skidding stop. What the lady is doing there, I don't know. (She may have been crying, hence the ripple.)

190

Top: *Marc Anthony expresses his negative opinion of a moving cereal bowl.*
Middle: *Lady of the house comments off screen.*
Bottom: *"Where's my kitten?"*

supposed to be—and is—a funny film. Comedy and tragedy really are closely allied. As Joseph Conrad said, there is no such thing as comedy or tragedy; tragedy prevails if you are writing tragedy, and comedy prevails when you are writing comedy, but each contains a little of the other.

Effects such as this cannot be achieved by trying to anticipate audience reactions. I had to put myself in the position of that dog, to understand how I would feel—how anyone would feel—in a similar situation. I had to care.

All the kitten had was the ability to love, so drawing him was comparatively simple. A kitten's ears are much bigger in relation to the face than an adult cat's, and as in all young mammals, his forehead is very high. I wanted him to be so darling that you feel you must pick him up and hug him, which is precisely what I wanted Marc Anthony to want to do.

When Bob McKimson drew Sylvester, Jr., he didn't try to make him look young; all he did was make a small version of Sylvester, with Sylvester's head unchanged on a tiny frame. This is the technique seen in so many Renaissance paintings, in which the Virgin Mary is shown holding a small adult human being rather than a baby.

Marc Anthony's emotions are very complex, and they demanded subtle drawings. When, for example, the kitten is kneading his back with its claws, as if it was a rug, Marc Anthony breaks out in a painful sweat. At the same time he feels an ambivalent happiness, easily understood by any parent or pet owner. This is a complex emotion for an animator to try to convey, but it is certainly worth a try.

All worthwhile pictures present a series of such problems. The only dialogue in the film is the ordinary woman's voice. Marc Anthony conveys everything he

191

feels by his expressions, and it is these expressions that make the animation so special. When the woman asks, "What are you up to now?" he points to himself with a look of exaggerated innocence. If anybody had looked in my wastepaper basket at the end of the day I did that drawing, they would have found fifty or more rejected drawings. I needed *that* drawing, and I knew it was somewhere between my memory and the tip of my pencil, but there was a sort of cornucopia of unsuitable drawings before I finally got the right one.

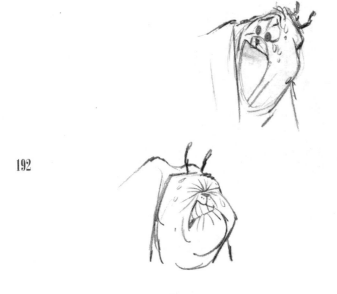

A Parable: A very rich man came to a famous Japanese artist. He wanted a painting of a stork. The artist told him it would cost ten thousand dollars. The rich man agreed but privately thought it was a very high price. The artist told him the painting would be waiting for him in two months.

He returned two months later, only to learn that the painting was not yet ready. In another two months he came back again. "I am ready," the artist said. "Please sit down." To the rich man's surprise, he took out his ink pad and set of brushes, prepared his inks, dipped the point of his chosen brush into the ink, and drew with deftly simple, beautiful strokes a magnificent painting of a stork. "Finished," he said.

The client was insulted. "Ten thousand dollars for that? It took you no more than ten minutes!" The artist didn't say a word. He walked across the room to a large cabinet and pulled open the doors. Thousands of drawings of storks fell out.

Well, I didn't do a thousand drawings of Marc Anthony's look of exaggerated innocence, but I did do at least fifty before I got it right, and that doesn't count the thousands of drawings I had done when I was learning how to draw this dog, after learning how to draw *any* dog, after learning how to draw.

Moments like these call upon the artist's unwillingness to do anything less than the best he or she can. Rough sketches are always necessary, if only as a loosening-up process, but when you sit down to draw, you should apply the utmost effort to making the best drawing you know how. If you cannot bring yourself to do that, find another occupation.

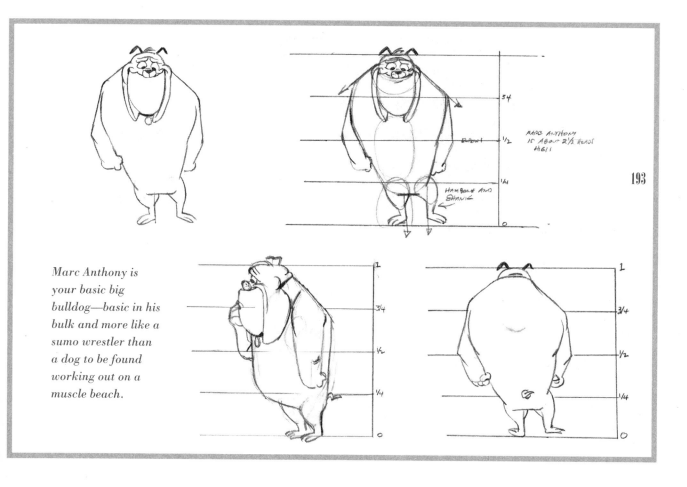

Marc Anthony is your basic big bulldog—basic in his bulk and more like a sumo wrestler than a dog to be found working out on a muscle beach.

193

Wile E. Coyote being careless with an explosive tennis ball—Acme, of course.

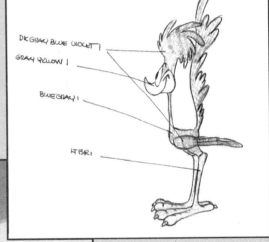

Very early model sheet of vertical Road Runner, from FAST AND FURRY-OUS *(1949).*

Top-of-the-line Acme product.

WILE E. COYOTE AND THE ROAD RUNNER

I am completely ill at ease with any machinery more complicated than toenail clippers, so I have no difficulty in understanding Wile E. Coyote's problems.

Comedy is always concerned with simple problems that everyone recognizes or has encountered: not agonizing love, but how to get a date; not agonizing starvation, but the hunger for a doughnut, a hot dog, a pickle; not an agonizing, parched death in an endless desert, but where to get a coin for a soda-pop machine; not a struggle for life itself, but the effort to get some of life's goodies. Comedy is the frustrating pain of trying to get your share; tragedy is teetering on a tightrope between life and death. Tragedy is walking through hell with Medea, King Lear, and Judas. Comedy is sharing a boiled shoe with Charlie Chaplin.

I see nothing in the Coyote that I can't find in almost any human being. Most of us share his desire for something small and special, be it diamonds, doughnuts, or Road Runner. Wile E. Coyote devotes enormous ingenuity and energy to chasing the Road Runner. People wonder what good it would do him to catch the Road Runner as there's obviously very little food on that scrawny frame. A rabbit would seem to be more nutritious prey, but Wile E. considers roadrunner to be a luxury item on the coyote's food chain. There are delicacies as yet unknown to the human palate, and one of them is this apparently succulent avian.

Even his loyalty to the Acme Company—in spite of the uncertain quality of the product—is solidly based on human behavior. I know many people who will buy a car, curse it for three years, and then trade it in for another of exactly the same make.

*Obviously
an Acme cliff.*

Without the Acme Co., where would Wile E. Coyote be? And, for that matter, where would the Acme Co. be without Wile E. Coyote? It is what is called in some quarters "a perfect symbiotic relationship," which Noah Webster defined as: "A couple of different living things living together in close association for mutual benefit." What the Coyote needs in terms of equipment, supplies, or armaments in his diligent and admirable pursuit of the Road Runner, the company is symbiotically ready to supply. Is it jet-propelled roller skates? Electrified tennis shoes? Steam-driven pogo sticks? Boulder pills ("Amuse your friends, be a boulder")? Leg muscle vitamins? Earthquake lozenges? Or any other et cetera?

The sheer beauty of the matter is that neither party is in the relationship for gain. Money is never involved. What the Coyote wants from his source, the Coyote gets—for free. What does the Acme Co. get for its participation? Why, a market for its products. Where else is there a probable customer for these special tennis shoes, pogo sticks, and highly specialized pills? Who else would have immediate need for such products as The Acme Little-Giant Kralfazz-

Driven Liquid Carbon-Dioxicized Super Coyote-Carrying Rocket?

As a matter of record, this happy relationship continues because it has never been established whether the high malfunction rate of the Acme products is due to poor workmanship or pilot error. Until it is, the Acme/Coyote symbiotic romance will continue to be one of the prettiest in the annals of primal behavior.

A villain should have a goal that is identifiable, that we can recognize as achievable, and that is so meaningful to the villain (we don't have to know why) that he or she will do anything inside or outside the law to achieve it. This is the essence of the fun, the delight and the fright of villainy. In the villain we suddenly and perhaps subconsciously recognize ourselves. Then we begin to sympathize and ask, "Why can't the poor Coyote ever catch the Road Runner?" When we cannot help asking that, we do indeed have a winning villain.

A Road Runner cartoon is basically a series of separate blackout gags with an underlying structure, as the Coyote returns obsessively to the fray. Mike Maltese and I found that we needed about eleven gags to make a film, and the trick was to proceed in a more or less orderly fashion up to a strong climax. Gags varied considerably in length and could be as short as four seconds, as long as four minutes, or almost as long as the film itself.

The ending might pick up something that happened—or failed to happen—earlier in the film. For example, the Coyote might set a trap for the Road Runner, such as a steel plate inside the road, designed to spring up and stop the passing bird. It doesn't go off, of course, and we forget about it until the end of the film, when the Coyote himself comes racing round the corner and runs smack into the

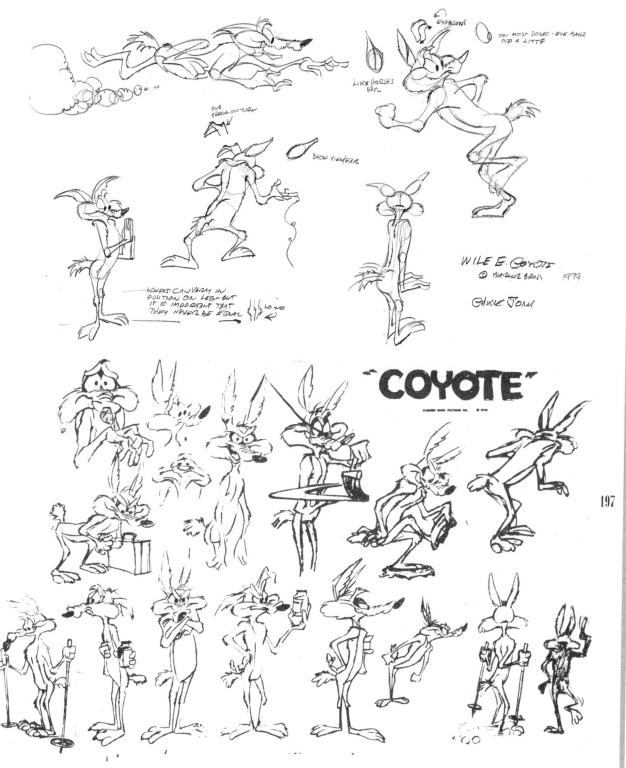

197

My character model sheet of the Coyote (anatomy alone is not enough).
This is the definitive Coyote, used to this day.

sprung trap. The Coyote's life is full of such backfire situations.

The nature of the gags changed over time. We used explosive gags more in the early pictures, then gravity became and remained the Coyote's primary problem. If you fall off a cliff, then obviously you represent a force that can be converted into another kind of force, like a teeter-totter with a rock on one end, and we shamelessly exploit this principle of physics.

Other physical laws we adapted. When the Coyote falls into the ravine, his body goes first, followed by his neck and finally his head. It's rather like a line of cars waiting at a traffic light. Most drivers stop within a couple of feet of the car in front, but when the lights change to green, each driver will wait until the car in front has driven about a car's length before following. In a line of ten cars, the first could be a hundred feet along the road before the last one moves. Why this is so, no one knows. But I am willing to learn from every foible of human behavior.

Audiences became so used to the idea that there was no practicality in whatever the Coyote was doing that we could introduce plans that seemingly had no point and no hope of success, such as the Coyote dropping an unlikely piano on the passing Road Runner, or strapping a helmet on his head with a little wheel on top, designed to slide down an angled wire to the road below. A dexterous and admirable circus act no doubt, but hardly a practical way to catch a Road Runner.

Humor is often a series of sensible statements ending in an unexpected oddity that completely changes the meaning of the scene. The Coyote has built a rickety construction all the way up the side of a hill, similar to a flume carrying water downhill. "It looks like he built it himself," the audience thinks, as we follow its path up the hillside, "and it's built to carry something lethal down to the road below." Sure enough, when we reach the top we find the Coyote putting a lighted match to a bomb, getting ready to send it on its way—and it immediately blows up, before it can utilize the long, carefully designed ramp.

Remember: Gravity is no danger unless you look down.

The bomb explodes in the audience's face as much as in the Coyote's. Nobody expects that explosion. Even I don't expect it; I am *still* surprised when that bomb explodes.

Most humor is fraudulent in that it lures the audience astray, and the gags in the Wile E. Coyote pictures mislead the audience in various ways. The flume-top explosion is an end the audience has no hint of. Other gags work because things do not go the way the audience expects, and the more carefully we reveal the evidence that a certain event is going to happen, the more dramatic the final reversal.

A variation involves pointing the plot in a particular direction, then changing it around to show that is not what you meant at all, before finally springing the original ending on a bewildered audience. Take the classic banana-peel gag, for example, in which everything leads up to a pratfall: a man is established as somebody we would like to see slip on the peel, then the banana peel is planted in his path; he comes walking along, unaware of the danger, reaches the peel . . . and steps safely over it. Then he takes one more step and falls down an open manhole. The moment of disappointment felt at the non-slip sets up something even more dramatically satisfying.

Animals' tails can be very expressive, from Pepé le Pew's confidently erect and swaying brush to the Coyote's ragged appendage. I read that you can see indecision in a cat's tail. On a rainy evening, when he wants to go out because he is a cat, but he doesn't want to get wet, he will stand in the open doorway flicking his tail. Whenever I draw an animal's tail, I am aware that I see only its outside, the way the fur

or hair hangs on it. Inside there is a bony structure, and believability is destroyed if I draw anything that intrudes into that solid area.

The Coyote's ragged tail (see page 201) was inspired by Japanese paintings of ocean waves, and Maurice Noble's background designs for the Road Runner cartoons were also influenced by Japanese thinking. Japanese artists use perspective in a different way from ours; for example, if a boat is about to crash on the rocks, and there are people watching from the safety of the shore in the foreground, they will be drawn smaller than the sailors in peril. Don Graham said that our Road Runner cartoons were the only ones he had seen in which the space was identified by the movement of the animals through it. There is no perspective, and distance is established only by the characters moving through the desert landscape.

*"By trying we can easily learn to endure adversity—
another man's, that is."
—Mark Twain*

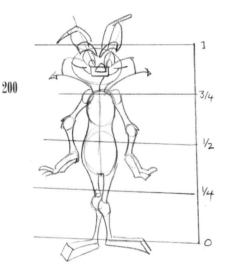

THE COYOTE IS QUITE AN ELEGANT CHARACTER, BUT BECAUSE OF HIS BUILD HE HAS A PROBLEM CONVEYING WHAT HE FEELS HE IS. IN SILHOUETTE HE LOOKS LIKE A DISSOLUTE BUGS. HIS ARMS AND LEGS ARE MUCH BONIER THAN BUGS'S (WHEN PEOPLE ARE SKINNY, THEIR ELBOWS AND SHOULDERS LOOK BIGGER), BUT THEIR BODY SHAPE IS THE SAME. THE TWO CHARACTERS HAVE IDENTICAL SKULLS, BUT THE COYOTE'S CHEEKS STAND ABSURDLY PROUD, WHEREAS BUGS'S ARE CONFIDENTLY CONTAINED. EVEN THE EARS ARE SIMILAR, WITH THE DIFFERENCE THAT THE COYOTE'S ARE A LITTLE BIT BROKEN. WILE E.'S HUNGRY LOOK IS COMPLETED BY A LITTLE POT BELLY.

THE MAIN CHANGE IN THE WAY I DREW THE COYOTE OVER THE YEARS INVOLVED THE KNEES. WHEN HE COMES TO A STOP IN THE LATER FILMS, ONE KNEE IS A LITTLE HIGHER THAN THE OTHER, ADDING TO HIS RAGGED LOOK. THESE KNEES AND THE POT BELLY ARE USUALLY ENOUGH TO IDENTIFY THE COYOTE. AND I USUALLY GIVE HIM AN EXTRA TOENAIL (I LIKE TO LEAVE ONE HANGING OUT).

THE WAY I DRAW THE COYOTE'S FUR ADDS TO THE UNKEMPT

Front view of Coyote: The nose is not right.
Anatomical view of the Coyote: The nose is still not right.
Side view of Coyote: The nose is right!

IMPRESSION. THE FUR IS SHOWN NOT OVER ALL THE BODY BUT ONLY WHERE IT CHANGES DIRECTION OVER A JOINT OR A CURVE IN THE FACE. FUR IS NOT OBEDIENT TO THE BODY; IT WILL CLING ONLY AS LONG AS THE SURFACE REMAINS FAIRLY FLAT. THE COYOTE'S HAIR IS PERFECTLY WILLING TO CLING TO THE UPPER PART OF HIS CHEEK, BUT IT PEELS OFF IN THE BREAK, JUST AS IT DOES ON BUGS BUNNY'S FACE. IN THE SAME WAY, EXCESS FLESH CREASES IN THE FOLDS OF A HEAVY ANIMAL'S BODY.

THE RAGGED TAIL WAS INSPIRED BY JAPANESE PAINTINGS OF STORMY OCEANS. WHEN THE JAPANESE ARTIST WANTS TO MAKE A BREAKING WAVE FRIGHTENING, HE DRAWS IT LIKE HOSTILE CLAWS RATHER THAN IN THE SOFTER WESTERN WAY. IF YOU HAVE A BOAT HANGING ON TOP OF A WAVE IN A JAPANESE PAINTING, YOU KNOW IT IS GOING TO GO OVER. THESE ARE WAVES TO DIE ON, NOT TO SURF ON. THE NORMAL WAY TO DRAW THE TAIL OF ANY ANIMAL, FROM A SQUIRREL TO A DOG, IS TO MAKE IT ROUND AND SOFT LIKE THE WESTERN WAVES; REVERSING THIS CREATED THE COYOTE'S TAIL. IT IS THE DIFFERENCE BETWEEN CONCAVE CURVES AND CONVEX CURVES, BETWEEN THE CUDDLY AND THE RATTY.

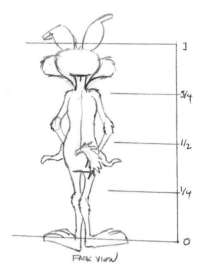

(Back view)
Best view for a Road Runner.

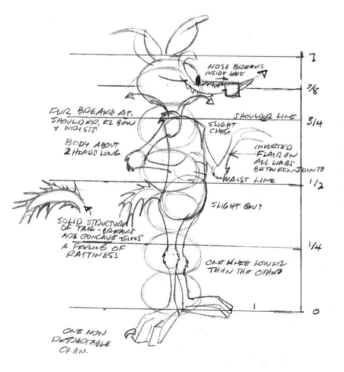

Detail of Coyote. Note attention to single, non-retractable claw.

Detail of tail.

201

Both the Road Runner and Wile E. Coyote emerged fully formed in *Fast and Furry-ous,* their first cartoon. But one of the advantages of working on a series of cartoons with the same characters was that I could develop them. The Road Runner did not change a lot visually over the years; he has very little personality, as he is a force. I tell students that the secret of drawing the Road Runner is learning how to draw dust: just draw a cloud of dust and hook a Road Runner onto it.

In his few speaking roles with Bugs Bunny, the Coyote is a different character. In these films he is an intellectual—"Wile E. Coyote, Genius"—involved in an intellectual struggle with Bugs and confident of success since, he claims in *Operation: Rabbit,* "I am a genius, while you could hardly pass the entrance examination to kindergarten."

Bugs Bunny is the Coyote's adversary in the speaking pictures, but Wile E. Coyote is forever linked with the Road Runner. My Road Runner is a rare case in which the animated animal is almost exactly like its living model. It has a small body, a long neck, a large tail, and wings that look as if they should work but don't. The head shape of the real roadrunner is slightly different, and it does not have such a prominent crop (except when excited), but body and neck are pretty accurate. My Road Runner has legs like elongated chicken legs, and a high forehead gives the bird a youthful look. It has a chest and a pelvis, just as we do, and the backbone extends a little at the tail. I think the tail makes things fairly rough for the Road Runner, as he must support this sizeable tail on a tiny bone structure, like a peacock. ("Honey, I'm sorry, I can't spread it. You just don't understand.")

Many people do not know there is such a creature as a roadrunner outside Warner Bros. cartoons. An ornithologist at the University of Iowa, who is a roadrunner expert, told me that the first question asked by her students every year is, "Does the true roadrunner really go 'beep-beep'?" and they do not believe her when she tells them that it doesn't.

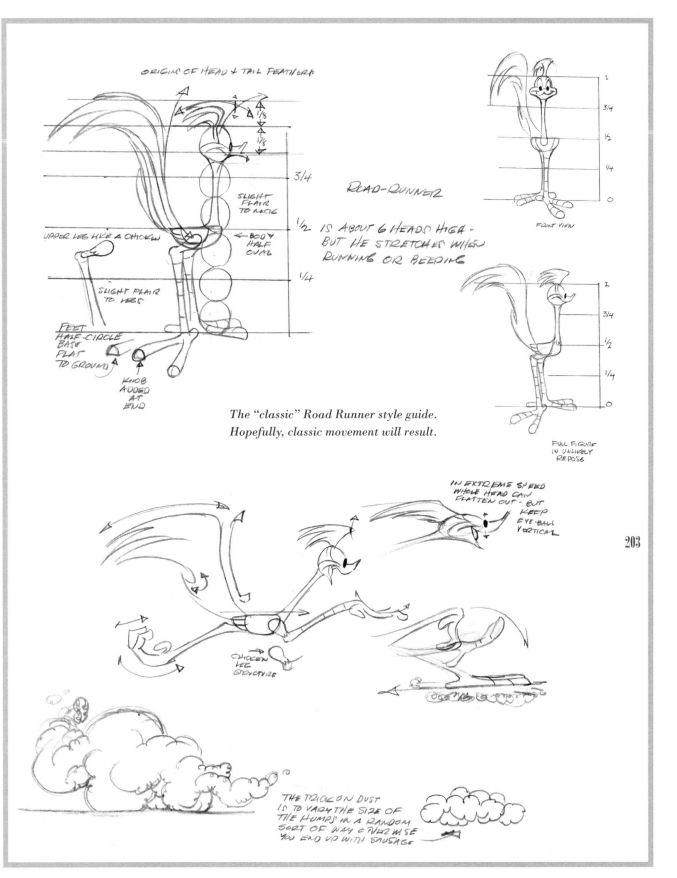

ORIGINS OF HEAD & TAIL FEATHERS

SLIGHT FLAIR TO NECK

UPPER LEG LIKE A CHICKEN

←BODY HALF OVAL

SLIGHT FLAIR TO LEGS

FEET HALF-CIRCLE BASE FLAT TO GROUND

KNOB ADDED AT END

ROAD-RUNNER

IS ABOUT 6 HEADS HIGH - BUT HE STRETCHES WHEN RUNNING OR BEEPING

FRONT VIEW

FULL FIGURE IN UNLIKELY REPOSE

The "classic" Road Runner style guide.
Hopefully, classic movement will result.

IN EXTREME SPEED WHOLE HEAD CAN FLATTEN OUT - BUT KEEP EYE-BALL VERTICAL

CHICKEN LEG STRUCTURE

THE TRICK ON DUST IS TO VARY THE SIZE OF THE HUMPS IN A RANDOM SORT OF WAY OTHERWISE YOU END UP WITH SAUSAGE

203

The alert yet relaxed sit.   *The determined first step.*   *The confident swagger.*

The Road Runner's immortal "beep-beep" was an accidental find, inspired by the sound Paul Julian made as he blindly tried to clear a route for himself along a Termite Terrace corridor (see *Chuck Amuck*). It seemed unimaginable to ask anybody but Paul to record this sound, so we invited him into the studio, and it is his voice that is heard in every Road Runner cartoon, although Mel Blanc is given credit for it. Paul would have made a fortune if he had belonged to the Screen Actors Guild.

The sound effects in this series of cartoons could be bewilderingly inventive. At the end of *Zoom and Bored*, the Coyote is dragged across the desert by a harpoon gun, and hardly a single sound effect is "correct," or even possible. Treg Brown used horns, broken bottles, and springs, but never the natural sound. What you see and what you hear are completely opposite in logic. For some reason, it works, and it's a good way of getting a laugh when you may not expect one, a technique Don Graham would call a ten-dollar trick.

Everything creative is a happy accident, as it always involves doing something you haven't done before. Sometimes it is only a question of recognizing and seizing on a creative mistake, and the faraway crash of the Coyote on the canyon floor provides a perfect illustration.

Three editors were involved in dubbing sound on a typical Wile E. Coyote cartoon. One controlled the music, one was responsible for the sound effects, and the third looked after dialogue (he was rarely very busy in these cartoons, as the dialogue was usually limited to "beep-beep"). These were nightmare sessions for the director, as the sound was invariably

The egotistical trot.   The all purpose-canter.   The irresistible all-out gallop.

turned way over the top, with people yelling at each other, music screaming, sound effects bellowing.

We were still in the fairly early days of sound, and editors kept their effects in the foreground, feeling that if a sound effect was there at all, the audience should hear it, no matter what it was or where it was supposed to be happening. They also believed that loud was always funny in a cartoon. So when the Coyote hit the ground, no matter how far away, the sound would be turned up LOUD.

We had arrived at the point where the Coyote falls off the cliff, and Robert North was in charge of the sound effects—a little slide whistle for the fall, followed by a short silence and a final loud crash. At that time, editors' controls were rheostat-like dials called *pots,* which they rotated to increase or lower the volume. Bob inadvertently had his pot turned way down low, so all we heard at the end of the drop was a distant "plop."

This was the only time I ever heard Bob laugh, and he laughed so hard he fell out of his chair. But being a professional sound effects man, he recovered himself, jumped up, and announced, "We've got to fix that." "Bob," I said, "if you touch that, you are a

dead fixer, and you will never mix another picture at Warner Bros. or anywhere else, because you won't have any hands."

BOB: But we've got to get it right.

DIRECTOR: What, Bob, is the purpose of an animated cartoon?

BOB: To get people to laugh.

DIRECTOR: In all the years we have worked together, you have never laughed before. Why did you laugh?

BOB: It must have been very funny.

DIRECTOR: And you want to take it out, don't you?

BOB: O.K. *[He was unconvinced.]* But I may get hell from Jack Warner.

The sound effect stayed. It was a happy accident, but I had to be ready to recognize it. It may never have happened again.

Bob had little to fear from Jack Warner, as he saw our cartoons only when he sent for some to amuse guests at his house. Jack's method of evaluating a feature film was based on the number of times he would halt his viewing to go and urinate. Ordinary films

U. S. NAVAL STATION
SAN DIEGO 36, CALIFORNIA

Address Reply To:

And Refer To:
CRS:ae
26 June 1952

Warner Brothers Cartoons Incorporated
1351 Van Ness Avenue
Hollywood, California

Dear Sirs:

We of the Enlisted Ship's Company Personnel, Administrative
Department, U. S. Naval Station, San Diego 36, California,
would like to commend the Warner Brothers Cartoon section on
the splendid cartoons they have been producing for some time.

On the 25th of June, 1952, it was our pleasure to view, with
our main attraction, one of your cartoons entitled, "BEEP BEEP".
Without exception, this was the most hilarious, most wholesome
and entertaining cartoon many of us have ever had the privilege
of viewing. The expressions, the action, the thought and work
put into it were superb.

We sincerely hope there will be more of these "BEEP BEEP" series
in the future.

CHARLES R. SHARPE
YNSN, USN
Representative

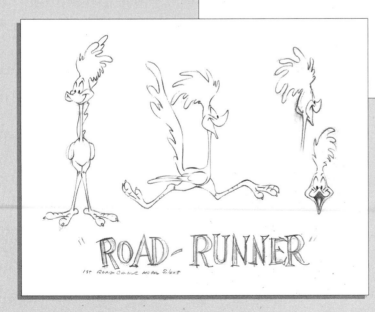

ALL ANIMAL ACTIVITY—AND HUMAN BEINGS ARE ANIMALS TOO—
IS CONCERNED WITH ONLY ONE PROBLEM: MOVING THE ANIMAL AND/OR
ANOTHER OBJECT FORWARD, BACKWARD, SIDEWAYS, UP, OR DOWN.
AND THE ONLY IMPEDIMENT TO THIS ACTIVITY IS GRAVITY.

IN ORDER TO OVERCOME GRAVITY, THE ANIMAL MUST PUT
ITSELF INTO SOME KIND OF TENSED POSITION—SIMILAR TO A
COILED SPRING OR A COCKED BOW. THIS IS THE ONLY WAY ANY
LIVING THING—AN ANIMAL, THAT IS—CAN PREPARE TO MOVE.

THIS IS NOT ONLY TRUE OF A FOOTRACE OR A SOCCER
GAME, IT IS ALSO TRUE OF POINTING YOUR FINGER OR KISSING
YOUR LOVER. WITHOUT CLIFFS AND WITHOUT GRAVITY
I DON'T KNOW WHERE I WOULD BE.

might rate perhaps three or four pees, but *Treasure of the Sierra Madre* was a seven-pee picture—meaning he didn't like it at all. I believe he didn't feel comfortable judging six-minute short subjects, because even Jack Warner was unable to pee more than once in a six-minute window of opportunity, and this restriction prevented him from appraising cartoons.

Eddie Selzer hated the first Road Runner cartoon, *Fast and Furry-ous*, because it had no dialogue. "Goddamit," he fumed, "we pay Mel Blanc and you should use his voice." He sulked about it. I told him that the film wouldn't work with dialogue, but he persisted: "I don't give a damn if it would work or not—WE PAY MEL BLANC!"

Management hated anything they had never seen before, and they had never seen anything like *Fast and Furry-ous*. When the film was released, they demanded we wait and see if anyone liked it or

not before we made another one, and the second Road Runner cartoon therefore did not appear for another three years.

I heard nothing about the fate of *Fast and Furry-ous* after it left the studio, until a letter arrived from a psychologist studying pilot behavior at the Pensacola naval base. His letter reported a new and peculiar phenomenon. As he was listening in to some pilots making practice runs in torpedo bombers on an old destroyer anchored off Pensacola, he heard the lead pilot saying "Red Fox: we are going in for the kill," and off he went, singing "beep-beep, beep-beep." And all the other guys went in after him.

"What the hell's the matter with these guys?" the psychologist wondered, thinking they had all gone Section 8 and would therefore have to be shot out of the sky. It turned out that *Fast and Furry-ous* had been screened at the base the night before, and these pilots had been so enchanted that they demanded it be shown again the next night. Everyone on the base came to this second show—about 8,000 people—so they had to run the film about eight times. Then the entire base stood up in unison and walked out of a Doris Day feature, which we thought indicated good taste.

I told Eddie Selzer about this incident, and he said that it couldn't happen again. In fact, the series turned into a chase that has already lasted more than forty years.

Before returning to the chase in 1994 with *Chariots of Fur*, I had made twenty-six Road Runner cartoons between 1948 and 1962, and I never ran out of material. On the contrary, I reached a point where I could write them almost as fast as I could write. *Chariots of Fur* was the first film produced by the young animators in the new Chuck Jones unit. They were all familiar with the Road Runner and Wile E. Coyote, who were ideal characters to introduce our method, as they are primarily physical, unlike the more complicated characters, such as Bugs or Daffy.

The Coyote has not changed since we met him last. If it works, don't fix it. (I very much doubt if that motto is hanging in the Coyote's living room.) The Road Runner, on the other hand, has loosened up a little. He now seems tickled by what he is doing, rather in the manner of Harpo Marx. Instead of simply vibrating when he comes to a stop, he may now do a rapid turn with one leg sticking out and laugh *with* the audience, giving him more personality. We shall see.

Termite Terrace was essentially a group of young people creating cartoons, and I want to revive that

208   BELIEVABLE ANIMATION ALWAYS INCORPORATES ODDITIES, WHETHER YOU ARE DRAWING CHARACTERS OR INANIMATE OBJECTS. ANIMATING A BOUNCING BALL IS A GOOD EXERCISE. WHEN YOU THROW A RUBBER BALL UP IN THE AIR, THE PULL OF THE EARTH SLOWS IT DOWN FROM THE MOMENT IT LEAVES YOUR HAND UNTIL IT COMES TO A STOP AND BEGINS TO FALL. AS IT FALLS, IT SPEEDS UP AGAIN, UNTIL IT HITS THE EARTH. BEFORE IT CAN TAKE OFF AGAIN, IT HAS TO *FLATTEN.* LOOK AT A HIGH-SPEED PHOTOGRAPH OF A FOOTBALL BEING KICKED, AND YOU REALIZE THAT THE FOOT GOES COMPLETELY INTO THE BALL BEFORE IT PULLS AWAY. THIS COMPRESSION IS WHAT GIVES THE BALL ITS ENERGY. TRY KICKING AN IRON BALL AND SEE WHAT HAPPENS.

It's contrasting views that make dramatic situations.

spirit. I was eighteen when I entered the animation business, and the old man of animation was Walt Disney, who was twenty-nine years old. At that time, I thought a bunch of old men in their forties or fifties were running the movie business. Today, in my eighties, I see that it was run by a bunch of *young* men in their forties or fifties.

When I was given the chance—at age eighty—to again produce cartoons for Warner Bros., I had no interest in reinventing Leon Schlesinger, Ray Katz, or Eddie Selzer, the most agonizingly unrealistic villains of my life. When I formed my new unit, I decided that I needed a producer I could trust. The only one I was certain I could trust was the producer I had worked with on *Mrs. Doubtfire*—my own daughter, Linda. So I made her my producer, and this has hamstrung me terribly, because I can't hate her—I have loved her too long for that. When she makes a judgment I don't like, all I can do is go away and sulk (which she used to do to me when she was little, so she's just getting it back).

I always wanted a producer I could kiss instead of curse, and now I have one: Linda Jones Clough (left), producer of CHARIOTS OF FUR *(1994),* ANOTHER FROGGY EVENING *(1995),* SUPERIOR DUCK *(1995), and more. Beautiful baby, funny and darling child, lovely and intelligent woman. How lucky can one get?*

209

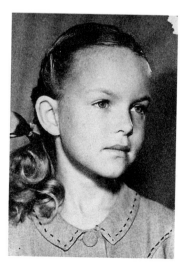

Linda at 12.

The beautiful Marian and the baffled Chuck at the Oscars (1996).

My daughter Linda and I had worked with Robin Williams on Mrs. Doubtfire. *I asked him to introduce me, knowing that if I fainted, he would catch me in a funny way.*

The New York Film Festival, 1982.

Films have much more in common with music than they do with easel painting. A painting is complete when the surface, whatever its dimensions and whatever its shape, is covered to the satisfaction of the buyer. The size and shape can be almost anything, from a postage stamp to the ceiling of the Sistine Chapel.

Film, however, has only a fixed space discipline contained in the oblong frame in common with much graphic art. Beyond that, like music, it depends on a series of successive impacts on a human sense: for music, the ear; for films, the eye. And films, like music, also depend on the retentive quality of that sense, for without memory of the preceding notes or the preceding frames, neither music nor motion picture exists at all. Both are progressive experiences, unlike painting, which is a stable experience.

When the last frame flashes before the viewer's eye, the film is gone. It is not only progressive, it is amorphous. It can be repeated only by replaying it, again like music. A recording of a violin concerto is just like a roll of film; it enables the listener to reexperience a progressive phenomenon, and the common factor is time.

A roll of film can be made to appear as a progressive experience over and over again, but it remains bewilderingly ungraspable when compared to a painting.

The filmmaker must therefore be aware that it is time he is dealing with, and that his emotional impacts must almost absolutely rely on time. Even his most beloved graphics are dramatically meaningful only if he leaves them on the screen for the number of frames needed to achieve emphasis.

A film unprojected is like a painting in the dark—it simply doesn't exist.

211

Lewis Browne said, "There are no judges, only people judging, no tramps, only people tramping." So it is that "there are no sheepdogs, only dogs guarding sheep, and only coyotes [wolves] hunting them."

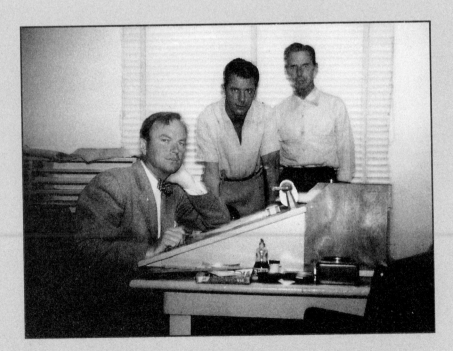

(From left): C. Jones, Lloyd Vaughan, and Ken Harris.

SAM SHEEPDOG AND RALPH WOLF

Ralph Wolf was a storyman at Warner Bros. cartoons, and he gave his name to the red-nosed version of Wile E. Coyote.

In pitting Ralph Wolf against Sam Sheepdog, I was trying to discover if I could do the opposite of the chase at the heart of the Road Runner cartoons. The Road Runner is moving all the time, and at great speed. I therefore wanted the wolf's opponent not to move at all. And that is exactly what happens—or doesn't. Sam just sits very solidly on the ground. He doesn't move; he is there.

The Sheepdog is always aware of Ralph's every move, but I don't know how he sees through that curtain of hair. I could have drawn long hair only over his nose, but I felt that his hair should be long everywhere. Even his feet are hairy, and when he sits

down, I put a little fringe of hair where his bottom meets the ground.

The story of Ralph and Sam comes down to Lewis Brown's idea that there are no judges, only people judging, no tramps, only people tramping, and so on. What does a judge do when he gets home at night? He is probably treated with the same disrespect as any other husband and father. Walt Disney's family could judge him only as a father, not as the father of full animation (which he was). When my daughter, Linda, was a little girl, she had real trouble convincing other kids in the theater that her father had drawn the Bugs Bunny cartoon they were watching. They simply didn't believe her. On one occasion when she saw my name on the screen, she pointed to it and exclaimed, "That's my father." The child next to her said, "Yeah, sure, and *my* father's Clark Gable." Linda does not know to this day whether he was or not.

Each of us has our way of judging other people by our relationship to what they do. In the Wolf and Sheepdog cartoons, there are no sheepdogs, only dogs guarding sheep. Guarding sheep is Sam's daytime occupation, and stealing them is Ralph's. They will have a friendly lunch together when the noon whistle blows, and at night they go home just like everybody else. Ralph lives across the street from Sam, and in the morning they come out together chewing doughnuts, greet each other, walk to work, punch the clock, and take up their professional positions. During the working day, just like the rest of us, they have a job to do.

214

Sam seldom trots and never runs to work. He rarely changes expression, either. (Hello, Buster Keaton!)

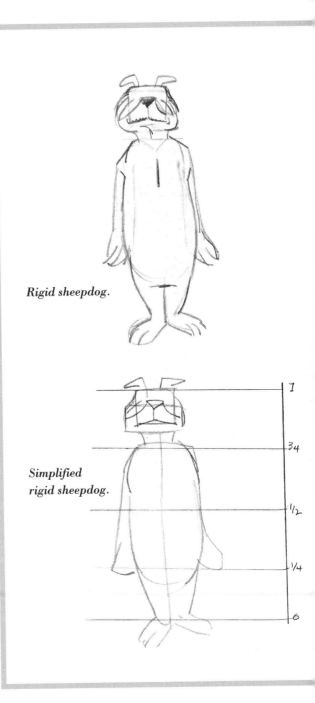

Rigid sheepdog.

Simplified rigid sheepdog.

Sam Sheepdog.

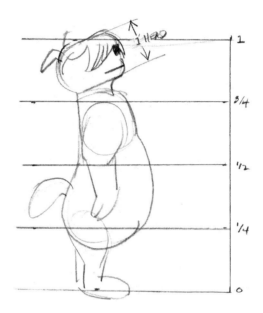

Sam Sheepdog quartered.

Determined coyote/wolf.

"Bye" before the fall.

Papa Bear in a calm moment.

This ideal American
family appeared years
before Archie Bunker
and company.

Mama Bear,
slovenly in an
endearing way.

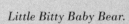

Little Bitty Baby Bear.

THE THREE BEARS

The Three Bears are fun characters to work with but hard characters to draw, because their *form* reflects their character in a way that Bugs's or Daffy's form does not. Papa Bear has to be ready to explode, and sometimes he does. Mama Bear must look like a slattern, and Junyer appears to be what he is— an oversized baby.

In their traditional role, the Three Bears are paid, in a way, to go out and be the Three Bears with Goldilocks, but they also have a home life, which is what we encounter in the cartoons. Not only does the bear family contrast with our idea of normality, the three bears are in contrast to each other as well. They are the negative of the ideal American family, a prefiguration by several years of such early dysfunctional-family television sitcoms as *All in the*

Family. There is the same small, angry father, the same dowdy mother, and the big, dumb child.

Father Bear is a recognizable figure for people of my generation, who grew up in a world where the father of the house was still considered the master, and fathers were opinionated. Like all fathers, Father Bear is trying to find a way out of an awkward financial position. My own father was forever attempting to rescue his family from financial straits, although I think he desired to solve our financial problems only so he could feel free to run for the hills.

Papa Bear reminds me of Eddie Selzer, who was similarly small and volatile; when Eddie couldn't do anything else, he got angry. As he yelled, he flushed red, throwing the white hairs that dotted his nose into relief. (These were hairs so spiny that if you were drinking a martini, you could have kept your olives spiked on them.) When Papa Bear yells, his nose merely lifts a little, but his eyes come together when he is really mad, and the entire face is squeezed tight.

Papa Bear has no neck, and in this respect he is a forerunner of Michigan J. Frog. The head emerges a little above his body, and the line of the shoulders is curved, making the whole body seem to focus on a point where the furious eyebrows meet above shadowed eyes and a discontented mouth.

Short arms both add to and express his frustration. These arms hang stubbily down, ending in scrunched fists that increase the impression of fury. I gave him a little T-shirt, which lifts when he raises his arms, revealing that he does not have much of a waist. If he is not feeling very happy with the world—his usual condition—his toes face each other, so that the whole body is held in a ball of rage.

The main thing I could never understand about real-life bears is why their clothes don't fit better. The average bear wears an oversized hide that would look sloppy on an elephant. An elephant's clothes fit badly enough, goodness knows, but the elephant's pants don't sag halfway down to his knees in the way a bear's trousers do. In the circumstances, it is really quite understandable that your run-of-the-mill bear looks querulous and a little anxious.

I did not use Mel Blanc's voice for the Three Bears. Billy Bletcher—a short man with a bellicose voice—was a natural for Father Bear. The role required no acting for him. I had no voice for Baby Bear until the eighteen-year-old Stan Freberg walked in with his

218

"SHE'S THE SLATTERNLY TYPE."

Art Heinemann explaining the subtleties of character design to the director.

manager and his wonderful, powerful voice, like Lon Chaney, Jr.'s Lenny in *Of Mice and Men.*

It is doubly frustrating for Papa Bear to have sired somebody as large as Junyer, who has to bend down in order to enter a room. Papa's seething frustration can lead to violence, but when he takes a swing at his son, he usually misses. Once in a while a smack lands on its target, but since he aims at Junyer's head and the head is so far up, there is little force behind the blows.

Junyer is huge, but he is like a baby. His eyes are sleepy, which is an endearing feature in little babies but hateful when children are five. When he is thinking of nothing, Junyer's mouth tends to drop, and I can remember driving my mother crazy with that same expression. His ears will not behave—one is usually droopy, and the other has a certain look to it that doesn't fool Mother Bear but that makes Dad angry. His legs are also slightly bowed, and whose knees would not buckle with the weight of that body on top?

Like many babies, Junyer is all stomach, and he is drawn so that we are looking *up* at the top of the chest and *down* at the bottom of the stomach, illustrating Don Graham's lesson: "Don't ever be so foolish as to think that you can't have an up view in part of a drawing of a human figure and a down view in another part." You can look up at the rib cage, down the thigh, and up to the eye. It is a way of *explaining* what you are drawing. A drawing of a woman's breasts looking down on one nipple and up at the other gives a much clearer understanding of the space, not to mention the beauty.

When Junyer's arms are folded across his belly, the important thing is to convey a sense of the droop around his vast stomach. If he uncrossed the arms and let them swing down, they would practically touch the ground, which would be absurd. On occasions like this, it is senseless for an animator to attempt to be accurate, even though the animator must always think dimensionally.

Because of pressures of time and money, suggestive details were sometimes all we could put in a drawing. For example, we could not always draw the characteristic bags on Junyer's cheeks, but a little line on each side of the nose seemed to be enough to give his face the desired look.

Unlike his father, Junyer has a neck, even though it is not very long. Audrey Hepburn, like many slim women, seemed to have an unusually long neck, but the illusion of length came from her having practically no trapezius muscle. In a football player, this muscle is highly developed, making the neck seem shorter, and Junyer has the neck of a football lineman.

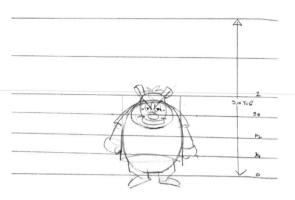

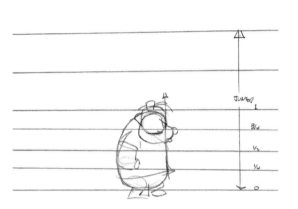

Above: *Relative sizes of the members of the most elegant of bear families.*
Right: *Paw would fit nicely into a potato sack.*
Opposite page, left: *Maw looks something like a lightbulb in a mob cap.*
Opposite page, right: *Junyer. Think of an oversized sweet potato, and you're half there.*

Birthday card for my mother (late 1930s).

220

Mama Bear shares her husband's necklessness, and the structure of the two is similar. But where Papa Bear holds himself rigid with anger, everything droops on his wife: her upper body droops, her lower body droops, her upper lip droops, her ears droop, even her hat tries to droop, but it can't get beyond the brim.

Because of the bulk of her bosom, Mama Bear's dress would hang wide over her lower body if left to its own devices, but I pull it in below the hips, giving it an awful look that any fashion designer would disown. I think she would probably be rather proud of her collar, and I don't know where she, like so many old-fashioned ladies of her class, bought slippers like that, which are easy on feet swollen by hard work.

My own mother would put on a mobcap like

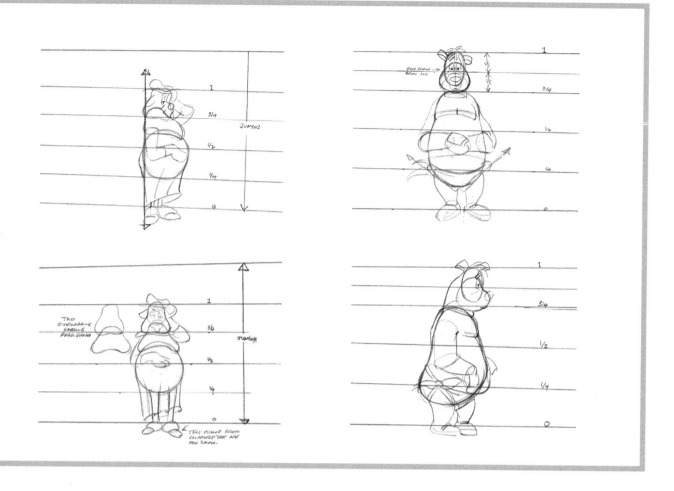

Mama Bear's when she was spring cleaning. On these occasions, anybody who came to the house was lassoed into helping, and there never seemed to be a shortage of mobcaps.

My own experiences as a father inspired at least one of these cartoons. *A Bear for Punishment,* in which Baby Bear forces his father to submit to the dubious joys of being pampered on Father's Day, is based on my own efforts to escape a Father's Day breakfast of scrambled eggs lovingly prepared for me by my daughter, Linda, when she was about six years old.

Ken Harris's animation of Mama Bear's stage performance for her fuming husband in *A Bear for Punishment* is a masterpiece. Every movement is correct. Ken was a fine dancer, and we could also call on Mike Maltese's excellent memory for vaude-

ville when we were planning her act. Mike showed Ken some old vaudeville routines, such as jumping back and forth over the other foot, as Mama Bear does in the show. The whole scene was beautifully done, and it is incredibly funny.

NOSE
DROPS A LITTLE
IN FULL FACE

*Pepé is the individual I always
wanted to be, so sure of his appeal
to women that it never occurs to
him that his attentions might be
unwelcome or even offensive. I
tried to make Pepé's confidence a
part of my own personality, hoping
to share in his sexual success.
On the screen it worked.*

PEPÉ LE PEW

If you can't do it yourself, animate somebody who can—Pepé le Pew, for example. Pepé's sexual confidence is absolute. He sees rejection as no more than a temporary setback, and every pursuit as an interesting variation on the road to inevitable success. (For myself, as an eighteen-year-old I took every expression from every girl as a rejection. If I couldn't find a rejection I liked, I would invent one.)

Pepé is the individual I always wanted to be, so sure of his appeal to women that it never occurs to him that his attentions might be unwelcome, or even offensive. I tried to make Pepé's confidence a part of my own personality, hoping to share in his sexual success. On the screen it worked.

The skunk may at first sight seem to be an unlikely lover, but these films would never succeed if the hero were a human being with bad breath, underarm odors, or smelly feet. Boot odors are simply not funny. It is only when an animal such as a skunk is *unaware* of his problem, which is built in and instantly obvious to everyone else, that the situation has comic potential. Pepé fit quite nicely into this role.

Pepé *cannot* know that he smells. He is clearly shocked to be informed about his odor in *For Scentimental Reasons*, so shocked that he pulls out a gun and threatens to shoot himself ("I missed, fortunately for you").

The situation would not work if the object of Pepé's pursuit was a female skunk, as a member of the same species would not find his smell unpleasant—otherwise there would be no more skunks. From the very first Pepé le Pew cartoon *(Odor-able Kitty),* he

223

Pepé en route to a rendezvous.

was always chasing a cat with a temporary white stripe along its back, and for me the main problem with these stories of sweet miscegenation was getting that stripe on the cat's back every time in a natural or at least logical way.

When Pepé is pursuing a female, I raise his behind a little high and keep his tail up. In the chase, he moves with a springy little bounce in which all four feet hit the ground at the same time. The more precise this movement—known as a pronk—the sharper the contrast with the fleeing cat, who looks increasingly upset and disheveled. She does not know that Pepé's desires are legitimate in his own mind; she does know that she has no wish to be assaulted by a lovesick skunk. She is panting, exhausted, as Pepé's easy bounce brings him ever closer. There is an inevitability to the end.

I first met this pursuit technique as a child, when a group of Mexican marathon runners came to Los Angeles in 1932 for the Olympic trials. They had gained their proficiency in long-distance running by hunting deer. Their method was not to shoot the animal from a distance but simply to follow it, tracking it remorselessly over a period of days, until the poor deer

wore out and just fell down. Pepé has similar confidence and a similar technique. I couldn't have him race madly after the girl. He has no need to hurry, for he knows that the fleeing object of his affections will eventually wear out and, in his opinion, joyfully succumb.

When somebody is chasing you, it is terrifying to look back and see that they are coming along at an easy pace, not even remotely tired. In *Roughing It*, Mark Twain described a dog taking off after a coyote. This was a city dog, with a pretty good opinion of his speed. He is only a snap behind the coyote, but he cannot gain, however hard he tries, which bothers him. Finally the coyote looks back at him as if to say, "I'm sorry, bub, but I can't spend all day fooling

Friz Freleng's drawing psychoanalyzes Chuck's frustration.

224

Bernyce Polifka's flattering view of Chuck's appeal. Pepé, as comic hero, represents dreams and ideals. To dream of yourself as admired and see yourself as admired are two different things.

Gene Fleury misreading a comment by his wife, Bernyce Polifka, on Chuck's drawing style. (Drawing by C. Jones.)

"BUT YOU HAVE, CHUCK-
YOU HAVE A WON
DERFUL TECHNIQUE!"

Eddie Selzer saw nothing funny in skunks speaking French, but in 1950 he took home the Oscars for FOR SCENT-IMENTAL REASONS *and* SO MUCH FOR SO LITTLE, *triumphantly taking credit (below) for two films directed and co-written by C. Jones. Opposite page: Well, we were allowed to hold the Oscars for a while.*

around with you." There is a zip and a sort of crack in the atmosphere, and the dog realizes he is alone. He begins to understand something about speed, limps back to the wagon train, and crawls under a wagon.

In the next chapter of *Roughing It*, Twain describes the jackrabbit. When *he* takes off, he just vanishes, leaving a trail of smoke as he disappears in the direction of San Francisco. This passage gave me the idea of pure speed and inspired the action of the Road Runner.

Maurice Noble created both the Road Runner's desert environment and the delicate French backgrounds for Pepé le Pew's European exploits. These backgrounds look as if Watteau had been crossed with Raoul Dufy, and our choice of Dufy as a model was deliberate, primarily because he demonstrated in his paintings that anything shown by color need not also be shown by line. Dufy would define the spirit of his subject by blocks of color, then he would draw over them, almost disregarding the limits of the

colors, so that, for example, lines depicting houses might be drawn partly over the sky.

Characters always start with an idea rather than a drawing. Before I drew Pepé for his first appearance in a cartoon, I knew something about his character, and I knew he was a skunk, but I did not know what he looked like. Live-action directors call casting sessions at this point to find an actor to match their notion of a character, but I begin drawing—my casting session. I did more than 200 drawings of Pepé before I was confident he would work according to our conception of him. From that moment on, he was as much subject to the limits of his physical ability as I am.

When we were writing *Odor-able Kitty*, in which Pepé made his first appearance (under the name Henry), the odious Eddie Selzer tried to block the project on the grounds that skunks talking French are not funny. (The French themselves find these cartoons very funny.) But when *For Scent-imental Reasons* later won an Academy Award, Eddie Selzer contentedly collected the credit and the Oscar, which he took home.

I had very low opinions about the Academy Awards until I won one, and then I realized how truly distinguished its recipients are. *For Scent-imental Reasons* won an Oscar, but it led to the loss of another award. Soon after the release of the film, my daughter, Linda, was involved in a junior high school spelling contest in which she was asked to spell

"sentimental." This was a word she knew she knew; after all, she had seen it on the screen, dignified by its presence in a film title: "SCENT-IMENTAL." She came home furious.

The only time I made a picture because I had a title was *A Scent of the Matterhorn.* I woke up in the middle of the night with the idea of separating the *A* from *Ascent.* I couldn't discard a title like that, so I made a picture. So much for inspiration.

On one particular Pepé le Pew picture, I told Ray Katz that he really should view the first color print of the completed cartoon, because I had spotted something in it that bothered me. In just one frame of one scene in which Pepé has the object of his pursuit pinned in a passionate embrace, the animator and I had contrived to make this an actual sexual relationship. "My God," Ray spluttered, "we have to change it!" I pointed out that this policy would involve altering all 2,500 prints of the picture. Money being a higher priority than propriety, Ray decided against the cruel cut, and the offending frame stayed.

Whether advised to move to Europe by his art school dreams, or inspired, perhaps, by the French backgrounds from his sketches in our Pepé le Pew cartoons, the great background artist, musician, and ventriloquist, John McGrew, went to live in France. Forty years after we worked together, I met him at his home near Lyon. He remains a supremely skilled artist, actively engaged in teaching and creating trompe l'oeil murals. His latest mural is some 300 square yards of baroque architecture and landscape.

• • •

Skunk One

Pepé le Pew is an insistent, if not an insidious presence in my life. He refuses to go away. Almost thirty years after I directed what I thought to be my last picture with him, he was still able to make his presence felt.

"Darling." It was my wife speaking in that level, undisturbed voice she employs in the face of dripping faucets, earthquakes, floods, and fire. "Will you stir over here, please?" Expecting no less than a tsunami, I saw instead an elegant young matron skunk daintily emerge from under the boards of our back porch. She seemed completely at home under and atop our veranda. She radiated self-satisfaction, which was soon justified by the appearance in her wake and on her train of three elegant infant skunks, with fluffy tails flaunting their confidence over bodies about the size of tennis balls.

230

They paid no attention to us, and Marian and I lived in peace and pleasure with them, but only as long as the glass door was between us. Their presence restricted our access to the veranda somewhat, but when below decks they bothered us not at all. An understood truce lasted for a few weeks, until the day the mother skunk came out on deck at teatime without moppets. They had, no doubt, gone off to boarding school, leaving mother free to take up her charitable duties and her bridge club in the adjoining canyon, known as Buck Gulley.

Knowing Pepé, it is quite obvious to me why she chose our house as a retreat where she could produce her brood. I'm certain that while strolling innocently through the park one spring day, she encountered this charming, handsome, gallant, sexy skunk with the elegant manners of a troubadour and (although she did not know) the moral code of a tomcat. Pepé may not have been disgruntled by his resulting fatherhood, but he was really not gruntled. Ever the pragmatist in such matters (even though a devoted romantic), Pepé quickly and gallantly took charge. "Go," he said, "to the domicile of my colleagues, Chuck and Marian Jones; they will take care of all the details. Go, my dear, to Chez Jones and bear with all my blessings our beautiful children. Au revoir, and look the other way in the future when some Lothario suggests that you couchez vous avec him. Be distant, remote; there is a great deal of lax morality lurking about."

That, I believe, is the way that Sherlock Holmes would have pieced together the whole, happily sordid matter.

Pepé celebrating our betrothal.

231

That look may not have launched a thousand ships, but it conquered —by not conquering— the devotion and love I could not have known really existed.

Skunk Two

One of the great character designers I had the privilege of working with was Art Heinemann. Heywood Broun may have looked like an unmade bed at the Algonquin, but Art looked like an unmade sleeping bag rented to a gopher, which has nothing to do with the fact that Art found himself one spanking summer morning sitting on the porch of a lakeside house in Coeur d'Alene, Idaho, letting the sunlight, wildflowers, rippling waters, and general lassitude engulf him. Even without Pippa passing, or a thorn goosing a passing snail, all seemed to Art to be pretty right with the world.

Entranced by nature busting herself to bring peace to his soul after eleven torturous months of working under the whip of Chuck Jones—the Torquemada of animation—he was amused to see in the distance a small, sweet-looking skunk, single-footing its way down the road paralleling the lake. Chuckling

Art Heinemann pointing out a secret. New director lurking about?

232

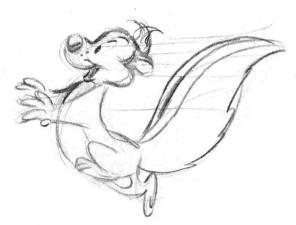

quietly to himself, he watched the little creature make a sharp, almost military turn up the gravel walk, trot up the few stairs to the porch, make another deliberate turn toward the now paralyzed Heinemann, and with a confident flip of its tail in one fell swoop—or swell foop—land on Art's lap and settle down to a peaceful nap.

Paralyzed? Petrified? Frozen? The English language has a paucity of appropriate words to handle Art's reaction to a disaster of such enormity. He later confided in me that finding yourself with a ticking stick of dynamite in your lap while strapped in an electric chair might give you some idea of his feeling that day.

He didn't *have* to think about the dangers in the situation, but he did: an aroused skunk, he had heard, would be able to pollute the air from Coeur d'Alene to Vladivostok, and an irritated skunk had teeth with which to painfully nip, and—this occurred to him also—the saliva of a skunk carried small, angry germs possibly full of Rocky Mountain Spotted Fever, not to mention the fact that a skunk is covered by a hirsute forest in which herds of ticks browse. As Julius Caesar said, "A coward dies many times before his death," and Art claims to have broken the record for imagined demises that morning.

He was working out his 1,253d death and trying to sweat *without* raining on the occupant snoozing in his lap, when his hostess appeared out of the kitchen door and said, "Well, I see you've met Mildred."

"Mildred?

"Mildred! This creature who has produced in me a mindless death of pure funk is *Mildred?*"

"Mildred is our house skunk," she explained. "We had her deodorized, flead, and fixed when we pulled her half-drowned out of the lake."

"Bewitched, Bothered, and Be-Mildred. Thank you for this, Walt Kelly," said Art. "At least I know what was the matter with me—I was be-Mildred!"

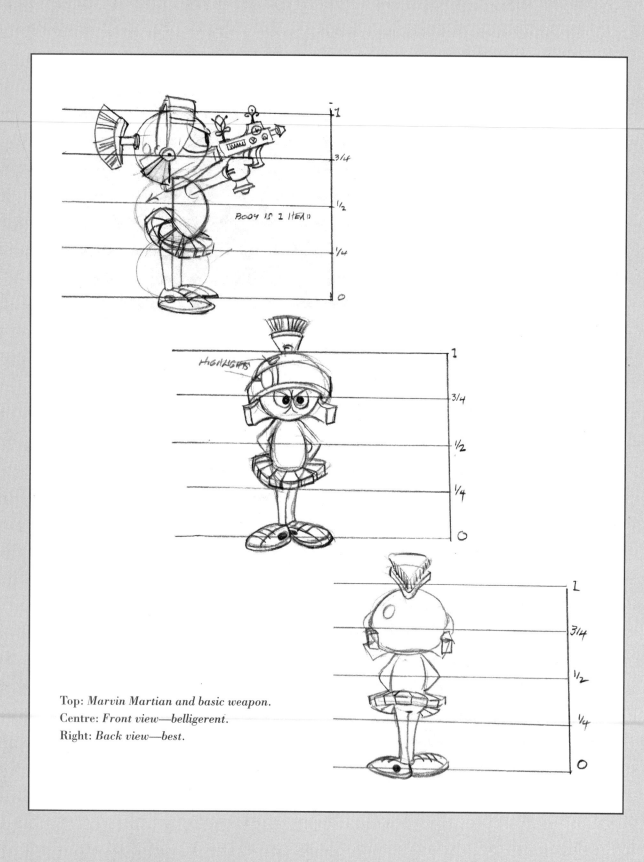

Top: *Marvin Martian and basic weapon.*
Centre: *Front view—belligerent.*
Right: *Back view—best.*

MARVIN MARTIAN

Marvin is one of those mysterious creatures that come out of the sky or up the stairs late at night. You don't know what he thinks, and you don't *want* to know. It is not simple happenchance that he appears to have no character. He is a Martian, and you cannot expect to find much personality in there. I gave him a certain amount of gesture, but he expresses little passion; instead of howling with anger and excruciating pain when his plans lie in ruins, he merely and carefully says, "Oh dear; back to the old drawing board."

Because he is a Martian, I decided that Marvin should be *dressed* as a Martian. My first step in creating the character was therefore to draw the curiously tufted helmet worn by Mars, the Roman God of War, although Marvin could take his version of the helmet off and shine his tennis shoes with it.

Abominable snowman and Martian, showing relative sizes.

Then, I figured, black ants are scary, so I put an ant-black face and a couple of angry eyes inside his helmet. The Martian has no evident mouth, but people are rarely aware of that. I then decided that a metal skirt was suitable wear for the God of War, and—suitable or not—putting tennis shoes on an ant seemed like a good idea, so I gave Marvin a pair of tennis shoes, like a lot of my characters.

Gossamer the monster is just a strange mass of orange hay also in tennis shoes, and Marvin's dog, K9, shares his master's taste in footwear. K9 looks like Charlie Dog in tennis shoes and a small helmet, plus an occasional flag flying on his tail. Some mar-

velous Martian characters accompany K9 and Marvin in these films, among them the birdlike things with bulbous bodies and short arms, which I believe I borrowed from Tyrannosaurus Rex.

For some reason, the manufacturers of Marvin's shoes, which we all wore as kids, believed that we were likely to run into things with our ankles, so a pad covered the ankle. My father knew better, and he always tacked a piece of protective metal around the front of any new shoes before he allowed us to wear them. This effectively delayed our kicking the toes out.

My father gave each of his children a fresh pair of tennis shoes every spring, by which time our leather winter shoes were pretty shabby. Each year, when I pulled these new shoes on and tightened the laces, they felt like Mercury slippers (Ray Bradbury agrees)—I thought I could fly, and I probably could. I ran and ran, and it felt wonderful. By the end of summer, the shoes were looser, toes were showing through, and it was time for winter shoes again.

*Faithful K-9
(Marvin Martian's associate)
flying Martian flag.*

Maurice Noble felt that
even the trees should reflect
the X in Planet X.

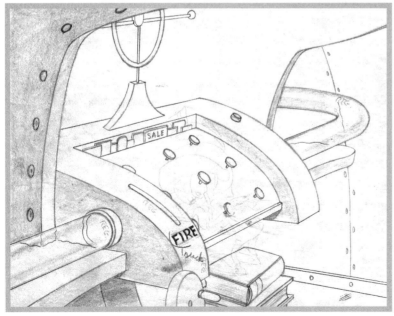

Marvin's ultimate secret
weapon.

Top: *The witch's candy-cane domicile
in BEWITCHED BUNNY (1954).*
Centre: *Witch Hazel in an inquisitive pose.*
Left: *C. Jones directing the great
June Foray as Witch Hazel and the equally
great Mel Blanc as Bewitched Bunny.*

WITCH HAZEL

AH HA HA HA HA HA HA

I like Witch Hazel. She gets such a kick out of herself, laughing uproariously as she zooms away, leaving behind her a cluster of hairpins in midair. Hazel's hovering hairpins were in fact a personal statement from me to the pennypinchers at Hanna Barbera, who would have their characters leave only little linear whorls in the air when they zipped out at speed. I thought that if you were going to leave something, it should be something interesting, like hairpins or, if the bull in *Bully for Bugs*, horseshoes.

When I began thinking about the character of Witch Hazel, I first tried to imagine what the witches in *Macbeth* would look like, and I decided that they were big. Witches also have hats, and Hazel has hers. It is an odd one. I wanted the hat to be shapeless and insubstantial, looking as if it might explode in a cloud of dust at any moment. Adding to the strangeness is the fact that Hazel's head doesn't continue up into the hat at the front; it just stops, as if part of the head had been lopped off. This oddity is not readily no-

ticed, but it was an important part of the character.

Nor did many people notice a curious feature in Hazel's mouth. A single tooth juts up from her lower jaw, and I felt there should be a place for this tooth to rest when she closes her mouth, so I drew a little socket in the lip above it. It seemed the right thing to do.

In contrast to the disheveled dentistry and hat, she has rather elegant hands with long fingers. Her clothes cover her body completely, and I assume that she is the same shape as the outfit she is wearing. When she went out, she put on bloomers and high-heeled shoes, which I wanted to look like a drawing rather than a three-dimensional form.

Witch Hazel is a vivid example of the fact that beauty is, thankfully, deeper than skin, and that outward appearances can, in her case, be trusted.

The incredibly talented June Foray did three different voices for three different Witch Hazels: one for Disney, one for MGM, and one for us. National consensus endorses ours as the best.

239

*Like the
infant Chuck Jones,
"nobody understands"
Ralph Phillips.*

RALPH PHILLIPS

Ralph Phillips was named after the animator Jack Phillips. We knew Jack as "Japanese Ace" in World War II, because he wiped out five American aircraft single-handed while training. Jack was, to put it mildly, an inept pilot, but he *looked* so precisely like everybody's idea of the perfect all-American pilot—including the unnecessary white silk scarf wound rakishly around his neck—that none of the generals could ever believe he was not what he seemed, and they kept on promoting him.

Audiences responded to Ralph—recognizing his desire to do something dramatic to impress his teacher—and to Maurice Noble's designs, which reinforce the films' realistic but dreamlike quality. If we took his name from Jack Phillips, Ralph took his character from Chuck Jones. I had no trouble writing dialogue or creating drawings for the Ralph Phillips cartoons, as Ralph is Chuck Jones as a child.

And the frequent focus of the six-year-old Chuck Jones's daydreams was Blossom Mills . . .

. . .

Love Is a Many-Splintered Thing

If Blossom Mills is still alive—and I have every reason to believe she is, since she was so beautiful, vibrant, pink, and lovely the last time I saw her, in 1920—I want her to know that I loved her then and indeed that I love her now.

The only thing I knew about girls when I was eight years old was from observation of my sisters. In other words: nothing. And from their dolls, which I thought might give me clues about girls who were not my sisters, such as Blossom Mills. But dolls were very secretive about their mysteries.

It simply never occurred to me that Blossom had a body underneath her clothes. I was not suspicious, curious, or knowledgeable about such matters, but I did know this: beautiful dolls had beautiful pink and white faces and hands—and so did Blossom Mills.

241

PAINT INDIANS
VERY RED...
THIS IS A SMALL
BOY'S IDEA OF
AN INDIAN...
(RED-SKIN, THAT IS)

Phillips's last stand. But the mail got through, and the mortgage money was safely and dreamily delivered to his teacher's cruel landlord.

The idea that there was a naked girl under all that clothing was an idea that didn't occur to me until six years later. But even unto this day I cannot conceive of Blossom Mills as any other than she appeared to be: a sort of small, beautiful, padded impossibility. This was about as close as I could have expressed it, if I'd had the intellect to express anything. I never heard her speak, so if she said "Momma" when tipped I cannot say, but otherwise I had—and

have—her perfectly memorized. Where her slender neck met the exquisite curve of her head, there were four tiny wisps curled randomly against her perfectly swept-up hair. Four? Yes. I, who had the eyes of a kingfisher and could count an ant's legs a block away, could equally and easily dwell with enchantment upon these wind-borne wisps from across the street (about the closest I ever got to Blossom Mills). The thought of those golden curls still brings adoration to my heart and tears to my eyes.

Blossom Mills, her adorable white-ribbed stockings—stuffed with what?—bulging a hundredth of an inch over patent-leather, ankle-covering shoes.

Ankle? No!! Wherever anyone else would have had ankles, knuckles, knees, elbows—why, Blossom had dimples. I assure you, she had dimples in her shoes. I can attest to it, having observed these enchanting leather dimples with far more loving intention than I attended to an ant's knees.

The shape of the rest of her clothing could best be described as a sort of tea cozy. Waists were not in that year for little girls—or dolls, for that matter. Suffice it to say that she usually had a circlet of red patent leather around the area where waists existed on larger girls.

Ah, yes, there was a nutmeg-dust of freckles across her alabaster nose and cheeks; tans were unknown to girls in 1920. Her lips justified the term *bee-stung*—they could not have ever opened to admit the passage of food. I would have been astounded if anyone had so suggested, and fortunately for my sanity and theirs, nobody did.

In those days little girls—big girls too—often carried parasols of dimity, pink-dotted swiss, and

Swinging young mice.

243

other exotic substances, and Blossom Mills, who was never an exception to the beau monde, carried one too. Her violet eyes (copied later by Elizabeth Taylor, who knew a good thing in irises when she saw it) in the subtle shadow of a parasol, as my Uncle Lynn would have eloquently noted, were "as pretty as a spotted puppy pulling a red sled through the snow."

Blossom Mills certified to me for all time the absorbing, mysterious, and exhilarating recognition that girls were indeed and in fact a great deal more than soft boys.

Bob Gribbroek's seamy theater from ONE FROGGY EVENING.

There must be some advantage in a singing frog.

Early sketches of Michigan J. Frog (no neck).

TAPPING IN THIS POSITION?
SEE MIKE

MICHIGAN J. FROG

A CASE HISTORY

In full animation there are two basic forms. The first is used in films such as *Bambi, The Lion King*, or our own *Rikki-Tikki-Tavi*, in which the animated creatures move like the real animals, but can talk to one another; and curiously enough, all the different species understand each other. In the second group are the *humanized* characters—Daffy, Bugs, and the rest—who do not move like real ducks and rabbits but are characters in the ancient tradition of Aesop and La Fontaine.

Besides directing and animating rabbits, ducks, and pigs who look and act completely unlike rabbits, ducks, and pigs, I have, under the peculiar pressures of my profession, been forced to animate cobras, elephants, horses, bulls, and mongooses (it's not "mongeese") who look and act as closely as possible

like genuine cobras, elephants, horses, bulls, and mongooses (still not "mongeese"). But Michigan J. Frog presented a special problem, since he belongs to both groups. He had to act and move as a genuine frog and yet, in ways bewildering and frustrating to his owner, he had to sing and dance and prance like an amphibian Pavarotti somehow crossed with an avocado-colored Fred Astaire.

Why?

Because the above idea was inserted into my imagination like a bee in my libido by that Mephistophelian writer Mike Maltese, creator and irritant extraordinaire. And once inserted, it wouldn't go away.

Well, if you're going to produce an animated cartoon about a frog who will exercise his glorious tonsils in glorious song, from "Michigan Rag" to "Fi-

245

garo," but only in the solitary presence of his owner, while persistently appearing to the rest of the world as an ordinary slop-legged, run-of-the-pond, standard frog whose sole oral accomplishment is "ribbit"—how do you get started on this impossible dream?

First things first. You must begin by designing a believable, fresh-off-the-assembly-line frog, apparently no different from any other frog in form and action. So, the frog that the construction worker first

discovers is a real, believable, standard frog, who for some astonishing reason is able to suddenly sing and dance. It would surprise nobody if Bugs Bunny burst out singing—we would take it for granted. But a realistically formed frog who suddenly bellows, "Hello my baby—"? It is—at least—unusual.

I got together with the animators and we talked real live frog. Frogs have this kind of lumpy body, like a plucked quail with sloppy, slippery legs. When you pick up a frog, as every boy knows, the legs just hang

sloppily slipperingly down and dangle, and that's how I drew him, just one slippery little body.

The first and most obvious recognition by the animator is that the basic frog lacks one of the essential features common to most vertebrates, from the pocket shrew to the giraffe and including Bugs Bunny and Daffy Duck, among other fabricated yet *living* characters: the frog doesn't have a neck. This shortcoming was described most accurately by John L. Lewis, president of the United Mine Workers' Union, when

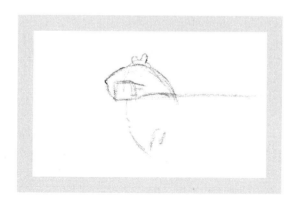

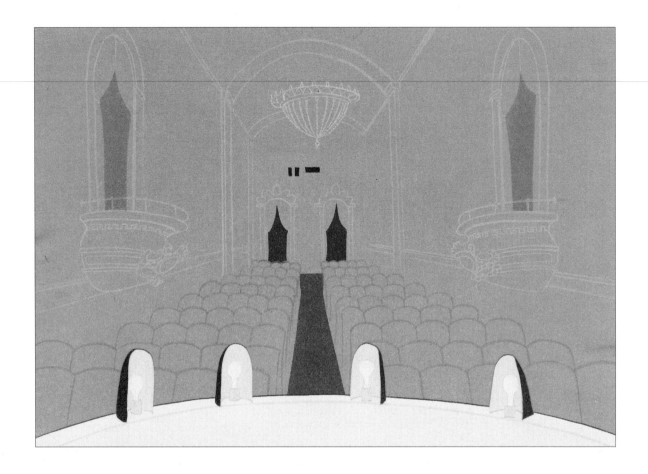

speaking in unflattering terms of William Green, the president of the AFL. "Green doesn't have a head. His neck just grew up and haired over."

Yes, that's a splendid description of every frog (except, of course, for the hair).

To explain the rest of the frog's torso, we must turn to another human being—the great television master of comedy, Ed Sullivan, who (among other minor accomplishments) introduced the Beatles to America.

Ed Sullivan's body didn't bend anyplace, either at the neck or the waist. Everything turned at once, as though the whole mass was cemented together. When he raised his arm to point at the Beatles or anyone else, the arm was riveted at a right angle like an old railroad semaphore.

So, if you can imagine a cross between William Green with unhaired neck and the body of Ed Sullivan with the sloppy, loose-hinged legs of a moribund toad, you can see how simple our job was. All we had to do was animate him like all furry animated characters, from a little pig to a lion king. I felt I had to make the frog believable in a very short time, so when he pulls himself out of the tin he slips a little bit, and when he blinks he blinks upward. That may sound ridiculous—who knows that is the way amphibians blink? *I* know it, so I have to put it in, and you'd better be impressed! As a director you *have* to believe the character yourself. He must move in your imagination like a frog, must "ribbit" like a frog, and must appear at an unexpected moment, as did a small frog I once cleverly inserted into my older sis-

Right: *Bob Gribbroek's sketch of Michigan J. Frog on the high wire.*

ter's lunch box. (Her response was the utmost gratification of my eighth year on this sorry planet, and my father's physically imposed displeasure in no way dimmed that joy.)

Our frog (not yet "Michigan J.") must appear just as unexpectedly to the audience. However, unlike my sister's failure to appreciate her good fortune, the discoverer's reaction to the frog in this case must be surprise without alarm. He must see a distinct—in fact, an overwhelming—possibility of financial gain and fame in the appearance of this frog.

Why should he so respond? Because, in his glorious way, this frog can dance and sing! Oh, come now, what's surprising about that, when we have a skunk singing "Tiptoe Through the Tulips" and a rabbit singing Wagner, to mention only a couple? How to make it believably surprising to the discoverer and the audience that this is a really-o, truly-o frog, and yet it can dance like Bill "Bojangles" Robinson and sing

in a voice Placido Domingo would die for? Answer: The environment from which he appears must be logical, the man who discovers him must be logical, that man must be doing something logical, and the frog must first be a completely logical, Green/Sullivan, slop-legged frog.

We must achieve a believable and lively locale. As we all know, there is nothing more appealing to your average audience than destruction. The sight of something blown down, blown up, or exploded fuels the interest of all and any audiences. So, we arouse interest by tearing down a building with the help of the Acme Demolition Co.— borrowed from Wile E. Coyote for the purpose—and we do it convincingly. This is a real building being really torn down, so when we come to an ordinary

249

Dramatic down shot of singing and balancing frog.

worker prying the top off the old cornerstone, the audience should be lured by all this believability and be ready to be surprised by any untoward event.

Now for believable action. With a powerful heave, our worker pries the top off the cornerstone, (naturally) peers down into the shell, and (curiously) pulls out a canister containing a document planted there many years ago. Blowing the dust off (again believably), he reads: "Be it known that this document . . ." All right, are you now comfortable? Nothing unusual to puzzle or discomfit you? Nothing but an ordinary man doing an unusual but completely believable task.

But look down at that long, oblong, gaping tin box at the bottom of that cornerstone. Two eyes appear. And a head. A quick, surprised response from our worker. A standard frog fumbles, slippering his way up onto the open lid. The eyelids blink up. He "ribbits" just the way he is supposed to.

We're still establishing ourselves in the realm of the believable. And before we can ask, "What the hell is a frog doing in that tin? Has he been in there since the

building was constructed?" the frog grabs a top hat and a cane, whips into a dapper cakewalk and begins singing. Then, just as suddenly, it drops back down to the Green/Sullivan crouch and becomes a standard frog again.

Hopefully the audience—and certainly our worker—is stunned, surprised, and perplexed. But wait a cotton-picking minute! There must be something valuable here, something exploitable, something with a thousandfold greater dollar potential than knocking buildings down for pennies! He envisions *himself* in top hat and tails, holding the frog, standing proudly and confidently in front of Carnegie Hall surrounded by dollar signs. Or, yes, La Scala! With a glittering marquee screaming: "THE WORLD'S FIRST SINGING FROG! THE ONLY NIMBLE-TOED, GOLDEN-VOICED AMPHIBIAN TO TREAD THE BOARDS OF THE STARTLED THEATER WORLD."

But this is a story, and the essence of this story is of course that Michigan J. Frog (since we now may call him by his proper name) is either unwilling or unable to perform before anyone but his owner. To the world beyond, this treasure is simply and sloppily a frog, his vocal range extending from "ribbit" to "galumph." And—in a very loose way— this becomes the plot.

The story develops, the frustrations mount, our worker-turned-entrepreneur's pitiful hopes of grandeur are dashed one by one by booking agents, audiences, the police force, and psychological behaviorists. Through incarceration to absolute hopeless frustration, he comes finally to the wan recognition that his only hope might be in F.A. (Frogs' Anonymous) and to the realization that only in another cornerstone of another building under construction can such a frog be disposed of.

Our tattered, saddened friend drops Michigan J. in his tin sarcophagus and into the first cornerstone

he can find, thereby unknowingly assigning the same frustrating fate to some future worker of the twenty-first century.

The film then quickly passes to the middle of the next century, where it is demonstrated that avarice is still alive and well. The worker of that era sneaks just as stealthily off to his doubtful destiny, as the frog in his tin canister sings again.

Fade out.

In 2056, an Acme building disintegrator (opposite and above) *discovers a singing frog in a cornerstone* (right), *and the faint gleam of momentary avarice rears its twenty-first-century head—ugly as ever.*

*Richard Williams,
having stolen the great
Ken Harris (seated at work
on A CHRISTMAS CAROL),
here seen unrepentant with
the author.*

*Flattering portrait of the
contemporary Jones drawn on
a napkin by the brilliant
Richard Williams.*

A director is awarded his star on the Hollywood Walk of Fame (left and below), almost a decade after Bugs's star appeared on December 21, 1985 (above). A star is a thoughtful convenience for those who know not where to deposit their chewing gum.

Egotistical frog—
much enlarged.

Key poses of Michigan J. Frog at work in his glorious reappearance in 1995's ANOTHER FROGGY EVENING. When you get far enough away from a picture—about forty years away, to be safe—you begin to realize that things could have been done differently. So in 1994 I decided to do another froggy picture. In the original cartoon, Michigan J. Frog comes out of the past and goes into the future. The new cartoon goes back in time to find him in Neanderthal times. Drawings by Tom Decker.

Early storyboards of *One Froggy Evening* included talking characters, but that just didn't work. There is no dialogue in the completed film; the only audible voice is the frog's. Having eliminated all dialogue, I finally realized how I wanted to tell the story. Imposing that discipline on myself made my work tougher, but it helped me pare away the fat to reach the essence of the film, which is that a man discovers a frog who can sing but who will not sing in front of anyone else. That is the story, *all* the story, and if I had allowed anything else to intrude—such as people discussing this singing frog—the frog's voice would no longer have been the dominant element. When, for example, the man takes the frog to the theatrical agency, the scene takes place behind glass. You can tell they are talking, but you do not hear the agent.

Keeping the frog from talking as well as singing was a problem at first, because I thought of him as having a full personality. But the more I worked on the film, the more I discovered that he has no personality beyond his appeal as a vaudeville performer. We don't know or care who he is backstage when his performance is over; we can't converse with him, we can only applaud. The unfortunate man who finds him is really his agent, trying to sell him to a cynical public.

The frog has no name in the picture, but we started calling him Michigan J. Frog after the "Michigan Rag," the song Mike Maltese and I wrote for the frog when we needed a ragtime song and could not find one we liked. And that is, I've heard, where Steven Spielberg found the idea of a hero whose name was a state—Indiana—linked to an animation director—Jones.

256

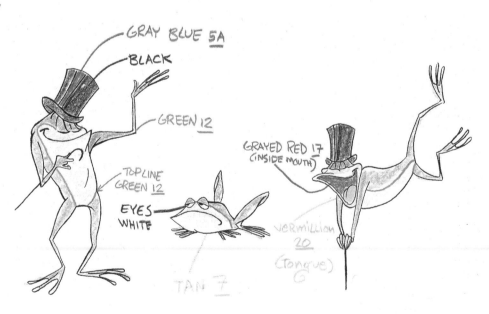

This old green frog is just what he used to be, ANOTHER FROGGY EVENING *(1995).*

Chuck Jones Film Productions is now back on the Warner Bros. lot, reviving the energy of Termite Terrace with a new team of young animators. Working with the great layout artist Maurice Noble, the unit's first film for Warner Bros. was CHARIOTS OF FUR, which premiered as a theatrical release in 1994.
Right: What do you catch with an Acme Giant Mouse Trap?
Below: Wile E. Coyote has had little luck with Acme springs.

It started one froggy evening in 1955, with one man's belief that a frog could sing (above).

Forty years later, Michigan J. Frog made his second appearance, in ANOTHER FROGGY EVENING (1995). The critics in ancient Rome are as harsh as ever, in spite of Gene Siskel and Roger Ebert's two thumbs up. Left to right: (back row) Tina Raleigh, Don Arioli, Rose Long, Chuck Jones, Michel Breton, Ben Jones, Herman Sharaf, Warren O'Neill, Greg Whittaker, Tod Polson, Lawrence Marvit; (middle row) Steve Fossati, Bob Givens, Linda Jones Clough, Greg Duffell, Tom Decker, Jill Petrilak; (front row) Charlie Puzzo, Ted Bemiller, Mike Polvani, Stan Freberg.

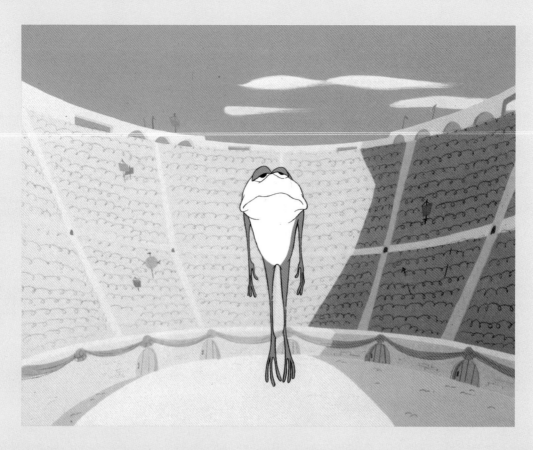

Michigan J. Frog makes a brief and songless appearance before the Emperor in ANOTHER FROGGY EVENING.

This oil painting displays the difference between performers Bugs and Daffy: Bugs plays the piano; Daffy attacks it.

In WHAT'S OPERA, DOC? (1957) the metal slats of Elmer's skirt make no sound as he jabs at Bugs's hole, irritating me every time I see the film. There is no such problem in an oil painting.

The Grinch peers down on Who-ville from Mount Crumpit. The Grinch's body is a sort of huge, sagging, pear-shaped structure, with arms, legs, elbows, and bony knees not unlike those of the Coyote. In fact Dr. Seuss felt that my Grinch looked more like me than like his Grinch. Like all fully animated characters, the Grinch has an implied skeletal structure and muscles; once decided, his skeleton had to be respected, to avoid rubbery inconsistency and unbelievability.

The Grinch hatches his plot to stop Christmas in Who-ville.

Once we knew something about how the Grinch would move, we made preliminary sketches to familiarize ourselves with him, so that he would act in ways consistent with his personality. All three sketches on this page are mine.

The Grinch's dog, Max, has a much bigger role in the film than in the book, because we needed a character to be both victim and observer. Max was directly inspired by a sad little fox terrier my father once tried—and failed—to train.

The downhill sleigh ride brings real excitement to the opening of Act 2.

The sounds of Christmas come to Who-ville. To some extent we are all Grinches about Christmas—all that noise, all those unwanted presents, all those thank-you letters to write.

Whenever I rented a car around the time
HOW THE GRINCH STOLE CHRISTMAS! (1967)
first appeared on television, it was invariably
Grinch-green, which was a popular color for cars
at the time. I didn't like it, and frequently had
to upgrade to a more congenial color. The Grinch
himself changes color slightly, turning a friendlier
green when he has his change of heart.

These two early
sketches show the
Grinch, with no
time for niceties,
collapsing the
Christmas tree
umbrella-style.

You're a mean one, Mr. Grinch!

Cindy-Lou Who surprises the Grinch. I drew Cindy-Lou to appear like a great-grandchild of the Grinch, but with everything right where he is wrong.

"Christmas Day will always be, just as long as we have we."

C. Jones in his lush Hollywood office at Sunset and Vine in 1965.

The little Who children asleep
in their bed. Note the ominous shadow
on the bedspread.

The evil Grinch even
steals ice cubes and lightbulbs.
(His soul is full of garlic.)

Opposite: The Grinch grinchily
absconding with all the Who toys.

How the Grinch Stole Christmas!

A CASE HISTORY

After thirty years at Warner Bros., I left in 1962 as naked financially as the day I started. No residuals. No royalties. No job. As there no longer seemed to be a market for six-minute theatrical cartoons, I had to find a way to do the only thing I knew how to do reasonably well—draw, direct, and time some kind of animated films—or perish. So I went out without much hope, found a new market that I hadn't known existed, and called together my old unit. We produced *How the Grinch Stole Christmas!*, *Horton Hears a Who*, *The Cricket in Times Square*, *Rikki-Tikki-Tavi*, *Mowgli's Brothers*, and several other TV specials, because television now held the money to pay fair wages for a fully animated product.

After thirty years at Warner Bros., I left in 1962 as naked financially as the day I started. No residuals. No royalties. No job.

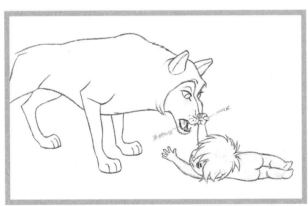

Mowgli and father wolf, from MOWGLI'S BROTHERS (1976).

Both these films (above and right), as well as HOW THE GRINCH STOLE CHRISTMAS! (1967), HORTON HEARS A WHO (1970), THE CRICKET IN TIMES SQUARE (1973), and others, were produced for television—an emerging market for fully animated films.

Boy meets mongoose in RIKKI-TIKKI-TAVI (1974).

From my Uncle Lynn I long ago accepted a rule that I have found to be useful in obtaining the attention and respect of a child. I try never, no matter what the incentive, to exclaim to a child how much he has grown since I last saw him, and I try never, no matter how tongue-tied I may feel in his presence, to ask him what grade he is in. Children may be young, but they are not fools, and they immediately recognize these questions for what they are: pat words uttered in place of genuine interest or just because we adults do not know what else to say. Such questions belong in the class with adult references to the weather and mode of travel. "How did you get here, drive?" is certainly a banal question to someone you have just met or are seeing again after a long time.

Fortunately for us, we are essentially courteous, and we recognize hesitancy for what it is and ice-breaking questions or statements for what they are. A child has no such sophistication. He is simply aware that he is hearing an ancient and oft-repeated question, and he tiredly gives the expected answer, but he surely does not warm up to the questioner.

There is always something interesting about a child, something or some aspect of his appearance, manner, or geography that can elicit some interest. George S. Kaufman provided an ice-breaker at dull dinner parties that will do as well as any other, if you are stumped by an unresponsive dinner partner: "Do you know how to get bloodspots out of a buffalo robe?"

Another line I would like to

I can't think of a single good "children's" picture that intelligent adults can't enjoy, and I see no reason why we should not respect our children at least as much as we respect ourselves.

—Pauline Kael

protest, with all the intense vehemence that hundreds of generations of indignant moppets would like to voice, is the "I've-got-a-little-boy-at-home-just-like-you" bit. This sounds about as sensible to a child as a similar line would sound to an adult: "I've got a little man (or woman) at home just like you."

Children think of themselves as individuals, with all the fierce devotion that anyone else does. To be categorized as a nine-year-old child, as though all nine-year-old children were the same, transcends the idiotic. It is frankly insulting, and the only difference between insulting a child and insulting an adult is that the child has no recourse.

"Have you ever been bitten by a bee?" is, in my mind, a far better question than, "My, what a pretty hair ribbon! Did your mommy buy it?" The first is an honest one and can generate mutual interest, while the latter is simply contrived and no real answer is possible. We have all either been bitten by bees or considered the painful possibility. It is something we can share with each other, no matter what our age differences.

In the same way, there is no such thing as a "children's book." Some time ago, the late Ted Geisel (Dr. Seuss) and Maurice Sendak, meeting in San Diego, agreed upon this. So did P. L. Travers (who wrote *Mary Poppins)*, and, I am sure, so did L. Frank Baum, Lewis Carroll, and Robert Louis Stevenson.

The absolute and only proof of what constitutes a "great" children's book or film is this: from *Peter Rabbit* to *Stuart Little,* each can be read again and again with pleasure by adults *and* children. Why? Be-

261

A large and rather snooty Mrs. Kangaroo reads the riot act to a sad elephant in HORTON HEARS A WHO *(1970).*

cause all great children's books and films, like all great books and films, are based on character. How many book plots or film plots can you remember? Even in whodunits, the works of the masters of this genre (James Cain, Raymond Chandler, Dashiell Hammett) evoke memories of brilliant characters. When assigned to do the screenplay of *The Little Sister,* Chandler himself confessed that he couldn't figure out his own plot.

If you believe in the character—"you" meaning both the director and the audience—you will believe or be in sympathy with what the character does and says.

• • •

Dr. Seuss could not draw a great crested grebe or a bowerbird, but ornithologists and zoologists throughout the world stood in awe of his unparalleled accuracy in sketching with absolute detail a Sneetch or a Lorax.

He eschewed the haunts of the great basking shark or the mating ground of the electric eel, but marine biologists could only gasp in envy at his knowledge and his piscatorial description of the denizens of McElligot's pool.

He enlightened us not about life in the Middle Ages or the plague years; he spent no time describing the Champs-Elysées, the Bourse, or Threadneedle Street, but no social scientist ever examined a thoroughfare as thoroughly as he examined Mulberry Street.

What Jane Goodall is to baboons and Dian Fossey to gorillas, Dr. Seuss is to the mind and heart of the male elephant. *Horton Hatches the Egg* is his monograph on the touching parental attitudes of the great pachyderm he so patiently studied.

His scholarly paper on organic compounds such as "oobleck" is certainly the definitive authority on this rare substance.

Writing in collaboration with B. Cubbins, he demonstrates with his treatise on hats that no subject was too trivial for his enquiring and investigative mind.

His compassionate study of the social structure and interpersonal relationships of the Whos of Whoville is equal if not superior to Margaret Mead's *Coming of Age in Samoa,* and only he was able to

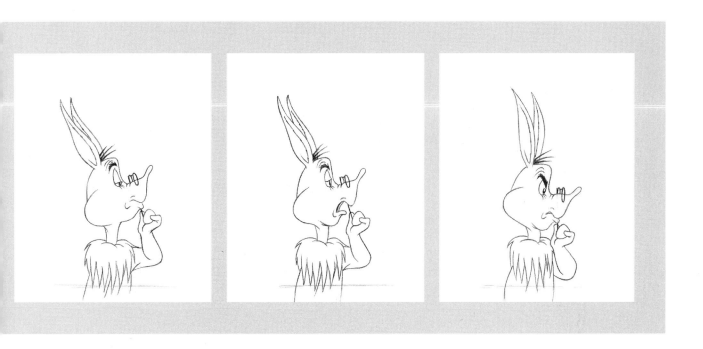

identify and classify (as those seeking Bigfoot and the Abominable Snowman were not) that curious, ominous, and antisocial, anti-Christmas creature: the Grinch.

The first time I met Captain Theodor Seuss Geisel was in 1943. We were brought together by a fracas called World War II, not *the* World War of 1914–1918, which did not require a number since we believed (Theodor at twelve, Charles at six) that this was the war to end wars. There are few enough positive elements to any war, but for me World War II opened the opportunity to work with one of the brightest, quickest, funniest minds of this or any other century.

Dr. Seuss was then Captain Geisel, in charge of the animation and documentary arm of the first motion picture unit, commanded by Colonel Frank Capra, quartered in the old Fox Studio on Sunset Boulevard and Western Avenue and fondly remembered throughout World War II as "Fort Western," as distinct from Fort (Hal) Roach where

Lieutenant Ronald Reagan picked up his ribbons for good conduct with oak-leaf clusters.

Our introduction and long acquaintance stems from some short training films designed to depict the trials, tribulations, and trepidations of the worst soldier in the Army, Private Snafu. *Snafu* is an Army term probably going back to the Crusades (where Woody Allen's ancestor served as a spy), meaning **S**ituation **N**ormal **A**ll **F**u--ed **U**p. *Fubar*—meaning **F**u--ed **U**p **B**eyond **A**ll **R**ecognition— came later.

The *Snafu* stories and rough storyboards were concocted at Fort Western by a group of ex-Warner workers and Disneyites, including Otto Englander, Phil Eastman, Dave Rose, Eugene Fleury, and Dave Hilberman. The boards were then taken to the Warner Bros. (Schlesinger) cartoon studio a few blocks away at the old Warner lot at Van Ness and Fernwood to be directed and animated.

263

Technical fairy, first class, from U.S. Army training film (1944).

Our films apparently inflicted no wounds and provoked no friendly fire on our allies. Their purpose was survival under conditions to be met in the Arctic, the Tropics, the Persian Gulf (yes, the *same* Persian Gulf), and other hostile zones. This was the only time I really knew what the audience was like for any of my films. Anyone who has ever been in the army knows how bad training films can be, and at that time they were terribly bad. Animation proved to be a very good medium for a training film.

DIRECTED BY CHUCK JONES

•

COMING SNAFU

SPIES

THE INFANTRY BLUES

PRIVATE SNAFU VS. MALARIA MIKE

LECTURE ON CAMOUFLAGE

GAS

GOING HOME

OUTPOST

IN THE ALEUTIANS

IT'S MURDER SHE SAYS

NO BUDDY ATOLL

SECRETS OF THE CARIBBEAN

264

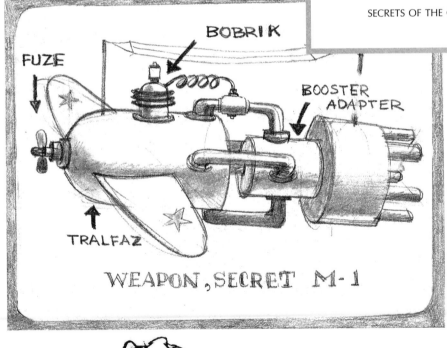

So that's what a secret weapon looks like?

Cuckoo and a Loon.

Common Swallow teaching a young Swallow its trade.

I HAVE ALWAYS BEEN FASCINATED BY THE WONDERFUL NAMES OF BIRDS. I HAVE NEVER MET A GREBE, A PUFFIN, A BOOBY, A HORNBILL, A GOATSUCKER, OR A NUTHATCH, BUT THEY ARE ALL MEMBERS IN GOOD STANDING (OR FLYING) OF THE AVIAN FRATERNITY. ALL THE BIRDS I HAVE EVER DRAWN ARE FICTITIOUS, BUT THE NAMES ARE USUALLY LEGITIMATE, TO BE FOUND IN A DICTIONARY. I FEEL THAT I AM AT LIBERTY TO DESIGN BIRDS TO FIT THE NAMES, JUST AS ADAM FELT FREE TO NAME THEM IN THE FIRST PLACE.

BOOBIES, KITTIWAKES, GOONIES, STARLINGS, BOWERBIRDS, GANNETS, MOURNING DOVES, MERLINS, CHICKEN HAWKS, AUKS, LARKS, TURTLEDOVES, SHRIKES, COWBIRDS, THE GREAT CRESTED GREBES, THE LESSER TOMTITS, THE KILLDEERS, KIWIS AND DODOS, SANDPIPERS AND SANDERLINGS, ERNS AND TERNS AND CRESTED JAYS, CUTWATERS AND SWIFTS, CASSOWARIES, TRUMPETING SWANS AND HOMING PIGEONS, PRAIRIE CHICKS, HELLDIVERS, MOCKINGBIRDS AND FLICKERS— THESE ARE A FEW THAT IMMEDIATELY COME TO MIND.

Western Fly-catcher with its fly caught.

A Grouse   Grouch   and two small grumbles.

I'M A CAT-BIRD   I'M A CAT-BIRD

Cat-bird.   *Mockingbird.*

* * *

After the war, *Major* Geisel retired to his home in La Jolla, hoping, I do believe, to escape Hollywood chicanery; he was robbed of the writing credit on an Academy Award–winning documentary (as many others have been) and was denied proper recognition for writing the Oscar-winning UPA animated cartoon *Gerald McBoing-Boing*. He was given a very meager credit, no share in the film's glory, and $500, which was all the payment he ever received. Even this $500 must have appeared generous in comparison to the $50 that Leon Schlesinger paid him for the rights to *Horton Hatches the Egg*. Unsurprisingly, Dr. Seuss was not eager to have more of his books made into film, but I climbed the mountain to meet this wonderful hermit and persuaded him to allow the Grinch off the hill.

266

The Grinch, with his horrible, wonderful smile.

There is nothing children like as much as a couple of good villains.

—*Beatrix Potter*

How could anyone—how could I—not love the Grinch? I have a section of my heart reserved for villains: for Long John Silver, for Captain Hook, for the Wicked Witches of East *and* West (I am not prejudiced on the compass points or on wickedness), for the cold Duke of James Thurber who said, "We all have flaws, and mine is being wicked." And finally, for my own tribe of miscreants: Wile E. Coyote, Marvin Martian, Daffy Duck, Friz Freleng's Yosemite ("Ah hates rabbits") Sam, etc., etc.

You can say that a Grinch wants to steal Christmas, and you don't need to know anything more about him—he is just a villainous Grinch who hates Christmas. A human being cannot be that simple. If a human villain—an old man, for example—wanted to steal Christmas, we would have to go deeper into the character, to find out whether he hated Christmas because of his age, because he lived alone on a mountain, or because he loathed kids. What we do shamefully recognize, of course, is that we are all a bit like the Grinch, for we all hate Christmas a little. Or a lot.

Even children hate Christmas a little. As a child you worry that your brother or sister might be given better presents, and you rarely receive all you asked for. And when it's all over, it's worse—there's the dull work of dismantling the tree, and above all there are the endless thank-you letters to write. My personal problem was forgetting what anybody had given me, and I would write to my grandmother complimenting her on knowing my size, when she had given me

Theodor Seuss Geisel appears to be an undercover agent rather than Captain Geisel of the U.S. Army.

a jackknife. Ted Geisel had no children, and he shared the Grinch's grumpiness about Christmas—all those kids racing around making a noise.

I was ready for *How the Grinch Stole Christmas!*, and the following is the story of how we nursed, cursed, stroked, anatomized, and gently traumatized the perfect villain into what, at first, seemed to be a reluctant screen life. In the book, Dr. Seuss had already carefully determined *who* the Grinch was (or is). Our job as animators was to find out how to match in movement the believability of that character.

The following rules for good animation are those we applied to all of our films, including, of course, *How the Grinch Stole Christmas!* All right, repeat after me.

1. *All living creatures, fictional or not, have anatomy. Equally true of an amoeba, an angle worm, a mastodon, and a Grinch.*

2. *If you want believability in your characters, you must have visual consistency. In animation, each character must move according to its own anatomical limitations: Daffy Duck must move with Daffy Duck's anatomy, Donald Duck with Donald Duck's structure. The amoeba's anatomy seems to have only one restriction—its bulk; like an inflated balloon, it can vary its shape, but it cannot change its volume. That is, if you want a believable amoeba.*

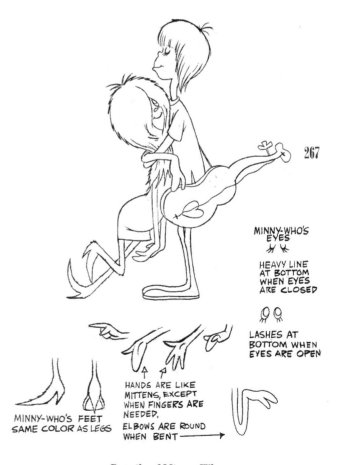

267

MINNY-WHO'S EYES

HEAVY LINE AT BOTTOM WHEN EYES ARE CLOSED

LASHES AT BOTTOM WHEN EYES ARE OPEN

MINNY-WHO'S FEET SAME COLOR AS LEGS

HANDS ARE LIKE MITTENS, EXCEPT WHEN FINGERS ARE NEEDED. ELBOWS ARE ROUND WHEN BENT ——→

Details of Minny-Who.

3. *All animals—humanized animals or animalized humans—must appear to stand, walk, run, or skip under the stabilizing pressure of gravity in order to achieve believability.*

4. *There is no sympathy without believability, no real laughter without sympathy.*

5. *In the sympathetic recognition of any character there must be some evidence of one's own self, one's own weaknesses, one's own mistakes, no matter how well self-concealed, buttoned down, or pigeonholed.*

6. *The filmmaker as well as the viewer must be able to find the character within himself. We cannot fashion personalities from what we suppose another person to be.*

7. *If you start with character, you probably will end up with good drawings. If you start out with drawings, you will almost certainly end up with limited characters, caught in the matrix of your limited drawing. Therefore . . .*

8. *It is not what or where a character is, nor is it the circumstances under which he finds himself that determine who he is. It is only how in a unique way he responds to that environment and those circumstances that identifies him as an individual. Hopefully, an interesting character becomes interesting because of that uniqueness among his contemporaries.*

9. *For identity, you do not draw differently, you think differently. It is the who of the character, not the what, that counts. Walk-through circus clowns depend upon what they look like for their brand of comedy. That is what they are. Comedians depend upon how they move for comedy and pathos—their wonderful who-ness.*

10. *As the writer John Buchan said, you will never succeed in playing a part unless you convince yourself that you are it.*

11. *Animation means to invoke life, not to imitate it.*

12. *No great children's book, film, or fable was ever written for children. It was written for the writer, the artist, the filmmaker. Again, the mark of any "great work" for children, from one by Beatrix Potter to a book by Dr. Seuss, can be easily identified: if it can be read with pleasure by adults, it is probably a very good, possibly a great, children's book.*

13. *You cannot write down to an audience or to your subject. You must write up to them with the certainty*

Not a Halloween party, but C. Jones among a galaxy of Ringling Bros. and Barnum & Bailey clowns. Only walk-through circus clowns depend upon what they look like for their brand of comedy.

that you cannot ever do justice to your subject, but must bend every creative nerve and muscle of your heart and brain to its full capacity in an attempt to do so.

14. The least you owe an audience is the best you can do.

15. No art form can exist without restrictive disciplines. Most of the great paintings in history have been caught in the terrible discipline of the rectangle. The filmmaker finds himself trapped in the exact and severe disciplines of both the rectangle and time. Most cinema features are in a time warp of 90 to 120 minutes, most animated cartoon shorts in a confinement of 6 minutes, television specials (including How the Grinch Stole Christmas!) 24 minutes.

16. You must not complain of your restrictions. If you cannot live with them, find a discipline you can live with.

Bob Cannon's view of a happy Jones.

• • •

Mondrian disciplined himself almost completely to lines parallel to the frame edge and in a long life found stimulation, not stagnation, in this, the seemingly most restrictive of disciplines.

The net is the discipline of tennis, the horse that of polo, the hoop that of basketball. Formal ballet has but five foot positions; the trombone depends on the slide; the octave of the ivory keys is the discipline of the piano, just as surely as Everest is the discipline of the climber. The filmmaker must struggle along with but twenty-four frames to the second, which translates to twenty-four drawings to the animator.

Yes, with these seemingly restrictive rules, we, at my unit at Warner Bros., found ourselves able to provide life to Bugs Bunny, Daffy Duck, Elmer Fudd, the Coyote and Road Runner, Pepé le Pew, and many more. The rules followed me from Warner Bros. to MGM, where I brought the Grinch to life.

270   Unlike an average Warner Bros. animated cartoon, the story of *How the Grinch Stole Christmas!* was already clearly established before we started, as was the Grinch's personality and configuration. What had to be determined was:

How does each of these characters move?

What kind of voice should each have? What kind of voice for the narrator? For Cindy-Lou Who?

Since the reading time for the book ran about twelve minutes, how to lengthen it to twenty-four minutes without padding it?

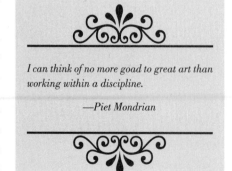

I can think of no more goad to great art than working within a discipline.

—*Piet Mondrian*

How to make a Christmas film without orthodox religion, without Santa Claus, without reindeer, snowmen, or the use of any of the classic carols?

The answers, in reverse order, turned out to be these:

Write our own new carols in Seussian Latin. After all, "Fahoofores, Dahoodores" seems to have as much authenticity as "Adeste fideles" to those untutored in Latin. And the first carol—"Trim Up the Tree with Christmas Stuff"—was written in square-dance cadence by the talented Albert Hague, and orchestrated and conducted by the equally talented Eugene Poddany. As to religion, the only line that *might* have come from the Scriptures, according to the networks, was: "'Perhaps,' thought the Grinch, 'Christmas doesn't come from a store.'" Better, far better, was: "Christmas day will always be, just as long" (joining hands) "as we have we." Poignant, but how lovely it would be if it were always ever so.

It was apparent to me from the beginning that the part of Max (the reindeer dog, as we came to know and love him) could and should be lengthened. We needed a character who could act as an observer—a role filled by Porky in *Duck*

If you cant appreciate what youve got, youd better get what you can appreciate.

—G. B. Shaw

Dodgers in the 24½th Century and *Robin Hood Daffy*—and we needed a *victim*. Max is both observer and victim, at one with the audience, who are also feeling victimized by this Grinch who wants to destroy one of our major refuges—Christmas.

Max represents all of us. He is a very honest, very decent, and very put-upon dog. Dr. Seuss described him as "Everydog—all love and limpness and loyalty." He also adds to the drama of

271

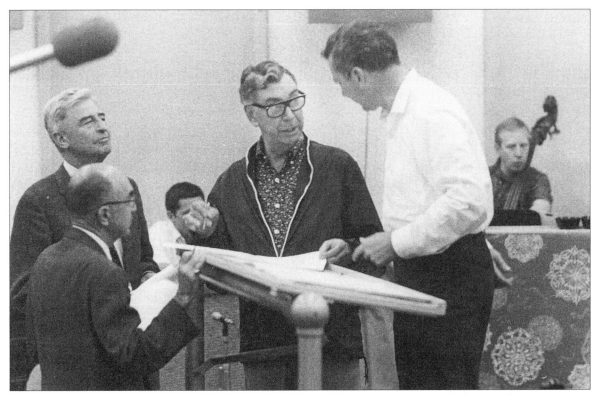

Dr. Seuss (left) *listening to a Thurl Ravenscroft* (center) *rendition of "You're a mean one, Mr. Grinch."*
The white-shirted figure is Eugene Poddany, conductor.

the story: the long downhill run that starts the second act brings real excitement and danger to that perilous sleigh ride.

As for Cindy-Lou Who, she was so appealingly small and innocent (I redrew her as seeming to be a great-grandchild of the Grinch in appearance) that we reluctantly held her part down, although it broke my heart to do so.

There was never any doubt in my mind that there was only one person to narrate this story and to be the voice of the Grinch: Boris Karloff. The recordings he had done of the Kipling stories and many others established him not only as the ideal actor but, in my mind and Ted's, as the *only* one. We had him read the entire script in his beautiful, rhythmic, caring voice, so that the rhythm would be consistent throughout the film. We then had our cunning sound engineers take the highs out of his recorded voice to create the gravelly grunt of the Grinch's voice. Finally, June Foray came in to record Cindy-Lou Who's voice. Having put on the earphones and listened to Karloff's reading, she captured its character completely as she brought Cindy-Lou Who to life. In this

way, the entire picture kept the cohesive rhythm that Karloff brought to it.

One of the few misconceptions about June is to think of her wonderful talent as "voice over." Nothing could be further from the truth. June is worthy of the gift-word: *actress*. She imbues a part with herself, be it a Mama Bear or the deadly cobra Nagaina in *Rikki-Tikki-Tavi*. As a vocal Grandma Moses, she brought the redoubtable Granny to life for Friz Freleng; for me, she did the loving mother seal in Kipling's *The White Seal*. She created three different witches named Hazel for Disney, MGM, and Warner Bros., all with different personalities but all with undeniable knowledge of Shakespeare's squacky trio. She could transfer her throat from a sweet Cindy-Lou in *How the Grinch Stole Christmas!* to a bellowing Red Riding Hood in *Little Red Riding Rabbit:* "I GOT A LITTLE BUNNY RABBIT WHICH I'M TAKIN' TO MY GRA'MA'S—TO HAVE! SEE!!!" From Natasha to (an asexual) Rocky, she dominated Bullwinkle and company for many years. Indeed, she is one of the few actresses I know who would understand John Barrymore's assertion that "an actor cannot say 'pass the

As for Cindy-Lou Who, she was so appealingly small and innocent (I redrew her as seeming to be a great-grandchild of the Grinch in appearance) that we reluctantly held her part down, although it broke my heart to do so. Voice by June Foray.

There was only one person to be the voice of the Grinch: Boris Karloff, photographed (right) *with Dr. Seuss at a recording session for* How the Grinch Stole Christmas!

Above: *Another villain, from* Water, Water Every Hare *(1952).*

butter' without understanding who said it, where it was said, and under what circumstances it was said." In fact—and I speak with the deepest respect for him—I can only compliment Mel Blanc by saying that he could be called a male June Foray.

"Show me the skeleton of any animal and I will show you how it must move," said Albert Hurter. Unfortunately, there are very few, if any, Grinch skeletons about, so we had to do with Dr. Seuss's careful academic drawings of the living Grinch.

All fully animated characters have implied, but very real, skeletal structures and the muscles to move themselves about. Once decided, the implied skeleton of Bugs Bunny, Daffy Duck, Pepé le Pew, or the Grinch must be respected, or it will become inconsistently rubbery and lose all claim to believability.

The Grinch fell well into this classic anatomical crew. His skull and enormous set of teeth are not notably different from Elmer Fudd's, only more so. His body is a sort of huge, sagging, pear-shaped, Porky Pig–like structure. His arms, legs, skinny elbows, and bony knees are not unlike those of the Coyote. So, we had a full-length portrait.

Cindy-Lou Who is a diminutive Grinch, where everything is right where the Grinch is wrong. Max the dog has a skimpy, scraggly, horizontal, pear-shaped body, a sad snout, and forlorn eyes.

Having identified the Grinch anatomically, we then considered how he *must* move. If children were to become involved in the story, the Grinch must move like a Grinch, not just be a drawing with arms and legs that move.

Max moves awkwardly. He was not the most graceful of dogs, and he was not built right to sit up. His toppling over when the Grinch uses him as a dress dummy harked back to a fox terrier my father once bought. This poor little fox terrier was the only dog I've ever known who was a complete nonentity. He would have had to move up to become a wimp. He could not sit up, he had a negligible tail, and his entire body came to a point. This fact was overlooked by my fa-

ther (who believed he could teach anybody anything) in his determination to teach this dog to "By God, sit up!" Father would prop the poor little thing up, stick his powerful finger at the terrier's nose, and bark, "Sit up!" Balanced on his bony coccyx, the sad little creature would topple slowly and inexorably over.

Several of these dismal failures only proved to my father that the dog wasn't *trying,* so he became harsher in his demands to "Sit!!" Then my mother advised him to try propping the dog up in the corner of the room. At that point, we four children were no longer able to muffle our hilarity, so turning savagely on us (figuring that we were to blame) he ordered us upstairs, while he duly propped the little dog in the corner. Upstairs we had the benefit of pillow and blanket to stifle our laughter, which became more and more intense as we heard "Sit!!" then a sliding sound, a thump, a curse, followed by another "Sit!!!!"

I was six years old, and I tucked this little dog away in my memory until I needed him to play the part of Max. I am often asked, "What is the source of your inspiration?" and after more than sixty years in animation, this is the only source I can honestly identify. So perhaps that sad, pointy dog served a purpose, after all.

Once we knew something about how our characters—the Grinch, Max the reindeer dog, and Cindy-Lou Who—were to move, we started doing some preliminary sketches to familiarize ourselves with them, so that they became a sort of visual family, and we could expect them to act in ways consistent with their personalities.

Unlike for most live-action films, we did not have a script. It is a time-honored tradition to present the entire story of an animated film in visual terms from the very beginning. A six-minute cartoon requires about 150 four-by-six-inch sketches. The director has to translate these sketches to the screen.

On a half-hour television special we are dealing with some twenty-four minutes—four times the length of the cartoons we were used to. We therefore had to have four times as many story sketches—at least 600. And the director had to do most of them, with the storymen doing the rest. In fact, I made more than 1,500 drawings.

During the long process (about two months) of converting *How the Grinch Stole Christmas!* to the finished storyboard, Ted and I worked together very closely, both at the studio (MGM) and at his glass-

The whole essence of good drawing—and of good thinking, perhaps—is to work a subject down to the simplest form possible and still have it believable for what it is meant to be. For example, an apple is almost square and has a deep indentation on top; an orange is round and has a shallower indentation; a bottle holds liquid and has a neck (if it has no neck, it is a vase or some other container); a tree has a trunk, and a bush sits on the ground.

Knowing these things makes drawing a much simpler matter. It is similar to the way natural scientists classify the world: when they see a moth, they decide which family it belongs to and then define its differences from other members of that family. It is no longer necessary to consider a violin as being different from everything else on earth; it is just different from every other instrument in its class—the stringed instruments. What Braque is suggesting with his cubist guitar is that all stringed instruments are based on one principle—a box (usually with a neck and hole) and strings. He divides the picture down the middle, showing all *stringed instruments on one side, this* particular *instrument on the other.*

enclosed eagle's nest in La Jolla. We brought my great scene and production designer Maurice Noble into our conferences to establish Who-ville, the Who-ville homes (within and without), the Grinch's hideaway, and the icy slopes of Mount Crumpit.

Ted was very patient with me, but we did have an occasional friendly argument about how to draw the Grinch. He felt that my Grinch looked more like *me* than like his Grinch.

Well, something had to give, so we ended up with a sort of mélange of all the Grinches. This is the way it came out and how we drew him in the film.

And so finally we were able to complete the storyboard, and with a pat on the back from Ted, I went off to New York to sell the idea to a sponsor. (Today you sell your film to the network; in those innocent days—1966—you sold to the sponsor, guaranteeing financial support, *before* you could proceed to the network.)

That sounded easy enough. After all, I could take great pride in the wonderful story and full professional storyboard, and I could—and did—act all the parts (even Cindy-Lou Who) while presenting the board—twenty-six times!

Yep. Twenty-six times I did my dog-and-pony, or rather dog-and-grinch, act for the icy-eyed acres of advertising agency people before I could find a buyer. The "omniscience" of those who refused *How the Grinch Stole Christmas!* demonstrates how clearly right Fred Allen was when he said, "A bunch of network or agency brass are men who alone can do nothing and together agree that nothing can be done."

At last, in the depths of my despair, success came from the most unlikely source of all: the Foundation of Commercial Banks!

You have to be kidding! The bankers bought a story in which the Grinch says, "Maybe Christmas *doesn't* come from a store"??!!

Well, bless their bankers' hearts. And I didn't even offer collateral.

Now all we had to do was to make a twenty-four-minute film out of the storyboard, which we did: finding the voices, recording them, writing the music, drawing hundreds of key character layouts (mainly my job), designing a couple of hundred backgrounds (Maurice Noble), painting all those backgrounds (Phil De Guard), animating more than 15,000 useable drawings (Ken Harris, Abe Levitow, Ben Washam, Dick Thompson), and having them inked, painted, shot, and dubbed (putting sound effects, music, dialogue, and film together).

At the dubbing session, it is difficult, if not impossible, for a director to accept that the sound technicians are not there to confuse and frighten him.

The model sheet for the Grinch. Ted felt that my Grinch looked more like me than like his Grinch.

Right: *A bunch of bankers
who eventually and with
some reluctance agreed
to sponsor* HOW THE GRINCH
STOLE CHRISTMAS!
*Jones and Seuss (in bow
ties) in attendance* (right
and below).

Their job (which they do superbly) is to balance dialogue, music, and sound effects into a coherent whole, in concert with the film itself. Nevertheless, as P. G. Wodehouse said, "Being scalped can never be an unmixedly pleasant experience."

You walk (walk?), creep (creep?), slither as innocuously as possible into this cavernous chamber of horrors, a huge room with empty seats for 500 invisible, leering people, each of whom seems to lean voraciously forward, ready to leap, to sneer, to criticize the very thought of *you* thinking you can direct an animated cartoon.

At the back of this room, under the projection booth, the three executioners sit along a long, evil, black, flickering pulpit, their talons grasping unknowable knobs, their tiny, red, piglike eyes concentrating on how to destroy any vestige of humanity or self-respect left in you.

278

Sketch of a guitarist made during the recording of music for HOW THE GRINCH STOLE CHRISTMAS!

The first run-through is a vile and turgid mishmash of all six or eight tracks played at full volume. Very much like a railway train loaded with bull elephants hitting head-on in the Holland Tunnel a train loaded with a chorus of banshees. This is to get your attention and deafen your ability to complain.

Silence.

"Is that second 'Grunt' on pot eight?" the head executioner asks.

Grunt.

The second running is somewhat quieter, the banshees obviously now being strangled by the elephants in a rather benign way. The executioners look approvingly at one another, nod at me as though to ask, "Any last words?" and then (always to my wondering eyes and ears) they run through an almost perfectly balanced, incredibly precise sound rendering of the completed picture.

We completed our film. Gestation period eleven to fourteen months, 15,000 useable drawings, 40,000–50,000 discards, 15,000 cels. Is it happenstance that animated life and human life are both composed of cel(l)s? Two hundred and fifty backgrounds, 250 background layout drawings, 1,200 character layout drawings, 4,500 unuseable and dispensable character layout drawings, sixty musicians for eight hours, a composer for six months, a sound editor for four weeks. Eight hours of dubbing in the pit where the pendulum never asks for whom it swings; it swings for thee.

The baby is born full-fledged. Whatever it hopes to be, whatever dreams it has are now forever etched in this granite statement: *Caveat emptor, cave canem,* which roughly translates to, "Careful what you buy, Jack, it might be a dog."

Here is a letter I sent to Theodor Seuss Geisel

We completed our film. Gestation period eleven to fourteen months, 15,000 useable drawings, 40,000–50,000 discards, 15,000 cels.

after a Festival of Dr. Seuss films that he had, regrettably, been unable to attend.

Dear Ted,

I have for years looked for an appropriate use of the word benison, *and at the Monday night tribute to Dr. Seuss I found the proper nesting ground.* Benison: a blessing or benediction. *There was an abundance of love as well, enough to easily reach and blanket La Jolla.*

It was only appropriate that you, who have warmed the cockles of so many hearts and stirred the imagination of so many of us, should in turn have your own cockles warmed to the boiling point by those of us who had the lucky privilege of working with you, as well as by those who knew you and loved you only through your books and films and who came out in droves to pay tribute and to bestow benison (see above).

It was a fascinating evening because we were able to see your private Seussean mythology inter-

preted in so many ways, from George Pal's surprising and touching attention to the essence of Seuss fables without being able, through the limitations of puppetry, to recreate the Seuss drawing style (The 500 Hats of Bartholomew Cubbins; And to Think That I Saw It on Mulberry Street), *to those of us who feel, and must feel if we are to contribute anything to the spirit and the intent of the story, that we are translating a book into a screenplay:* How the Grinch Stole Christmas! *(Chuck Jones),* Horton Hears a Who *(Chuck Jones),* The Lorax *(Friz Freleng),* The Cat in the Hat *(Hawley Pratt), and* The Butter Battle Book *(Ralph Bakshi), which alone seems to me to be the process of putting a book on the screen not as a screenplay, but as an extension of the book itself.*

The miracle of the whole evening, Ted, was this: Dr. Seuss came through in every case. The drawing styles varied, the intent did not. In every film the love and honor each director felt for the material came

Dear Chuck:

In a
completely inadequate
show
of
repricosity
for
~~that~~ great letter
you wrote
me
on November 28,
I have
dug up out of my
akhives
the floppy yellow
Bow Tie
~~that~~
you purchased for me
about a dozen years ago
and
I now wear it
every day
all day long
and on Monday, Wednesday
and Friday nights I wear
it in my beddie house.
* * *
With many, many thanks
for much!

Ted

through, lovingly and respectfully; the dialogue and the intent of both the dialogue and the action were as accurate as the varied talents could reasonably be expected to provide.

If all orchestral conductors led Mozart in exactly the same way, then the need for conductors would vanish. Art always can be subject to interpretation, providing the intent of the composer is respected. I think Monday night would have pleased, if not delighted, you. Each interpretation, though perhaps rife with small mistakes to you, was a tribute to the intent of your books.

As the one who, twenty-seven years ago, first lured you off of that lovely hilltop home in La Jolla into the maelstrom of television, I approached Monday night with some trepidation, but the evening was suffused with the kindred elation all of us felt who had shared in the remarkable privilege of working with a legendary storyteller; working perhaps with a living Hans Christian Andersen—well, that's close but perhaps not close enough.

Anyway, it was a lovely evening.

Love, Chuck

When *How the Grinch Stole Christmas!* was first broadcast it was, to the delight of the network and the bankers who backed it, a success. For me, the most significant event surrounding the Grinch's screen debut was a meeting with the reporter who came to interview Dr. Seuss for *TV Guide*. Although she declared a complete lack of interest in the animator behind the film, she was persuaded to talk to me. She is now my wife, Marian.

281

Marian

She smelled the way the Taj Mahal looked by moonlight.
—Raymond Chandler

Standing right there, just inside the door,
looking as sweet and contented as an angel half full of pie.
—Mark Twain

We were childhood sweethearts—but not with each other.

We met first, she contended, on the wharf at Santa Barbara; I not quite eighteen years, she not quite eighteen months. To be sure, I did in fact visit Santa Barbara about that time as a deckhand on the *Amy*, a 105-foot schooner my father had chartered on one of his last get-rich-quirk schemes (he had given up "get-rich-*quick*" as a footless fancy years ago).

Father had come to Santa Barbara, as Evelyn Waugh so redolently put it, to lure some of the "epileptic royalty from their villas; uncouth peers from crumbling country seats; . . . illiterate lairds from wet granite hovels" in the canyons, to join, for substantial fees, a cruise to Tahiti, or, as his brochure so poetically noted: "Two months of lazy loafing on sunny southern seas." This hell-ship did eventually put to sea, but that saga must wait impatiently for the good old nonce. Romance takes precedence.

Knowing Marian as I do now—or *think* I do

*Marian paints with photography
the world around and within her,
using her camera as a painter uses a
brush—a laughing, poetic, or dramatic
brush, always a delight and
in all ways a pleasure.*

*Photographs by Marian Jones.
Clockwise from top right:
THE THIRD EYE, BEGINNINGS I,
NUDE BARBIE DESCENDING A STAIRCASE,
THE PERSISTENCE OF PERSISTENCE.*

Beautiful wife and happy husband, 1983.

now—I cannot doubt that even at that cotton-panty stage of her raffish career she might indeed have cast a salacious eye at a stalwart young salt, 6'1", weighing in at nine stone. (A stone is fourteen pounds, a pood—in Russia—equals thirty-six pounds, so in poods and pounds I came in at almost exactly . . . 125 pounds for those who are, like me, weak in math.) An irresistible object of desire, no doubt, to one small girl who could walk under a Doberman pinscher without disturbing her hair ribbon.

I *do* remember stumbling over something soft on the wharf, so that must have been Marian.

Otherwise, I shamefully failed to recognize my destiny in this encounter, at a time when I was far more interested in silk panties than in cotton ones, at a time when Marian was still involved with maternal breasts and I was just getting involved with dry martinis (thirty-five years later, our attitudes were reversed).

Perhaps it is just as well that we parted: the slight disparity in ages is indeed meaningful when you are young. After all, I had just finished with high school, while she was still teething, and one thing I cannot stand is an irritable woman. Our culinary desires were somewhat incompatible as well. She was into Pablum and pacifiers, I into things under glass like hot dogs, hamburgers, caviar, pâté de foie gras, and anything James Bond might have ordered.

Conversation might have been strained, too. If your dinner companion is confined to observations such as "goo," "da-da," and "aw gone," there is a certain lack of sparkle to the atmosphere.

So, as she says, if we *did* meet, then too we sadly realized that we must bravely face the inevitable, a short separation of thirty-five years or so. Our brief encounter, therefore, was but a skein of dreams for the future.

Off we went to school—but not together. I to Chouinard Art School, Marian to Stanford. We got married—but not to each other. We had children—but without the benefit of each other's genes.

For many years, without each other, we practiced our hobbies: mine, driving producers insane; hers, driving editors mad.

In 1965 an unlikely Cupid in the form of a Grinch took matters into his own impatient hands and things began to happen, slowly but discernibly. She both interviewed me (for *TV Guide)* and interfered with my equilibrium (by being so loveable and lovely).

Time, as has been so succinctly stated, passed.

Then one day we both got married again—this time to each other—and I discovered something startlingly, incredibly wonderful: marriage is not necessarily a device expressly designed to annoy me. Living with Marian is to live in an atmosphere where I can, and do, flourish, where the joy of existing, working, and loving together justifies the whole matter.

I fell in love with her long before I met her, and made many drawings of the kind of grace and beauty that I rather helplessly supposed existed somewhere. Without her, this book could never have been; with her, it *had* to be written.

Mirrors have longstanding love affairs with Marian. I have never met a mirror so lackadaisically jaded or indifferent that it could resist the opportunity to smile back at her and glow and glory in the opportunity. I am one of those mirrors.

Yes, mirrors and I have that in common; we both adore Marian. And being in love with Marian is like going up in a pink balloon on the first day of spring with a basketful of jonquils, a jug of myrrh, a loaf of frankincense, a hatful of bubbles, and a thou—if that thou is thee, Marian.

Someday I hope to overcome my tendency to understate, and eloquently—even poetically—say how I really feel about her. Maybe that's what the next book will be all about.

At least I can be sure of one devoted reader. Me.